■ Divided We Stand

Divided We Stand

The Strategy and Psychology of
Ireland's Dissident Terrorists

John Horgan

OXFORD
UNIVERSITY PRESS

OXFORD
UNIVERSITY PRESS

Oxford University Press is a department of the University of Oxford. It furthers the University's
objective of excellence in research, scholarship, and education by publishing worldwide.

Oxford   New York
Auckland   Cape Town   Dar es Salaam   Hong Kong   Karachi
Kuala Lumpur   Madrid   Melbourne   Mexico City   Nairobi
New Delhi   Shanghai   Taipei   Toronto

With offices in
Argentina   Austria   Brazil   Chile   Czech Republic   France Greece
Guatemala   Hungary   Italy   Japan   Poland   Portugal   Singapore
South Korea   Switzerland   Thailand   Turkey   Ukraine   Vietnam

Oxford is a registered trade mark of Oxford University Press in the UK and certain other countries.

Published in the United States of America by
Oxford University Press
198 Madison Avenue, New York, NY 10016

Library of Congress Cataloging-in-Publication Data
Horgan, John, 1974–
   Divided we stand : the strategy and psychology of Ireland's dissident terrorists / John Horgan.
      p. cm.
   Includes bibliographical references and index.
   ISBN 978-0-19-977285-8 (hbk. : alk. paper)   1. Terrorism—Northern Ireland.
   2. Terrorists—Northern Ireland.   3. Irish Republican Army.   4. Irish unification question.
   5. Northern Ireland—Politics and government—1994-   I. Title.
   HV6433.G7H67 2013
   363.32509416—dc23
   2012016616

9 8 7 6 5 4 3 2 1
Printed in the United States of America
on acid-free paper

This book is dedicated to the life and work of Paul Wilkinson 1937–2011

CONTENTS

■ FOREWORD

Why will you find this book so valuable? Dr. Horgan has built up a remarkable database of open source intelligence on the republican terrorist groups that remain active in Ireland after the decision of the main body of the republican movement to eschew terrorism and commit to democratic politics. His material goes much further than anything else that is publicly available by not only tracing the actions of the multiplicity of splinter groups but also addressing the details of individual actors, by gender, local geography, employment, age, and much else besides, producing an enormous amount of data that he then subjects to careful scrutiny and analysis. Terrorism, as the term itself suggests, uses powerful emotions as its tools, and sometimes those who try to investigate it find their own analyses distorted by what they wish to believe or what they fear may be true. John Horgan insists on providing us with the material so that we can make informed judgments, but in addition provides his own scrupulous analysis of the history of the different groups and their emergence, their strategies, and their various trajectories of activity. Furthermore, he takes us beyond individual psychology, which has failed to shed much light on the problem, and starts to explore the psychosocial and group aspects of terrorism. We are not yet able to be definitive, but John Horgan uses his Irish data to take us down a path of proper scientific analysis as Marc Sageman and Scott Atran have done in South Asia and the Middle East and North Africa.

Progress and development in human affairs are more often the result of serendipity and paradox than is popularly imagined, but that is not to say that a scientific approach is not of value. On the contrary, it is precisely the careful, thoughtful, orderly observations of the scientist, in the social sciences as in the physical sciences, that reveal to us the unexpected results that we would not have noticed had we not rigorously followed the evidence where it takes us. In addressing the long-standing problem of terrorism and politically motivated violence in Ireland it had always been thought self-evident that secret intelligence and cunning propaganda were the essential tools not only of the terrorist, but also of the lawful authorities whose job it was to frustrate terrorism. So too it was believed that the majority of ordinary people and those for whom they voted could be brought to reach political agreements that would marginalize extremism and bring peace. Unfortunately, years of efforts failed to deliver the results on both fronts. Or to say it in another way, the observational evidence, however unwelcome, pointed in a different direction. On the political front the 1998 Good Friday Agreement grew out of the apparently contrary decision to construct an inclusive process that was open to the involvement of those groups that had prosecuted terrorist campaigns, so long as they were prepared to explore a nonviolent and democratic way of dealing with political divisions. On the security front too, prolonged failure to achieve an end to terrorism led to a new experiment in using openness and following the evidence wherever it takes, even if it was not politically welcome. The British and Irish Governments established an Independent Monitoring Commission in 2003 requiring it, by law, to produce regular six-monthly reports on paramilitary activity and its relation to the political parties, and to make recommendations for remedies that would deal with terrorist violence. The outcome was successful, and in this excellent book John Horgan outlines some of that work.

However, the significance of this book is that it goes so much further. The last regular monitoring report from the Independent Monitoring Commission (IMC) was published in October 2010 and the work of the Commission was brought to a close by the two Governments with the publication of a final review report in July 2011. Realizing the value placed on the IMC reports the British Government undertook to publish its own six-monthly accounts of terrorist activity. However, the first of these reports, when it was eventually published, was disappointingly thin, and so I was delighted to read the well-informed and detailed material in this book. I have no doubt that this will also be the reaction of all of those who follow the security situation in Ireland, and its implications for dealing with terrorism and violent political conflict across the world.

As if this were not enough, Dr. Horgan then discusses some of the implications for a counterradicalization program in Ireland and points to important questions for the future. You will understand why I found this a book that once started, demands to be read straight through, but then becomes a reference book, a compendium of useful information, and a data-mine of material for further study. Scholars and security buffs will not feel bereft of the IMC reports when this book comes into their hands, but they are likely to insist on further publications from Dr. Horgan, whose approach deserves to become a model for researchers of other terrorist campaigns.

The Lord Alderdice FRCPsych (former IMC Commissioner)
House of Lords, London SW1A 0PW

■ PREFACE

The peace process that culminated in the signing of the Good Friday Agreement of 1998 finally brought hope to Northern Ireland and to a people who have long suffered the consequences of a protracted conflict. After decades of dirty war, the various paramilitary factions finally allowed their political representatives to enter a process that would herald the end of terrorism in favor of the democratic process. The bullet was out. The ballot box was in. Yet, after all that progress, terrorism has returned to Northern Ireland. The peace and stability brought by the Good Friday Agreement are now being threatened by new and substantial security challenges.

This book is about the new breed of Irish Republican terrorists. It is about the terrorists' *terrorists*—the dissident voices that develop from within the ranks of terrorist movements. It is about people for whom there will never be a peace process, never a negotiated settlement, and who will never be satisfied by politics or appeased by mainstream opinion. They are the self-styled "dissident" Republicans, though they themselves reject this term. They span several groups and comprise a confusing array of titles, including the *Continuity IRA*, the *Real IRA*, *Óglaigh na hÉireann* (once a name used by the Provisional IRA, then the RIRA, and now a breakaway group from the RIRA), and, most recently, the Tyrone-based group calling itself simply *the IRA*. There are at least a dozen more "microgroups" that range in size, scope, and ambition, from ones that are little more than a few non-violent dissident protestors to others with close ties to former PIRA personnel now heavily engaged in promoting violent attacks against the Police Service of Northern Ireland.

This book seeks to provide an understanding of these Violent Dissident Republicans (VDRs). It explores questions such as the following: Who are the dissidents? What do they want? What are their strategic, psychological, and ideological driving forces? How do they organize and execute their activity? Where are they recruiting? What factors affect the growth and maintenance of dissident activity? And how can we help in preventing violent dissident Republicanism? The book attempts to make sense of this complexity by drawing on a major empirical enquiry into the dissidents—the result of thousands of hours of research into what the dissidents say and what they do. Of course, it is at best a challenge to write about unfolding events. At worst it is foolhardy. Yet the sheer volume of dissident activity, the massive surge in terrorist recruitment, and the ferocious escalation of intimidation, kidnapping, torture, shootings, bombings, attempted bombings, hoax events, and murders show no sign of abating. The dissidents, at least for now, are indeed here to stay.

This book does not seek to simply draw attention to the problem. It provides analysis of who the dissidents are, where they come from, what they want, and what they do in order to seek those objectives. In any assessment of the capabilities of VDRs, it is clear that they represent only a tiny minority of the Irish Republican community. However, this tiny minority has shown a formidable ability to disrupt the normalization process in Northern Ireland, often substantially. They have survived, regrouped, and are now an active terrorist force across Northern Ireland.

The VDR study, conducted over 2 years at the International Center for the Study of Terrorism (ICST) at the Pennsylvania State University, has seen a massive data collection effort on two distinct fronts: violent dissident *activity* and violent dissident *personnel*. The data used to inform the descriptions provided in this book are not drawn from secret or confidential sources. In an attempt to place this study firmly within a social science approach to the study of terrorism, the data are drawn exclusively from tens of thousands of items of open-source material. Our data points come from newspaper reports (ranging from national sources with international media coverage to the smallest of parochial town and village newsletters). We have assembled hundreds of statements issued by the dissidents themselves, their supporters online, and published interviews with dissidents and those tasked with responding to them. The ICST VDR study presents data on 662 personnel involved in dissident Republican activity. The CIRA, RIRA, Óglaigh na hÉireann, and other VDR groups are responsible for more than 1200 known acts catalogued in the ICST database. This book presents the analysis of those data.

In Chapter 1, I describe the context in which the dissidents currently operate and describe the research project from which the data in later chapters emerge. Chapter 2, with John Morrison, takes a closer look at the character of these groups, in particular tracing the historical factors that have contributed to the splits, schisms, and factions that now dominate the alphabet soup of groups and microgroups. In Chapter 3, we examine the volume, extent, and nature of dissident activity. Chapter 4 focuses on the people responsible for this activity as we examine who the individual dissidents are, where they are from, and where they go to commit terrorist acts. In Chapters 5 and 6 we consider the strategy and psychology of the dissident groups and try to make sense of who they are and why, despite a successful peace process and their overwhelming lack of public support, they are still here. Chapter 7, about responding to the threat, is presented with an understanding of the dissidents' strategy and operations in mind, and Chapter 8 offers some concluding thoughts with a look to the future.

John Horgan
State College, PA

■ ACKNOWLEDGMENTS

I am very grateful to the UK Government for its sponsorship of the Violent Dissident Republicanism (VDR) project since 2009 and for its recognition of the value of open source academic research on terrorism. I hope that the small contribution in these pages complements (and in some ways challenges) those analyses that must remain behind closed doors. Nothing that is said here should be interpreted as supportive of (or supported by) the UK Government or any of its policies.

Throughout the life of the VDR project, I benefited from the input of many skilled researchers. I am grateful to Dr. Paul Gill, who has helped me in several critical areas on the first iteration of the project in late 2009–2010. Since then, I am especially grateful for the input of Dr. John Morrison, Project Manager of the second phase of the project, and an encyclopedic brain on all matters Irish. His tireless research assistance and long hours working on various project tasks (he is also co-author of Chapter 2) were so extensive that there is no way this project would have been completed on time without him—thank you John. I am also grateful for the research assistance of Patrick McGowan, whose meticulous efforts from the beginning of the project ensured that we double and triple checked each and every database entry. Richard Watson, Anne Scaduto, Sue Mira, Nicole Zinni, and Su Chuen Foo helped with research throughout the life of the project. I am more generally grateful to my other colleagues at ICST and Penn State, Machelle Seiner, Bryan Carter, Mary Beth Altier, Kurt Braddock, Michael Kenney, Bryan McDonald, Peter Vining, James Piazza, Philip Schrodt, Sam Hunter, Lily Cushenbery, Rick Jacobs, Christian Thoroughgood, and Emma Leonard. I give special thanks to my good friend Philip Jenkins for suggesting the title of Chapter 6—see, I told you I'd use it!

In addition to recognizing John Morrison as co-author of Chapter 2, some material presented in Chapters 2, 3, and 4 is drawn from two key papers co-authored with Drs. Morrison and Gill, in particular, Horgan, J., & Gill, P. (2011). "Who Becomes a Dissident? Patterns in the Mobilization and Recruitment of Violent Dissident Republicans in Northern Ireland." In M. Taylor & P. M. Currie (Eds.), *Dissident Irish Republicanism* (pp. 43–63). London: Continuum Press, and Horgan, J., & Morrison, J. (2011). "Here to Stay? The Rising Threat of Violent Dissident Republicanism in Northern Ireland." *Terrorism and Political Violence, 23*(4), 642–669.

Abby Gross, Joanna Ng, and Lori Handelman at Oxford University Press were terrific to work with, while Scott Steedman's steely eye was most appreciated in the final stages (thank you Scott).

Any research project I conduct at the Pennsylvania State University is facilitated by multiple people. I am grateful to Christine Woods and Trish Alexander for their tireless patience with my grant-related adventures, as well as to Associate

Dean Denise Solomon and Dean of the College of the Liberal Arts, Susan Welch, and Professor Mel Mark, head of the Department of Psychology. I am also grateful for the support and friendship of Keith Karako, Kathy Stathakis, and Cliff Thumma, as well as unceasing support and encouragement from Mark Luellen and Ray Lombra.

Throughout the course of the research that both informed the development of this project and others since then, I have benefited from the knowledge and experience of far too many people to mention, including those who cannot be named. Suffice it to say, that those who cannot be thanked in these pages know precisely who they are. Others can be acknowledged. These are, in no particular order, Max Taylor, Mark Currie, Martyn Frampton, Ed Moloney, Jim Cusack, Sean O'Callaghan, John (Lord) Alderdice, and Frank Ritter. I am grateful to other researchers, colleagues, and friends with whom I shared ideas and who were always quick to lend me a view and those from whose research I have benefited over the years. I thank Randy Borum, Conor Lynch, Allison Smith, Danielle Hawkins, Paul Taylor, Padraig McGowan, Lisa McInerny, Maura Conway, Donald Holbrook, Jerry Post, Ariel Merari, Helen O'Leary, Leonard Weinberg, Philip Mudd, Gary LaFree, Gary Ackerman, Victor Asal, Karl Rethemeyer, Martha Crenshaw, Stevan Weine, Clark McCauley, Bruce Hoffman, Joe Rivers, Scott Stanley, Richard English, Arif Alikhan, Chris, Amy, and Phoebe Griffin, Mike Gelles, Mark Fallon, George Kesidis, Stephen White, Ali Soufan, Marc Sageman, Kathleen Carley, Tom Neer, Susan Sim, and Robert Fein.

The earliest supporter of the idea that gave rise to the project, which eventually would lead to this book, was Professor Paul Wilkinson. In July 2007, over a Scotch in his living room in Crail, I asked him his thoughts on a book about the dissidents. As with any proposal I made to Paul, he replied, "it's a wonderful idea, and I think you should do it." I benefited from his friendship, support, and encouragement in more ways than I probably realize, and he is greatly missed by everyone who knew him.

Closer to home, I am always grateful for the constant friendship and support of Barry and Michelle, Rick, Louise and Ryan, Ruth, Nelius and Killian, Martin, Bridget, Sophie, Ruby and Evan, and Tim and Jean.

Finally, to you Mia, my greatest champion, for everything that you are.

■ Divided We Stands

1 Here to Stay?

Was it for this the wild geese spread
The grey wing upon every tide;
For this that all blood was shed,
For this Edward Fitzgerald died,
And Robert Emmet and Wolfe Tone,
All that delirium of the brave?
Romantic Ireland's dead and gone,
It's with O'Leary in the grave.

From "September 1913" by William Butler Yeats

■ INTRODUCTION

On 15 June 2010, the Saville Report detailing the events that took place in Derry, Northern Ireland on 30 January 1972 was finally published. The report concluded that not only had British army paratroopers fired on unarmed civilians on what became known as "Bloody Sunday," but that those same paratroopers had fired the first shot, adding that "many of these soldiers have knowingly put forward false accounts in order to seek to justify their firing."[1] British prime minister David Cameron subsequently issued an apology on behalf of the state: "What happened on Bloody Sunday was both unjustified and unjustifiable. It was wrong. These are shocking conclusions to read and shocking words to have to say. But you do not defend the British army by defending the indefensible." Irish prime minister Brian Cowen acknowledged both the report and Cameron's words: "This is not about the re-opening of old wounds, but rather it is about the healing of the gaping wounds of injustice left behind by the terrible events."[2]

Exactly 1 year later, the families of those affected by another atrocity, the Kingsmill massacre, received a report of the enquiry into the events of 5 January 1976, when an Irish Republican Army (IRA) active service unit stopped a van carrying textile workers home from work. A masked gunman asked the passengers about their religion. The IRA ordered the single Catholic on board to leave, then shot dead the 10 remaining Protestant workers. This massacre is widely described as one of the worst sectarian attacks of the Troubles. The report into it, conducted by the Historical Enquiries Team (HET), confirmed IRA responsibility in addition to the fact that the group had targeted the workers on the basis of their religion. The IRA had used a cover name, the "South Armagh Republican Action Force," and one of its members had claimed that the IRA had no part in the massacre.[3] But Republican Action Force was simply one of a long list of convenient cover names used to mask IRA involvement from certain operations. On 22 June 2011, senior Irish Republicans finally conceded what had been known for 30 years even within their own ranks. The Sinn Féin spokesperson on victims, Mitchel McLaughlin, told the BBC: "I do not dispute the sectarian nature of the killings, it was entirely wrong and I have no problem in condemning what happened."[4]

Significant as these two events were, both will ultimately be overshadowed in the history books by another milestone in "healing"—Queen Elizabeth II's official visit to the Republic of Ireland. Delivering a key speech in Dublin Castle, the Queen drew admiration for directly addressing the legacy of a century of conflict and animosity between the neighboring countries. The Queen expressed "deep sympathy" for all those affected as a "consequence of our troubled past.... With the benefit of historical hindsight we can all see things which we wish had been done differently or not at all."[5] The visit was a remarkable testament to the normalization of relations between the two states.

All of these events and more have taken place against the backdrop of an ongoing peace process in Northern Ireland. They stand out as dramatic examples of progress in a region that has been plagued by conflict for generations. Perhaps the greatest testament to change in Northern Ireland is that two former sworn enemies, Sinn Féin and the Democratic Unionist Party, now share power in the Northern Ireland Assembly. Following a series of intermittent setbacks on discussions surrounding devolution leading up to December 2004, the St. Andrews Agreement of 2006 allowed political parties to hold elections and restore power-sharing in Northern Ireland in 2007. Justice and policing powers devolved to the Northern Ireland Assembly in early 2010. These events would undoubtedly not have happened if the Provisional IRA (PIRA) had not renounced its "armed struggle," and the strength of the cooperation could not have been sustained without the overall support of the respective represented communities. Beyond the transformed political climate, the signs of security normalization are visible to all. In 2 years, army troop levels in Northern Ireland were reduced from more than 14,000 to less than 5,000. The number of British Army bases dropped from 24 to 13, and all "observation and communication sites" (nine in total) were shut down.[6] The British military in Northern Ireland "had no continuing role in law enforcement and were no longer visible in border areas. Watch towers and protected installations had gone, as had frequent helicopter flights, and the border was generally apparent only because the style of road signs changed."[7]

In some ways, it is difficult to overestimate the scale of the change in Northern Ireland. The final report (released in July 2011) of the Independent Monitoring Commission (IMC) provides a wide-ranging summary of that change. The IMC was founded in late 2003 by the Irish and British governments to "monitor and report on the continuing activities of paramilitary groups" and to issue reports at 6-monthly intervals.[8] It notes that the major catalyst, if not cause, for recent progress "was the gradual removal of paramilitary activity as a cause of friction between Assembly parties, largely as a result of the changes within PIRA."[9] Those "changes within PIRA" were significant. On 6 April 2005, Sinn Féin president Gerry Adams called on the IRA to give their "total support to democratic politics": "Such decisions will be far reaching and difficult. There are many problems to be resolved by the people of Ireland in the time ahead. Our struggle has reached a defining moment. I am asking you to join me in seizing this moment, to intensify our efforts, to rebuild the peace process and decisively move our struggle forward."[10] Three months later, the IRA issued a statement in which it describes its leadership having "formally ordered an end to the armed campaign."[11] The statement added that "We are very mindful of the sacrifices of our patriot dead, those who went to jail, volunteers, their families and the wider Republican base. We reiterate our view that the armed struggle was entirely legitimate."[12]

The IRA statement, one of its least ambiguous, proved the catalyst for change across Northern Ireland's main Loyalist paramilitary movements. As the IMC reported, these changes included "the UVF's and Red Hand Commando's (RHC) announcement of the end of their campaign in May 2007, and the Ulster Defence Association's (UDA) similar announcement in November that year; the LVF's announcement that it was standing down in October 2005; between June 2009 and February 2010 the UVF/RHC, the mainstream and South East Antrim element of the UDA, the Irish National Liberation Army (INLA) and the Official IRA all decommissioned their weapons."[13] Perhaps the final IMC report put it best: "After less than a year, local control of policing and justice is already taken for granted. The people of Northern Ireland are putting the Troubles behind them and are moving on to build a new future."[14] In the words of a former Republican prisoner: "Who in their right mind would want to go through all that again?"[15]

The decline of the Provisional IRA has been long and complicated. Even in its death throes the movement's activities threatened to derail a peace process whose tendency to break down in acrimony now seems a distant memory. The PIRA's involvement in the £26.5-million robbery of the Northern Bank in December 2004, and in the murder 1 month later of Robert McCartney, provided good evidence to its critics that despite Sinn Féin's claims of commitment to democratic politics, the Republican movement had either difficulty or reluctance in shedding its paramilitary past. In many ways, character change has been a defining quality of the Irish peace process. The choreography that surrounded Sinn Féin's efforts to embrace mainstream democratic politics has involved constant maneuvering and repositioning. The July 2005 statement by the PIRA leadership was certainly the clearest prerequisite for Sinn Féin's full integration into the new political climate (and not least to satisfy a deservedly suspicious Democratic Unionist Party, with whom Sinn Féin would eventually share a political platform) that would emerge from the St. Andrews Agreement in 2006.

Much of the fallout surrounding the near collapse of the process at semiregular intervals can be directly attributed to Sinn Féin's previously ambiguous yet convenient relationship with the PIRA. In August 1995, at a Belfast rally of Irish Republican supporters, Sinn Féin president Gerry Adams delivered a speech in which he criticized the British government for not living up to its responsibilities as part of the burgeoning peace process. In frustration, a man in the crowd implored Adams to "Bring back the IRA," to which Adams infamously replied, "They haven't gone away, you know." Seven months later, the Provisional IRA ceasefire broke down amid fierce accusations that British prime minister John Major's government had, in the words of a former member of the PIRA Army Council, "prolonged the IRA ceasefire for as long as possible without giving anything in return."[16] A PIRA car bomb detonated in the London Docklands area of Canary Wharf signaled the end of the ceasefire and the start of a renewed bombing campaign in England. The PIRA would eventually renew its ceasefire in 1997 and its political wing, Sinn Féin, would ultimately steer the bulk of the Republican movement into mainstream politics via the Good Friday peace agreement of 1998. In July 2005, 7 years later (and 3 weeks after the al-Qaeda bombings in London that killed 52 people), the Provisional IRA formally announced the permanent end of its "armed struggle."

Adams' remarks from 1995 stand in stark contrast to the statements issued by him and the PIRA leadership 10 years later in which they announced that the PIRA's campaign had come to an end. But what he said to the Republican masses in 1995 became a cliché about the seeming inevitability of Irish Republican militancy. No matter what the peace process, no matter what the will of the majority of people on the island of Ireland, it seems guaranteed that in the absence of an Ireland united on Republicans' terms, there will always be some Irish Republican group eager to take up arms in advancing the Irish "cause." Even now, and against the backdrop of one of the most hard-fought peace processes in modern memory, splits, splinter groups, and breakaway factions are doing their best to destabilize normalization and threaten security across Northern Ireland. In fact, the guaranteed emergence of dissident factions is so synonymous with Irish terrorism that playwright Brendan Behan once remarked that the first item on the agenda at any Republican meetings was always the matter of "the split." Academic and IRA expert John Morrison has even asked whether this development should be characterized as "the affirmation of Behan?"

In one sense, the fact that dissident factions break away from the parent organization is not surprising. Splitting is a common process in any organization, big or small, "new" or "old," violent or nonviolent. Throughout the IRA's history there have been many splinter groups, ghost groups, and factions (temporary and long-lasting). Some Republican splinter groups have been short-lived, whereas others have lasted more than 20 years. Many are well known, but some defy the efforts of even seasoned IRA historians to characterize them as either true splinter groups or merely convenient fronts. Few will remember "The Avengers," a tiny group that described itself as "pro-Republican ... but not the Irish Republican Army" that was responsible for exploding parcel bombs (with 39-hour detonation delays) in London post offices in the early 1970s. The bombings were in retaliation for "harassment of ... Republican women in and out of prison."[17]

Scholars who study postconflict societies frequently remind us that it is normal to expect a certain level of violence as part of that transition. The years following the Good Friday Agreement have certainly seen some shocking events. Several of these were associated with the PIRA, and seriously threatened to derail the peace process. Mo Mowlam, the former Northern Ireland secretary of state, famously said, "the peace we have now is imperfect, but better than none."[18] Echoing

Mowlam's statement was the final IMC report: "Those who expected the immediate disbandment of leadership structures were not simply unrealistic; they were seeking something which would be counter-productive."[19] The IMC recognized that "change would be achieved only if the leadership remained in position and could continue to guide the organisation in the right direction."

Yet all of these sentiments reflected expectations surrounding the slow decline of the IRA rather than the emergence of a dissident movement. The security situation in Northern Ireland has worsened significantly since 2008, while at the same time becoming ever more complex. While the Provisional IRA has been relegated to the history books, a new wave of terrorism has swept the region. Those responsible for this violence are called "Violent Dissident Republicans" (VDRs) by some. But they are more widely known collectively as "the dissidents." They comprise several different groups. Some are overlapping entities across two or more groupings and others are proud to stand alone in defiance of their old colleagues in the IRA. Some of these groups, particularly the major factions of the Real IRA, the Continuity IRA, and Óglaigh na hÉireann (ONH), are organized and led by disaffected Irish Republicans once loyal to Gerry Adams and Martin McGuinness. These groups now view both Republican leaders as traitors who have compromised too much in their efforts to end the IRA's tactical use of the armed struggle and bring Irish Republicans into the mainstream political scene. Their unifying feature is their unequivocal rejection of the Good Friday Agreement and their belief that Sinn Féin's participation in the process that led to that agreement was fundamentally at odds with Republican ideals. Jonathan Tonge summarizes the raison d'être for the dissidents—the Good Friday Agreement, which because of its reliance on the principle of consent, does not necessarily guarantee a united Ireland: "The Agreement offers substantial internal change, but a reformed Northern Ireland under British jurisdiction was not the vision for which most Republicans had fought in a conflict in which almost 3,700 people died between 1969 and 1998."[20]

It was probably inevitable that Adams and McGuinness would never succeed in bringing with them all Republicans, but, and in the wake of the 1998 Omagh bombing, the reemergence of dissident activity in Northern Ireland has surprised even the keenest of observers. A cursory glance at recent news headlines from Northern Ireland and England reinforces this: "750 dissident bomb alerts in past two years," "Mortars found at County Kildare 'bomb factory,'" "Device 'could have caused carnage,'" "Policeman killed in Omagh car bomb attack," "Police confirm second bomb found in North Belfast," "Real IRA admit Londonderry gun attack," "Car bomb officer Peadar Heffron's leg amputated," "Irish Republicans 'aiming for more young recruits.'" Furthermore, the twenty-sixth and final report from the IMC, though reflecting on the positive legacy of the peace process, cautions about the increasing brutality of the dissidents[21]: "The seven years since [the IMCs establishment in 2004] have seen major adverse paramilitary events... [including] the resurgence of serious violence by dissident republicans in 2009 and 2010 in which four have been murdered." Pointing to "classic signs of insurgent terrorism," members of the Police Service of Northern Ireland (PSNI), the IMC warns, are "at greater threat than they were in 2004 when we first reported."

Although frustration, anger, and outrage typify the outward local reaction to the resurgence of terrorism in Northern Ireland, to those far removed from the dissidents' operational theater the reaction is one of incredulity—a common response being, "I thought that was all over." Northern Ireland, after all, has been transformed by a peace process that has brought relative stability and prosperity, and the overwhelming majority of people north and south long for the kind of stability and prosperity they have been denied throughout a 40-year campaign of violence. Many simply cannot believe that not only has terrorism returned to Northern Ireland, but that it is escalating in scope, volume, and intensity. There is little that can be said about the 1998 Omagh bomb that has not already been burned into the consciousness of those who survived an episode that many hoped would, at best, herald the end of those responsible. A common refrain is the hope that the latest victim of the conflict did not die in vain. Yet despite the detonation of a car bomb that murdered 31 people and injured more than 300 not only have the dissidents not gone away, they have grown in strength and number.

For most international observers, the dissidents' latest campaign came to the fore in March 2009, when members of two such groupings claimed responsibility for three murders. Within a period of 48 hours, members of the Real IRA shot dead two soldiers at Massareene Barracks and Continuity IRA gunmen shot and killed a member of the PSNI. In 2009, their tactics ranged from encouraging their members and fringe supporters to detonate incendiary devices and petrol bombs, to targeted assassinations of police officers in November. Yet the 2009 murders were not bolts from the blue. In hindsight, the outward signs of disaffected Republican rejectionists have been clear for a decade. Since 2001, a stenciled message painted on the entrance to St. Finbarr's Cemetery in Cork has read: "It's not over yet. Óglaigh na hÉireann." John A. Murphy, Emeritus Professor of Irish History at University College, Cork, explains: "Because just inside the entrance lies the railed-off 'Republican' burial plot which holds the graves of Cork's revered lords mayor Thomas MacCurtain and Terence McSwiney and of other patriots. The Republican plot is the mecca of numerous Nationalist commemorations and it also contains memorial tables to various IRA activists over the decades.... When you claim a place in the pantheon, you hope to legitimise yourself in the republic apostolic succession."[22]

By July 2008, the dissident threat was "confirmed" to former PSNI chief Sir Hugh Orde when he described "at least 25 attempts to kill...officers in the last 18 months." His remarks, a prophetic warning of what was to come less than a year later, seem now at odds with remarks conveyed by the twenty-first report of the Independent Monitoring Commission, which reported that the two senior dissident groupings at the time, the Continuity IRA (CIRA) and the Real IRA (RIRA), "do not...present some coherent organization like PIRA...much less do they have anything like the capacity to mount a consistent and substantial campaign." A similar evaluation, this time from a former PIRA member who is now a prominent nonviolent dissenter, Anthony McIntyre, echoed the IMC sentiment: "Some people think their strategy is to drive the British Army back onto the streets, but I'm not sure.... I don't think there is a strategic logic behind them.... I think they probably see the pool settling, and every now and then they'll throw something into it to create ripple effects—and embarrass Sinn Féin."[23]

Though the 2009 murders were the most dramatic examples of residual terrorism in Ireland since the Omagh bomb of 1998, they also signaled a dramatic turn in an already steady rise in activity that began in 2008 and continues today. In 2010 alone, high-level attacks ranged from the detonation of a bomb at a Newry courthouse in February to the targeting of a number of PSNI stations by dissident bombers throughout the year. On 2 April 2011, consistent with this overall rise in VDR activity, a car bomb planted by dissident Republicans murdered 25-year-old Catholic PSNI officer Ronan Kerr outside his home in Omagh, County Tyrone. In fact, the security situation in Northern Ireland has worsened so much that British home secretary Theresa May declared in September 2010 that the threat level posed by VDR organizations had risen from "moderate" to "substantial,"[24] and inferred that a VDR attack on the UK mainland was a "strong possibility."[25] This was echoed in the placement of the "activities of residual terrorist groups"[26] alongside international terrorism as a "tier one" security risk to the national security of the United Kingdom.[27] In the same month Jonathan Evans, the director general of the British Security Service (MI5), publicly acknowledged that the service has "seen a persistent rise in terrorist activity and ambition in Northern Ireland over the last three years."[28] In January 2010, MI5 revealed that it was monitoring more "life-threatening plots being prepared in Ulster than at any time since before the Good Friday Agreement," and that by 2010, there were more plots being hatched than by Islamic extremists in mainland Britain.[29] The 2011 review of Britain's *Prevent* counterterrorism strategy emphasized that "there remains a serious and persistent threat from terrorist groups in Northern Ireland. . . . The threat in Northern Ireland itself is SEVERE, which means an attack is highly likely."[30]

Dissident Republican activity goes far beyond plots aimed at police, soldiers, and targets of "national security." In recent years there has also been an increase in low-level activity, with the return of punishment attacks and other forms of vigilante justice in which, among others, suspected drug dealers and sex offenders have been targeted within traditionally Republican communities. The revelation that the paramilitaries continue to play any active function in the communities they once claimed to represent is frequently met with disbelief. Knox[31] reminds us that a "key element" of the Good Friday Agreement was a proposal to reform then existing policing and criminal justice systems. In the words of the agreement, the people of Northern Ireland could look forward to a new police force "capable of attracting and sustaining support from the community as a whole."[32] "[T]hat such criminal activity continues to exist in communities," Knox argues, "is an indicator of . . . support for, or at the very least acquiescence in, paramilitary tactics."[33] Lister[34] describes how "teenage boys [aged 14 and 15] from East Belfast were beaten and locked in a cupboard for several hours by the Provisional IRA after they were wrongly accused of smashing a window in a leisure complex." These beatings, many of which go unreported to the police, feed directly into another dark statistic: "Up to 13 young men in [North and West Belfast] have taken their own lives since Christmas after punishment attacks by dissident republican terrorists."

These incidents raise questions about both the legacy of the Troubles and the vacuum left by the mainstream paramilitaries (namely, the Provisional IRA and the Ulster Defence Association) in the wake of the various peace agreements that have seen both major groupings surrender armed conflict as a means of political struggle. It is certainly plausible that former paramilitaries connected to the PIRA are still be involved in this activity.

■ **ASSESSING THE THREAT**

So what does all this mean? Certainly, the threat from the dissidents resists easy characterization. We can find a broad range of contradictory views from knowledgeable figures on all sides of the political and security spectrum. For those too hardened or cynical in their coverage of Northern Irish events, there is a sense that "it's not so bad." There have been accusations and political recriminations that argue that really, on the basis of a relatively low fatality rate (compared to the scale of the attacks), the threat from dissident Republicans is probably overblown, and is in no way comparable to the threat posed by the Provisional IRA at its height. Some have even attempted to describe the 2010 bombings as "out of character"[35] for the dissidents, alleging that much of the high-level dissident activity was in reality "false flag operations run by MI5." Conspiracy theories notwithstanding, threat assessments that invoke comparisons with the Provisional IRA are at best misleading and at worst uninformed. We would do well to appreciate the lessons of history when it comes to assessing threats posed by terrorist groups. On 20 November 1971, *Irish Times* reporter Conor Brady described a research brief published by the Institution for the Study of Strategic Conflict.[36] The report, entitled "The Spreading Irish Conflict," described the then-fledgling PIRA's "clumsy," "amateurish," and "unimaginative" attempt to develop a terrorist campaign. Then it claimed that the PIRA's bomb attacks amounted to "nothing more than a man nervously lobbing a petrol bomb so badly made that the wick falls out before it reaches its target," and concluded that "They have failed to make any systematic attack on strategic targets…or to extend their campaign of selective assassination to senior officers or leading politicians." That report, now an historical curio, seems almost surreal with an assessment that could not have been more premature. Twenty-two years later, and 12 months before the 1994 ceasefire that would eventually herald the disbandment of the PIRA, over 3000 people were dead, with tens of thousands more injured, traumatized, or forever affected by "The Troubles." The PIRA was responsible for over 2000 of those deaths.

It would be equally premature, of course, to suggest that the threat posed by the dissidents is comparable to that once posed by the PIRA. Yet the dissidents stand alone in today's Northern Ireland and pose an ongoing threat to life in the region. In September 2009, the Northern Ireland Police Federation announced at their annual conference that within the space of 2 years, dissident Republicans had caused 750 bomb alerts, 420 of which involved "viable explosive devices."[37]

A common challenge in studies of terrorism is to avoid either underestimating or overestimating the threat posed by any group. On the challenge of "assessing," the IMC noted in their final report that, particularly in dealing with complex material, it was "often difficult to reach precise and confident judgements."[38] Several conflicting and wildly different answers have been offered to the question of whether the dissidents pose a serious threat to security. In November 2010, Ulster Unionist politician Basil McCrea claimed that the dissidents were at "97 percent" of the capability of the IRA, and that "the only thing stopping them doing it is an extremely efficient PSNI operation in terms of disrupting serious crime and these people."[39] McCrea alleged that he received this information via confidential intelligence forwarded to him in his capacity as a member of the Northern Ireland Policing Board. Nationalist and Unionist politicians alike protested the allegation, decrying it as "sheer madness" and "reckless scaremongering."

A different example of the challenge of threat assessment came in the wake of a publication by scholar Martyn Frampton. Before Frampton published his book *Legion of the Rearguard,* an exhaustive examination of the dissidents, he highlighted sections of it released in a report by the International Center for the Study of Radicalisation (ICSR) at King's College, London, entitled "The Return of the Militants." Veteran journalist and leading IRA expert Ed Moloney describes Frampton's claim that the threat from dissidents "is now at its greatest level in over a decade" as "alarming." Moloney issued a commentary following the release of the ICSR report, arguing that "[I]t would be wrong to overstate or exaggerate their potential. The threat from dissidents was actually much greater in 1998 than it is now."[40] He goes on to say that "Dr Frampton produces some 12 pages of dissident-linked incidents since 2009 to support his case, but closer examination reveals a preponderance of punishment shootings, hoax bomb-warnings and bombs that failed to detonate—always an indicator of possible security force infiltration. The violence committed by dissidents in the last two years could easily fit into a two- or three-week period when the Provisionals were active."

In Moloney's view, the "greatest flaw" in Frampton's analysis "lies in his failure to understand that the engine which sustained the Provisionals is not available to the dissidents. It is true, as he says, that the Provisionals and the dissidents share a detestation of the partition settlement of 1921, but it is not that which kept the Provisionals going for some 30 years. What nourished them was the support of a sizable number of Catholics who believed it was impossible to ever get a square deal within the Northern Ireland state." Moloney asserts that the dissidents' campaign actually more closely resembles the failed IRA border campaign of 1956–1962 "than a continuation of the Provisionals." Frampton's counterresponse[41] acknowledges that the dissidents' "adherents are not in large number," but that they are "here to stay," taking "solace from their ideological certainties."

Though each successful attack by the dissidents feeds a renewed exchange of polarized views, their features have been adeptly observed by commentators such as Jonathan Tonge.[42] He explains that not only are the dissidents small in number, but that their lack of cohesion is one of their defining characteristics. Given the outcome of Sinn Féin's participation in the peace process, Tonge is surprised that they have not attracted even more members:

[W]hat may be remarkable about the current peace and political processes is the lack of defection to Republican ultra groups, following the acceptance by Sinn Féin of the 1998 Good Friday Agreement. The deal fell substantially short of the Republican goal of a united, independent Ireland, a point acknowledged by Sinn Féin. The relative unity of provisional Republicans is even more startling in view of the PIRAs willingness to decommission part of its weaponry, a move unprecedented in the history of the IRA.[43]

Another IRA expert, Rogelio Alonso, suggests that it is surprising that the dissidents even exist. Their mere presence today can be contrasted with what Alonso describes as the "modernization in Irish Republican thinking" about the use of violence.[44] The origins of this logic, Alonso argues, can be traced to the series of PIRA ceasefires in 1975, when an understanding "gradually emerged within the movement that armed struggle would not be enough to force the British out of Ireland." The effectiveness of the PIRA's armed campaign was primarily, Alonso says, in its propaganda effects. It served to advance the agenda, "though without achieving the ultimate realization of their traditional aims." Of special significance is how Sinn Féin has transformed itself throughout the peace process and has since come to condemn the dissidents. Alonso cites Pat Doherty, Sinn Féin's Vice President at the time of the Omagh bombing, who said that "The attack was not about removing the British government presence from our country. It was not an attack on the British military establishment in Ireland. It was not an attack on a commercial target. It should not be allowed to be claimed as part of the legitimacy and honourable struggle for Irish Independence."

But the "dissident" picture has changed significantly since Omagh, becoming so complex as to be virtually impenetrable to those outside Northern Ireland. To characterize dissidents as "out of touch" and "living in the past" is as unhelpful as it is misleading, and does little to advance an assessment of the threat their movement poses. Whereas Sinn Féin tries to encourage forgetting the past to strengthen its current position, the dissidents rely on the unwavering certainty of, and adherence to, that same past. Alonso's claim reflects the logic used by the dissidents: Doherty's arguments, just like Adams's, have "no basis at all, since actions of the nature of Omagh are clearly justified in the republican mentality, having been a constant feature of the PIRA's strategy along the years."[45] Alonso continues: "When Gerry Adams branded public statements made by the dissidents as 'opportunistic PR,' he seemed to ignore that for decades propaganda had also guided his movement's strategy…his condemnation of Omagh was not followed by the rejection of IRA actions in the past. In other words, Adams simply censored one kind of Republican violence."[46]

The lifeblood of the dissidents is derived from their adherence to core militant Republican principles. They draw their strength from the same messages Adams and the PIRA leadership preached to their followers prior to the peace process to which Sinn Féin and the PIRA are now wedded. Alonso cites the opening words of Adams' presidential address at the 1983 Sinn Féin Ard Fheis (party conference): "There are those who tell us that the British Government will not be moved by armed struggle. As has been said before, the history of Ireland…tell[s] us that they will not be moved by anything else."[47] The dissidents, Alonso argues, "understand that their ideals have been betrayed by leaders like Adams and McGuinness, who have strategically controlled the movement since the 1970s"; in their eyes, the story of the "peace process" has also been a story of the continuing compromise of Irish Republican ideology. In Sinn Féin the dissidents now have a convenient near enemy to accompany the traditional far enemy of Westminster. The essence of the dissidents is that they are true rejectionists. In supporting the abandonment of the Republic's constitutional claim of territorial control over Northern Ireland (Articles 2 and 3), the dissidents believe it is Sinn Féin, not Unionists or even Nationalists, who have effectively ensured the continue partition of Ireland. This point is echoed in analyses of the dissidents by Frampton, Alonso, Tonge, and several others.

Alonso's view finds much support among nonviolent Republican dissidents. McIntyre laments the Good Friday Agreement as the "death of Republicanism" and characterizes the PIRA's campaign as having ultimately failed: "The political objective of the Provisional IRA was to secure a British declaration of intent to withdraw. It failed. The objective of the British state was to force the Provisional IRA to accept—and to respond with a new strategic logic to—the position that it would not leave Ireland until a majority in the North consented to such a move. It succeeded."[48] Alonso describes the peace process as representing "the success of pragmatism over principle in the republican mentality."[49] The dissidents' campaign then would not only seem to be unreasonable and wholly lacking in any pragmatism, but in the long run, utterly doomed to failure. Yet this has not deterred them.

■ **EXAMINING THE EVIDENCE**

Imagery, mythology, and a healthy dose of imagination have tended to substitute for real analysis of terrorism in Ireland throughout both the political process and civil society more generally. It might seem surprising that there has not been more research on dissident activity. Frampton argues there has been little more than a "fragmentary examination"[50] of the groups and suggests that such efforts have been "largely obscured by an emphasis on the mould-breaking nature of the peace process, which had encouraged a certain degree of myopia."[51] He also suggests that the belief that, for the most part, conflict has ended in Northern Ireland offers a "conceptual challenge."[52] The assumption may well be that despite short-lived successes brought on by highly sporadic activity, the dissidents are still due to go away, any day now. Yet there have been some insightful analyses of the dissidents. These include research by Henry Patterson,[53] Jonathan Tonge,[54] Robert White,[55] James McAuley,[56] John Morrison,[57] Margaret Gilmore,[58] John Mooney and Michael O'Toole,[59] and Mark Currie and Max Taylor.[60] Frampton's own analysis presents an exhaustively detailed trace of the ideology and activity of the dissidents.

Some of the most valuable insights into the labyrinthine transformation (and compromises) of Irish Republicanism since the ceasefires have come from leading Republican thinkers including former PIRA members Anthony McIntyre and

Tommy McKearney.[61] Other close perspectives come from journalists who have extensively covered events since the ceasefire and have attempted to sift through the associated "fog" of behind the scenes progress.[62]

Many of the existing analyses are descriptive in nature. Though no less valuable for this, it is apparent that much of the confusion around attempts to assess the threat posed by the dissidents stems from a lack of reliable data to inform this analysis. This book is different. It is not based on any kind of "insider" expertise and does not seek to supplant or challenge these existing accounts. What it does seek, however, is to provide what is missing from most existing accounts of the dissidents—a closer examination of their activity and personnel.

In this sense, this report, and the project from which it is drawn, is based on a series of core research principles. Sageman[63] describes some challenges in the study of terrorism and suggests three core recommendations:

1. The need to adopt a scientific approach, and consequently
2. The need to employ tried and tested social science methods
3. The need to examine all available data, and "not a biased selective sample."[64]

The core starting point for any good analysis of terrorism is data. Those data can take multiple forms. It can include reported events, statements issued by those claiming responsibility for those events, news media coverage of those events, and, of course, demographic and other data of interest on those who engage in terrorist activity. Consideration of data allows us to generate hypotheses, look for patterns, and ask questions such as the following: How much activity is there? How is it changing over time (in terms of frequency, intensity, lethality, etc.)? Who is responsible for it? Is the movement replacing imprisoned members with new ones? How are tactics changing over time, and is there a coordinated strategy to what the movement is doing? Answers to all of these questions are currently lacking in an analysis of violent dissident activity in Ireland.

Equally important is clear and consistently used terminology. The term "dissident" is as contentious as it is critical for understanding this phenomenon. Outside of Northern Ireland, the term conjures nobility, sacrifice, and hardship—rejection, but rejection for an "ideal." Notable dissidents from history include German Nobel laureate Carl von Ossietzky, prevented by the Nazis from leaving a concentration camp to receive his award,[65] a punishment echoed in 2010 when Chinese democracy advocate Liu Xiaobo was also prevented from traveling to Oslo to accept the same honor.[66] These and other political dissidents around the world are frequently admired for adhering to their principles in the face of repression, imprisonment, torture, and even death from those regimes they dare to criticize.

In Northern Ireland, "dissident" is most commonly used to describe splinter groups that refuse to accept ceasefires, but it is a term that can be applied to almost all Republicans (at one time or another). The answer to who precisely warrants the label of "dissident Irish Republican" is complex and varied.[67] Dissidents vary by tactics and strategy. Some are peaceful, whereas those under examination here are militant. To further complicate matters, in late 2010 a new collective term for the dissidents emerged: "residual terrorist groups." This is a phrase that has been promoted by representatives of the British and Irish governments as well as the PSNI.

The label was justified by concern about the apparent nobility associated with the term "dissident." In his previous capacity as Irish minister for foreign affairs the current leader of Fianna Fáil, Micheál Martin, actively called for the discontinuation of the word "dissident": "[It] is a completely inappropriate term.... [It] relates to people of conscience during the Cold War, and that term has no application to the kind of indiscriminate bombings which have taken place, or the murder of police officers or British Army personnel. They're betraying the republican tradition."[68] Tonge also rejects the use of the term "dissidents," and in its place refers to Irish Republican "ultras."[69]

A different perspective is offered here. A change in terminology is not only unnecessary and inappropriate but potentially misleading. "Dissent" does not convey a value judgment on the act of dissidence, any more than it does on what is being dissented. Consequently, use of the title "dissident" does not place any value judgment on an individual or organization but instead describes that person or group's defining characteristic. The question is not one of approval or disapproval, but rather whether the act of dissent is the defining characteristic of the organization under analysis. The answer to this must be Yes. Each of the groups under examination here have, through the act of schism or split, dissented from what is now accepted as "mainstream" Republicanism (while it is the case that ONH actually split from *other* modern-day dissident groups, their most defining feature is still their core assertion of a rejection of Sinn Féin and the mainstream politicization of Republicanism by its leadership).

All of the dissident groups (including the nonviolent dissidents) addressed here reject both the Good Friday and St. Andrews agreements. They do not accept the PSNI as a legitimate policing force for the six counties of Northern Ireland and consider Sinn Féin guilty of having strayed from the path of Republicanism. Though some of them view being a "dissident" as a sign of their credibility and commitment to basic Republican principles, they reject the label "dissident Republican." To them, Sinn Féin deserves the label "dissident Republicans," not those who have stayed true to the path. Their stated beliefs are that any political settlement short of British withdrawal from Northern Ireland and an independent united Ireland falls too far short of their Irish Republican goals and therefore cannot be used to justify the permanent cessation of violence.

That said, the use of the "dissident" label throughout these chapters in no way implies homogeneity of organization, ideological focus, or tactical repertoire. Within dissident Irish Republicanism there is ongoing competition and conflict between groups. There are also visible internal conflicts within specific groups, most notably the Continuity IRA. Although there have been actions, attacks, and statements[70] suggesting the possibility of a dissident coalition,[71] the overall picture remains one of competition. Though this does not negate the possibility of dissident cooperation on some levels, it does acknowledge a certain level of autonomy across the groups. Furthermore, that competition does not permeate only dissident Republicanism, but affects Republicanism and Nationalism on the whole. All of the currently active movements are in constant competition with each other to gain what little influence may be available within the Republican community to leverage both membership and support. Through their words and actions each

Republican organization proposes that *they*, and no other group, are the only legitimate Irish Republican group, the ones who will ultimately bring about a united Ireland (the prize that Gerry Adams and Martin McGuinness, they argue, have failed to deliver).

Clarification of this term is important for other reasons. Not all of the dissident activity documented in the databases that were built for the project that culminated in this book is illegal in nature, and many if not *most* of the individuals reported in media accounts of dissident activity have never been convicted of terrorist offenses. Thus, the relationship between nonviolent and violent dissident activity represents an important analytic challenge. As the following section will illustrate, the inclusion from open sources of individuals identified in either the event database or the personnel database or both should not be viewed as, or interpreted as, indicative of involvement in terrorist activity.

■ THE INTERNATIONAL CENTER FOR THE STUDY OF TERRORISM (ICST) VDR PROJECT

The research that is presented in this report began in October 2009. Called "the VDR Project," it was concerned primarily with analyzing the mobilization and recruitment of violent dissident Republicans in Northern Ireland. The study sought to understand the types of individuals participating in VDR activity and to provide a data-driven empirical research base that can inform efforts at the individual, team, group, and community level for preventing, disrupting, or hindering mobilization and recruitment to VDR groups. The study sought to answer the following questions:

1. How and why do dissident groups emerge?
2. How can the VDR phenomenon be characterized?
3. Who becomes involved in violent dissident Republicanism? What are the sociodemographic backgrounds of recruits to VDR?
4. What does VDR activity look like and how has it developed and changed over time?

The research involved identifying and analyzing data from multiple sources, including literature reviews, open-source media, and other sources.

The project involved the identification and collection of data on (1) VDR activity and (2) VDR personnel. VDR activity was collated based on an investigation of open-source media accounts, which led to the creation of an event database. VDR personnel were identified from these accounts and the results are documented in a second database. As above, not all of the events documented in the event database are illegal in nature. Some may be characterized as subversive in nature, whereas others (though not violent) may be indicative of an intent to engage in violence. By the same measure, not all of the individuals identified in media accounts were convicted of terrorist offenses. Many were charged with an offense but were never convicted. The term "dissident" should not under any circumstances be seen as interchangeable with "terrorist." The people charged but not convicted were often known to be involved with the dissident movement, but not engaged in illegal behavior. In some ways, the "charged but not convicted" subset of dissident personnel could be considered a type of control group. In the following sections, we make explicit the differences emerging between violent and nonviolent dissidents and reflect upon the significance of these differences. As will become clear during the analysis, the individuals included in our personnel database are not all currently active members of dissident groups.

Multiple data sources were consulted by the research team to confirm attribution and responsibility. Attribution is a complex and challenging task, both at the individual and group level. The IMC acknowledge this in an annex of their 2005 report in attempting to categorize "concerned" individuals. Their reports overall are a testament to just how difficult attribution is, even with access to a wide variety of confidential sources of evidence in addition to open-source material: "One of the more challenging issues we faced was the attribution of incidents, particularly when it was not fully clear how far members of paramilitary groups were acting on their own initiative and how far with the sanction or on the orders of the leadership, local or central."[72]

The analysis presented here considers as dissidents all those who have actively engaged in subversive and terrorist activity since the inception of the Good Friday Agreement in 1998 and onward.

Database Structure

The VDR event database catalogues dissident Republican activity. As of 8 July 2011, it catalogued 1244 distinct violent and nonviolent events (899 violent acts, 151 threats of violence, and 194 relevant but nonviolent acts). The database integrates information from four types of open sources (in order of relevance): (1) newspaper and media accounts; (2) Republican literature/propaganda; (3) publicly available government publications and reports; and (4) online terrorism event databases [e.g., the University of Maryland's START Global Terrorism Database (GTD) and the Oklahoma City National Memorial Institute for the Prevention of Terrorism (MIPT) Database]. Four fields cover the temporal aspects of each event and five fields track geographic information. Organizations tied to the event and whether they claimed responsibility (in the event of violence) cover a further two fields. The event type (meeting, bombing, shooting, riot) and weapons used (if any) are also captured in the event database. In the case of a violent event, a further five fields capture information on fatalities, injuries, and victimology. The final three fields tie individuals to events, provide a summary of the event, and chronicle the sources from which we garnered data.

The benefit of developing a dataset such as this stems from the sheer amount of information to be gleaned from open sources. Media reports are often exceptionally detailed, even for information on what might appear to be "active" members who have not necessarily been convicted of recent activity. A good example is how the British media identified former PIRA members who were deemed to have defected to the dissidents. Bernard McGinn, a 52-year-old former PIRA member and proclaimed "master terrorist,"[73] was said to have joined ONH in 2010 after becoming "disenchanted with Sinn Féin's policies and what they regard as the party's abandonment of traditional Republican values." While in the PIRA, McGinn was imprisoned in 1999 for 490 years for "three killings, conspiracy to murder, possession of firearms and involvement in bombings." He was freed from prison in 2000, under the early release scheme as part of the Good Friday Agreement.

The VDR personnel database catalogues individual members of dissident organizations. It is important again to note that not all those included have engaged in illegal activities—the main focus here is those who have been convicted. Dissidents involved in legal activities were included to provide a broader understanding of the movement and whether there are discernible differences between those engaged in legal and illegal forms of dissident activity. As of 8 July 2011, 662 dissident Republicans were identified from open sources, but 199 were convicted of offenses. The personnel database uses the same data-gathering method as the event database although there is far less reliance on online terrorism event databases. Published books provided insightful information on particular individuals. For each individual, the database captures multiple pieces of information. The individual's name, alias, gender, date of birth, and age are recorded in the first five fields. A further four fields list geographic variables (place of birth, known addresses, places of arrest, and whether these locations are in the North or South of Ireland). The individual's occupation, socioeconomic status, marital status, and whether he or she has children provide further biographical information. The database also captures information on the dissident organization(s) with which the individual is aligned, the subgrouping (unit, brigade, etc.) of the parent dissident organization with which the individual is associated, Republican groups with which the individual was previously associated, their current status (active, imprisoned, deceased, etc.), and the position/role the individual played within the organization. A further three fields code information on network linkages with other dissidents across friendship, family, and operational ties. A generic "other information" field captures other interesting data about the individual that may be added to newly generated fields as the project develops. The final field documents the sources from which the data were obtained. A complete breakdown of the database structure is provided in Appendix A. The database is an ongoing project, and by the time these pages are in print, will already have been updated further.

■ CONCLUSIONS

The Northern Ireland of today is significantly different from the one in which the Provisional IRA operated. Under the Good Friday Agreement and the subsequent St. Andrews Agreement, the main political parties are operating in a devolved power-sharing assembly in Stormont. Sinn Féin is the largest Republican or Nationalist party, with Martin McGuinness the sitting Deputy First Minister, working closely with the First Minister, Peter Robinson of the Democratic Unionist Party (DUP). Sinn Féin also has a strong representation in the Houses of the Oireachtas in the Republic of Ireland, and on town and county councils both sides of the Irish border. Within the greater Belfast area

Sinn Féin is, as of the 2011 local elections, the largest single party. Republicans across Ireland have therefore voted to have active representation in all the main governmental bodies across both states, and have accepted that the pursuit of a united Ireland must be done through purely peaceful political means. In doing so they have rejected the continuation of violence in their name and have dele-gitimized the claims of representation being made by the various VDR groups. Yet nobody can deny that terrorism has returned to the streets of Northern Ireland. In the next chapter, we examine precisely who these groups are and where they have come from.

■ **NOTES**

1. BBC News. 2010. "Bloody Sunday Report Published," 15 June.

2. Ibid.

3. Cusack, J. 2011. "A Bloodbath Lost Among Daily Slayings." *Independent on Sunday*, 26 June.

4. BBC News. 2011. "SF: Kingsmills Families Need Truth 'Like Other Victims,'" 22 June.

5. Sky News. 2011. "Queen's Historic Visit to Ireland Ends," 20 May.

6. Independent Monitoring Commission. 2011. *Twenty-Sixth and Final Report of the Independent Monitoring Commission: 2004–2011 Changes, Impact and Lessons.* London: The Stationery Office.

7. Ibid.

8. Ibid., p. 9.

9. Ibid., p.14.

10. RTE News. 2005. "Adams Calls on IRA to Support Peace Process," 6 April.

11. BBC News. 2005. "IRA Statement in Full," 28 July.

12. Ibid.

13. Independent Monitoring Commission. 2011. *Twenty-Sixth and Final Report of the Independent Monitoring Commission: 2004–2011 Changes, Impact and Lessons.* London: The Stationery Office. Pp. 12–13.

14. Ibid., p.14.

15. Community Foundation for Northern Ireland. "From Prison to Peace: Learning from the Experience of Political Ex-Prisoners." Belfast: Community Foundation.

16. Interviewed by the author in Co. Kerry.

17. *Irish Times.* 1973. "Pro-Republican Group Claims Parcel Bombs," 3 September.

18. Secretary of State statement, Northern Ireland Office, 27 August 1999.

19. Independent Monitoring Commission. 2011. *Twenty-Sixth and Final Report of the Independent Monitoring Commission: 2004–2011 Changes, Impact and Lessons.* London: The Stationery Office. P. 47.

20. Tonge, J. 2004. "They Haven't Gone Away, You Know": Irish Republican "Dissidents" and "Armed Struggle." *Terrorism and Political Violence, 13*(3), 671–693.

21. Independent Monitoring Commission. 2011. *Twenty-Sixth and Final Report of the Independent Monitoring Commission: 2004–2011 Changes, Impact and Lessons.* London: The Stationery Office.

22. Murphy, J. A. 2001. "Bomb Proves That It's Not Over Yet." *Independent on Sunday*, 5 August.

23. Walsh, J. 2009. "Could IRA Splinter Groups Bring Back Ireland's Troubles?" *Christian Science Monitor*, 23 October.

24. "Substantial" is the third ranked threat level in British security with the threat levels from lowest to highest being "low," "moderate," "substantial," "critical," and "severe."

25. RTE. 28 September 2010. "UK: Dissident Republican Threat Level "Substantial," www.rte.ie/news/2010/0924/ukterrorism.html. Accessed December 10, 2010.

26. This is a new term being adopted by the British government and others.

27. HM Government. 2010. *A Strong Britain in an Age of Uncertainty: The National Security Strategy*, 27–29.

28. Speech available at www.telegraph.co.uk/news/uknews/terrorism-in-the-uk/8008252/Jonathan-Evans-terrorism-speech.html. Accessed April 4, 2011.

29. Kirkup, J. 2010. "MI5: More Terrorist Plots from Irish Republicans Than Islamic Extremists." *Daily Telegraph*, 1 January.

30. HM Government. 2011. *Prevent* Strategy. June. UK: The Stationery Office Ltd, p. 14.

31. Knox, C. 2002. "See No Evil, Hear No Evil: Insidious Paramilitary Violence in Northern Ireland." *British Journal of Criminology, 42,* 164–185.

32. Ibid.

33. Ibid.

34. Lister, D. 2004. "Terrorists' Punishment Attacks at Record High." *Sunday Times*, 28 February.

35. *The Phoenix*. 2010. "MI5's 'False Flag' IRA Operations." *Affairs of the Nation*, pp. 64–65.

36. Brady, C. 1971. "I.R.A. Are Clumsy and Lacking in Imagination, Says Booklet." *Irish Times*, 20 November, p. 9.

37. *Irish Independent.* 2009. "750 Dissident Bomb Alerts in Past Two Years," 24 September.

38. Independent Monitoring Commission. 2011. *Twenty-Sixth and Final Report of the Independent Monitoring Commission: 2004–2011 Changes, Impact and Lessons.* London: The Stationery Office. P. 32.

39. BBC News Northern Ireland. 2010, "Dissident Republican Strength Claim 'Sheer Madness.'" 12 November. www.bbc.co.uk/news/uk-northern-ireland-11741503

40. Moloney, E. 2010. "Renegade Republicans Remain on the Margins." *Belfast Telegraph*, 30 November.

41. Frampton, M. 2010. "Dissident threat Hasn't Gone Away, You Know." *Belfast Telegraph*, 7 December.

42. Tonge, J. 2004. "They Haven't Gone Away, You Know: Irish Republican 'Dissidents' and 'Armed Struggle.'" *Terrorism and Political Violence, 16*(3), 671–693.

43. Ibid., p. 672.

44. Alonso, R. 2001. "The Modernization in Irish Republican Thinking Toward the Utility of Violence." *Studies in Conflict and Terrorism, 24,* 131–144.

45. Ibid., p. 138.

46. Ibid., p. 139.

47. Ibid., p. 135.

48. McIntyre, A. 1998. "We, the IRA, Have Failed." *The Guardian*, 22 May.

49. Alonso, R. 2001. "The Modernization in Irish Republican Thinking Toward the Utility of Violence." *Studies in Conflict and Terrorism, 24,* 131–144.

50. Frampton, M. 2010. *The Return of the Militants: Violent Dissident Republicanism.* London: International Centre for the Study of Radicalisation and Political Violence. P. 2.

51. Ibid., p. 6.

52. Ibid., p. 3.

53. Patterson, H. 2011. "Beyond the 'Micro Group': The Dissident Republican Challenge." In M. Taylor & P. M. Currie (Eds.), *Dissident Irish Republicanism* (pp. 65–95). London: Continuum Press.

54. Tonge, J. 2004. "They Haven't Gone Away, You Know": Irish Republican "Dissidents" and "Armed Struggle." *Terrorism and Political Violence, 13*(3), 671–693.

55. White, R. 2010. "Structural Identity Theory and the Post-Recruitment Activism of Irish Republicans: Persistence, Splits, and Dissidents in Social Movement Organizations." *Social Problems, 57*(3), 341–370.

56. McAuley, J. 2011. "'Not Like in the Past': Irish Republican Dissidents and the Ulster Loyalist Response." In M. Taylor & P. M. Currie (Eds.), *Dissident Irish Republicanism* (pp. 143–166). London: Continuum Press.

57. Morrison, J. F. 2010. The Affirmation of Behan?': An Understanding of the Politicisation Process of the Provisional Irish Republican Movement Through an Organisational Analysis of Splits from 1969 to 1997. Ph.D. dissertation, University of St. Andrews.

58. Gilmore, M. 2009. "No Way Back? Examining the Background and Response to the Rise of Dissident Terrorist Activity in Northern Ireland." *The Journal of the Royal United Services for Defence and Security Studies, 154*(2), 50–55.

59. Mooney, J., & O'Toole, M. 2002. *Black Operations: The Secret War against the Real IRA*. Ashbourne, Co Meath: Maverick House.

60. Currie, P. M., & Taylor, M. 2011. *Dissident Irish Republicanism*. London: Continuum Press.

61. McIntyre, A. 2008. *Good Friday: The Death of Irish Republicanism*. New York: Ausubo Press; McKearney, T. 2011. *The Provisional IRA: From Insurrection to Parliament*. Dublin: Pluto Press.

62. Rowan, B. 2003. *The Armed Peace: Life and Death after the Ceasefires*. Edinburgh: Mainstream Press.

63. Sageman, M. 2008. *Leaderless Jihad: Terror Networks in the Twenty-First Century*. Philadelphia: University of Pennsylvania Press. Pp. 13–16.

64. Ibid., p. 14.

65. Freedom House. 2010. "Planet Gulag." *Foreign Policy*, December 9.

66. Glasser, S., & Baker, P. 2010. "The Billionaire Dissident." *Foreign Policy*, May–June.

67. To be comprehensive, let us include Martyn Frampton's definition: "The term 'dissident' is ... used as a catch-all, to encompass those of an Irish republican persuasion who have broken with the 'mainstream' movement of Sinn Féin and the Provisionals. It is by their opposition to the peace process and/or the political status quo in Northern Ireland that they have come to be labelled 'dissidents,' though many within their amorphous ranks would insist that it is they who have stayed true to their beliefs, where others have not." (Frampton, M. 2010. *The Return of the Militants: Violent Dissident Republicanism*. London: International Centre for the Study of Radicalisation and Political Violence. P. 12.)

68. Simpson, M. 2010. "Visit Part of New Anti-Dissident Strategy." BBC, 12 October. Accessed 18 April 2011: www.bbc.co.uk/news/uk-northern-ireland-11521483.

69. Tonge, J. 2004. "'They Haven't Gone Away, You Know.' Irish Republican Dissidents and Armed Struggle." *Terrorism and Political Violence, 16*(3), 671–693.

70. In an interview on the "Prime Time" programme aired on Irish television broadcaster RTE on 20 April 2011, a Continuity IRA representative stated that "We have a cordial

relationship with all the armed groups throughout. Our volunteers as well will be aiding any operations that we are asked to join in. The war will continue and it will escalate."

71. The most obvious example of this is still the Omagh bombing of 1998, which saw the CIRA and RIRA working together.

72. Independent Monitoring Commission. 2011. *Twenty-Sixth and Final Report of the Independent Monitoring Commission: 2004–2011 Changes, Impact and Lessons.* London: The Stationery Office.

73. Mooney, J. 2010. "IRA 'Master Terrorist' Defects to Dissidents." *Sunday Times Online,* 4 April.

2

Interior Rebellion: A History of Irish Republican Splitting

■ WITH J. F. MORRISON

"We're going to make this state ungovernable. We intend to carry out major operations. We intend to cripple the state. We intend to show that there is no normalisation in the occupied six counties[1] at the moment"

—*Continuity IRA spokesman, 2011*[2]

▓ INTRODUCTION

To suggest that splits have typified the development of Irish Republican militant groups is an understatement. Throughout its history Irish Republicanism has continuously split and factionalized. These splits have not just shaped Irish Republicanism, they have led to some of the most significant and influential events in recent Irish history. A split led to the formation of the two historically dominant Irish political parties, Fianna Fáil and Fine Gael. Splitting has also been a catalyst for the intensification of paramilitary violence[3] and played a major role in the recent politicization of the majority of the Republican movement.[4] And the current dissident groups owe their origins to recent splits within the Republican movement.

The dissidents represent a clear case study in organizational complexity and heterogeneity. They vary in their size, geographic location, strategies, ideologies, structures, and, not least, personalities. This chapter provides an introduction to each of the major dissident groups. It presents a detailed examination of each group's origins, activities, and stated goals. In doing so, it provides a deeper context to the data analysis that follows in Chapters 3, 4, and 5. The focus will be on the three most active dissident Republican groups, the Real IRA (RIRA), the Continuity IRA (CIRA), and Óglaigh na hÉireann (ONH), as well as their political affiliates.[5] But it is important to note that there are many additional dissident groups. Most are quite small, and there is considerable confusion about their nature and significance. They are sometimes called "microgroups," and some of the lesser-known entities (often associated with only a handful of small events) are alleged to be proxy or even "ghost" groups.[6] Despite the apparent proliferation of these smaller dissident groups, the focus for this chapter outside the main dissident groups will be on Republican Action Against Drugs (RAAD), Republican Network for Unity (RNU), and Éirígí.

■ THE CONTINUITY IRA AND REPUBLICAN SINN FÉIN

The CIRA is the oldest of the Violent Dissident Republican (VDR) groups. It emerged as the result of the major 1986 split within Provisional Republicanism. The group's political wing, Republican Sinn Féin (RSF), also emerged from the same process. Ostensibly both groups formed in 1986 after the Provisional Republican movement voted to drop abstentionism to Dáil Éireann (the lower house of the Irish parliament) at both the 1986 Sinn Féin Ard Fheis and the Provisional IRA General Army Convention. Some analysts dismiss the significance of the process leading up to these votes, and miss the fundamental rationale behind the exit and the postsplit dominance of the Provisional movement within Irish Republicanism. Although the birth of the Continuity Republican movement may lie in 1986, its origins need to be traced back to the previous decade.

In the mid to late 1970s, in the aftermath of the 1969–1970 split that led to the formation of both the Provisional IRA and the Official IRA, a number of young northern Republicans were coming to prominence within the leadership of both the Provisional IRA (PIRA) and Sinn Féin. These "young Turks," led by Gerry Adams, Martin McGuinness, Danny Morrison, and others, called for the restructuring of the entire organization. They wanted the PIRA to become a cellular organization[7] to ensure its capacity of pursuing a "long war" strategy.[8] This proposed strategy would go hand in hand with a new form of political pressure via Sinn Féin.[9] For many it was obvious that this heralded a schism within the movement, one that is often described as a "north versus south" or an "old guard versus young guard" division. Young northern Republicans were slowly taking over from the old-guard leaders who had led the 1969–1970 split that saw the birth of the Provisional Republican movement in response to the perceived failures of the Goulding leadership.[10]

This "old-guard" leadership included people such as Ruairí Ó Brádaigh and Dáithí Ó Conaill, and was largely based in the Republic of Ireland. These leaders' popularity was steadily declining across the Republican movement, most notably due to their perceived mishandling of the 1975 ceasefire. During this ceasefire, which had started in February of that year and officially ended in November, the Provisional leadership led by Ó Brádaigh engaged in talks with the Northern Ireland Office (NIO) of the UK government, demanding British withdrawal from Northern Ireland. However, unrest grew within the Provisional movement about the leadership's handling of both the talks and the ceasefire. Many rank and file members believed the talks had been allowed to go on too long without any real benefits for the movement, and alleged that the leadership had been deceived by the British into thinking that they could achieve something by continuing with talks. Over time some members even broke the ceasefire, claiming responsibility for their actions with names other than the Provisional IRA. Gerry Adams recognized the organizational pressures this situation brought to the Provisional movement at the time: "When the struggle was limited to armed struggle, the prolongation of the truce meant that there was no struggle at all. There was nothing but confusion, frustration, and demoralisation, arising directly from what I call 'spectator politics.'"[11] The discontent was evident not only within the communities but also among Republican prisoners and internees. In fact, difficulties around maintaining focus and direction have in the past been more significant for the Republican movement than the lack of progress on the political front. These difficulties led to the decision to call off the 1975 ceasefire (and, 20 years later, similar reasons led to calling off the 1994–1996 ceasefire). But in 1975, even with the growing unpopularity of the leadership, the young northerners knew that they needed the support of some of the older members in order to bring about the changes they wished and to retain an air of Republican legitimacy.

In the 1970s and 1980s, the major means of communication for Republican points of view was newspapers. This tool was used to great effect by the prisoners of the period to broadcast their opinions on the current status of the movement as well as their beliefs regarding the future direction the movement should take. Most notable among these contributions were the *Brownie* letters, authorship of which is consistently accredited to Gerry Adams. Until January 1979 there were two Provisional newspapers: *Republican News* (based in the South under the editorial control of the southern leadership) and *An Phoblacht* (based in the North under the control of the northern leadership). In January 1979, when Deasun Breatnach stepped down as editor of *Republican News,* Danny Morrison, editor of *An Phoblacht* and a close ally of Adams, came to Dublin with his staff from Belfast and merged the two papers to form *An Phoblacht/Republican News.* This move proved significant as the young northerners now controlled the movement's propaganda and could push their opinions and beliefs without fear of alternative viewpoints within the movement being put forward. They used this tool to great effect throughout the 1980s and beyond, gradually getting the Republican community accustomed to their proposed changes.

The early years of the 1980s can accurately be described as crucial ones that shaped the Republican movement of today, both "mainstream" and dissident. In 1981, 23 Irish Republican prisoners took part in a staggered hunger strike, demanding that they be given political status within the prisons. The strikes lasted from March to October and led to the death of 10 prisoners. At the beginning, the Republican movement failed to generate significant levels of support. However, a high-profile and successful campaign to get Bobby Sands, the leader of the hunger-strikers, elected as Member of Parliament (MP) for the vacant Fermanagh–South Tyrone seat brought new levels of support and attention for the prisoners and the movement as a whole, not only within Northern Ireland but across the island of Ireland and internationally. Although this public support for the fasting prisoners waned with each death, support for political Republicanism rose throughout the hunger strike.

Support for the politicization of the movement can be seen in a number of election victories for Sinn Féin candidates both during the hunger strikes and in the 4 years that followed them, though it is clear that this support declined significantly with each year. But the initial dramatic rise in support did not go unnoticed by the Republican leadership and in the October 1981 Ard Fheis it prompted Danny Morrison to make his famous speech outlining his vision, and his allies' vision, for a Republican strategy embracing both politics and armed conflict. This strategy is often referred to as the "Armalite and the Ballot Box" because of Morrison's use of this phrase during his speech.[12] One of the emerging narratives of this defining period of Irish Republicanism is that of Richard O'Rawe. A PIRA prisoner within the Maze at the time of the hunger strikes who is now a vocal nonviolent dissident, O'Rawe claims that the Adams' leadership of the PIRA deliberately used and manipulated the elongation of the hunger strikes to their own tactical advantage to promote their goals and aspirations within the movement.[13]

The aftermath of the hunger strikes saw the Adams leadership intensify its campaign to change the movement and gain control of the Republican movement. Although they stepped up their campaign the group still implemented changes in a gradual manner. One of their first objectives was to cancel the *Éire Nua* (New Ireland) policy strongly supported by Ruairí Ó Brádaigh, Dáithí Ó Conaill, and other old-guard Republicans. Éire Nua was a social and economic program for the movement developed along with the formal structuring of the Provisionals in the early 1970s. It was approved as Sinn Féin and PIRA policy in 1971. The central tenet of the program was the federalization of a united Ireland in which the island would be divided into four federations, one for each province.[14] In the 1980s the Adams leadership believed this to be, and sold it as, a "sop" to the Loyalists and Unionists, as they would more than likely have command of the Ulster federation. Their first attempt to remove this policy came in the 1981 Ard Fheis, when they received a majority vote for its removal but did not meet the requisite two-thirds majority (which they did receive the following year).[15]

This constitutional withdrawal of the policy highlighted the growing tensions within the leadership and in 1983 Ó Brádaigh, Ó Conaill, and Cathleen Knowles McGuirk all stepped down from the *Ard Comhairle* of Sinn Féin. In Ó Brádaigh's resignation speech as president of Sinn Féin he highlighted his belief about the dangers of constitutional politics and the need for the Republican movement to stick to its "basic principles."[16] These resignations were vital in the Adams leadership gaining overall control of the movement, and in turn being able to promote their planned politicization as a united leadership.

With the visible decline in public support for Republicanism in the mid-1980s and the rise of constitutional alternatives such as the New Ireland Forum[17] and the Anglo-Irish Agreement,[18] Republicans believed that their movement needed major political reform. In response, they reopened the internal debate about the possibility of dropping the abstentionist policy. However, although the Goulding leadership of the mid to late 1960s had tried to change this policy for all three parliaments at the same time, the Adams leadership proposed dropping abstention only from Dáil Éireann (the lower house of the Irish parliament). This proved to be a key strategic move as it was the least objectionable of the three options in the opinion of a number of Republicans.

For many members of the then Republican movement, the abstentionist policy was more than a tactic—it was a defining feature of what it meant to be an Irish Republican. However, the proposal to drop only the policy while continuing with the armed struggle proved less divisive than the more comprehensive changes proposed by the Goulding leadership, which also included stopping all paramilitary activity. As with all constitutional amendments, this reform required a two-thirds majority. The young leadership understood that if it was to be successful they required the support of prominent Republicans from the PIRA and Sinn Féin, and most importantly from some old-guard Republicans, in order to legitimize their proposals and influence the overall membership. That they had that support was apparent in the range of speakers who spoke in favor of the change in the 1986 Ard Fheis of Sinn Féin. Supporters varied from the new leadership of Adams, McGuinness, and Morrison to other old-guard Republicans such as John Joe McGirl and Joe Cahill and prominent PIRA prisoners such as Gerry Kelly, who sent a letter of support from prison in Amsterdam. The support of these and other prominent individuals as well as a number of years of groundwork proved successful when the motion was passed. From then Sinn Féin members elected to Dáil Éireann were constitutionally allowed to take their seats in parliament.

With the passing of this bill, a small number of delegates walked out of the venue and left the movement. They "continued"[19] the Ard Fheis in a different location where they declared the establishment of Republican Sinn Féin.[20] Those who walked out were mainly old-guard figures that included Ruairí and Sean Ó Brádaigh, Dáithí Ó Conaill, Cathleen Knowles McGuirk, Des Long, and Joe O'Neill. Historical analysis may reveal a succession of very gradual changes leading up to this 1986 vote. From their lack of preparation, it has been suggested that the dissidents were not fully ready for the split, as they had not laid the groundwork for the development of a new organization. When the media asked them if they had an armed wing, Ó Conaill replied "not yet." Although this may have been true at the time, the development of a newly armed Republican movement was already in progress.

After the PIRA General Army Convention of 1986, where a vote to drop abstention to the Dáil was similarly taken, those opposed to the change, mainly from the outgoing Army Executive, met to develop a new armed movement. They contacted Tom Maguire, the last surviving member of the last all-Ireland Dáil and a member of the older, original IRA, and in 1987 he issued a statement[21] declaring the legitimacy of the Continuity Executive, the title of the new armed wing, as the *true* IRA, although discounting the claims to legitimacy of the ongoing Provisional IRA.[22] Although the existence of an armed wing was heavily suspected it was not until 1994, at a graveside salute at Maguire's funeral, that the Continuity IRA[23] came to the public's awareness. To this day it is widely believed that these two groups, Republican Sinn Féin and the Continuity IRA, are intrinsically linked, with a large proportion of their leaderships and memberships overlapping and the Republican Sinn Féin paper *Saoirse* acting as a host for CIRA statements. Neither group has ever gained the levels of support or membership of the Provisionals. However, they are to this day considered one of the most dangerous paramilitary groups in Northern Ireland.[24]

The modern-day focus of the CIRA has been on vigilante attacks and organized crime, although also targeting members of the Police Service of Northern Ireland (PSNI) through both bombings and shooting attacks. Their targeting of the PSNI, in particular Catholic officers, in parallel with an increase in hoax attacks is part of their strategy to disrupt the normalization of a post-Good Friday Agreement Northern Ireland. Although they have not been as active as the RIRA or, in more recent times, ONH (RIRA), they have illustrated their lethal intentions time and time again, most recently through the March 2009 murder of PSNI officer Stephen Carroll.

Since their inception the leadership of the Continuity movement has been steadfast in promoting themselves as the only "true" Republican movement that have not compromised on the Republican ideals or principles. The principles and vision of the movement are centrally tied to Republican Sinn Féin's founding president Ruairí Ó Brádaigh, who has been the group's dominant voice and figure since its inception. The origins of the movement saw Ó Brádaigh centrally tied to the promotion of Éire Nua and he has played a similar, central role in the establishment and promotion of *each* of the movement's policies, principles, and ideals since 1986. These have been strongly tied to his unwavering loyalty to the history of Irish Republicanism and the tactics and strategies implemented by his Republican forefathers. As detailed by Frampton,[25] for Ó Brádaigh, an issue such as abstentionism to the three parliaments is less a tactic and more a central principle of Republicanism, on which there can be absolutely no compromise. It is with great pride that Ó Brádaigh and the Continuity movement regularly announce that they are the only Republican group that has stayed true to these founding principles that can be traced back through the Republican lineage. In essence, it is just as important to Ó Brádaigh to stay true to historical Irish Republican principles in the search for a united Ireland as it is to achieve unity; in his mind, being "right" and true to his historical Republican principles are more important than being popular. This was the rationale for identifying the new military wing as the *Continuity* IRA. Given Ó Brádaigh's central role in forming, guiding, and shaping the Continuity movement in his image since its naissance in 1986, it is likely that it is only when he has truly disengaged from the leadership of the movement that any attempts for significant change can be made. Even though he is no longer RSF president he is still *the* dominant figure within the movement.

Although they are central to the existence and identity of Republican Sinn Féin and the Continuity IRA, these very same principles have, in the recent past, given rise to significant internal conflict within both the CIRA and RSF, which led to further schisms in 2010. It is believed that some recent attacks credited to the group, especially those undertaken since 2010, have been undertaken without the consent of the Army Council. This has included a growing number of punishment attacks being claimed by the CIRA. This "growing unrest" within the organization has reportedly taken root within the movement, where it is widely believed that some younger members view Republican Sinn Féin members as "dominating" the Army Council. The prevailing view is that those same younger members are holding the movement back and are reducing the chances for the organization to develop its strategies and tactics.[26]

The most recent divide occurred in 2010 when the paramilitary CIRA moved out from under the control of the RSF leadership, who they believed were stifling them militarily. Speaking on RTE's *Prime Time* a representative of the Belfast Brigade of the CIRA stated the following:

> We didn't split from any part. Republican Sinn Féin, who may have a say in the Continuity IRA, they split, they walked away. But the total army, the leadership from

top to bottom, are intact. Republican Sinn Féin no longer speak for the Continuity IRA. The Continuity IRA speak for ourselves.[27]

To confuse matters even further, this new CIRA is now referred to within Republican circles as the "Real CIRA."

Serial Splintering

Like most splits throughout the history of the Irish Republican movement, this 2010 paramilitary divide was accompanied by a similar splintering of Republican Sinn Féin. Although the new group still uses the name Republican Sinn Féin or *Sinn Féin Phoblachtach,* it is more commonly referred to as "Real Sinn Féin." This divide has been led by the Limerick branch of the movement, spearheaded by Des Long. The split came via an acrimonious response to the Ó Brádaigh leadership refusing to advocate a "Broad Front" approach to the Irish Republican struggle.[28] This was a proposal to work together with other dissident groupings such as the Republican Network for Unity. The traditionalist leadership refused to countenance this idea as they would not associate with those who had accepted the dropping of the abstentionist policy in 1986. The focus of much of the new group's press releases has been to discredit the leadership and membership of the *original* Republican Sinn Féin, now led by Des Dalton.[29]

This is a regular attribute of splinter groups. They attempt to justify their existence—and, essentially, their move away from the parent organization—by first systematically discrediting the original group. The majority of VDR groups use the same tactic, concentrating much of their time on attempts to discredit the actions and members of Sinn Féin in order to justify their own positions.

Although this most recent split appears to be a national divide, not all schisms have affected the entire movement. At times, splits within RSF and the CIRA (both together and separately) have tended to happen at a much more localized level. As described by Frampton, this is particularly relevant to the CIRA because of the localized nature of its operational membership and activity, and therefore its overdependence on the strength of local units and leaders.[30] This has at times led to localized division within the group. The most potent example of this is the emergence of the Strabane-based splinter group that moved away from the Continuity IRA in 2006 and adopted the name Óglaigh na hÉireann (ONH). Not to be confused with the ONH that is now associated with the Real IRA, it might be more appropriate to refer to the Strabane group as ONH (CIRA). They are thought to have virtually ceased activity since 2009.[31] During their short existence, the group carried out a number of operations, including at least twice targeting the Strabane PSNI station with pipe bombs and the murder of alleged RIRA member Andrew Burns in Donegal in February 2008.[32] It is likely that some, if not all, of its members have rejoined the CIRA since the separation from the traditional leadership of RSF.

■ THE REAL IRA AND 32 COUNTY SOVEREIGNTY COMMITTEE

Of the currently active VDR groups the most dangerous has been the RIRA. The RIRA came into existence in October 1997 after a split in the Provisional IRA. This divide was nominally due to the rejection of the Mitchell Principles by key core members of the PIRA leadership, most prominently the PIRA's quartermaster general, Michael "Mickey" McKevitt. The split coincided with the separation from Sinn Féin of key former members. The latter went on to form the 32 County Sovereignty Committee (renamed the 32 County Sovereignty *Movement* upon separation from Sinn Féin), a group commonly thought to act as the political voice of the RIRA. The RIRA is best known for the Omagh bombing of 1998 and the murders of British soldiers Patrick Azimkar and Mark Quinsey in March 2009.

As with the origins of the CIRA, the RIRA emerged from a long process involving the gradual politicization of the Provisionals that culminated in the current peace process. As a result of the strong vote of approval gained by the Adams leadership in the 1986 Ard Fheis and Army Convention, they were able to continue with their politicization process without concern of imminent internal factionalism. As a result, in 1987, Sinn Féin published "Scenario for Peace," a document that called for an all-Ireland constitutional conference while also replacing the central Republican demand of "Brits out" with one of national self-determination.[33] The following year, one of the major advances on the road to a peace process took place with the initiation of talks between Gerry Adams and John Hume, the leader of the constitutional nationalist Social Democratic and Labour Party (SDLP).[34] Although there was denial on behalf of the PIRA of the possibility of a ceasefire coming from the talks, these meetings clearly showed the intent of the Republican leadership to look beyond the exclusive use of force. The Hume–Adams talks were to prove important as they showed both to Republicans and Nationalists the possibility of a pan-Nationalist front,[35] a concept the Adams leadership needed to develop.

Throughout the late 1980s and early 1990s there were significant advances made within the movement to facilitate the eventual disengagement from armed activity. These advances allowed the leadership to enter into (often secret) negotiations with the British and Irish governments. The public meetings between Adams and Hume were a precursor to secret talks that began in 1990 between the British government and Sinn Féin. "Adam Ingram," a representative of the British government, entered into direct contact with Martin McGuinness. Although the Republican movement put forward their proposals to the governments in the form of a document developed throughout the process of the Hume–Adams talks,[36] Albert Reynolds and John Major[37] in 1993 negotiated a separate document that became known as the Downing Street Declaration.[38] This declaration was initially seen as a setback in the Republican movement. It deviated from Hume–Adams in that it placed a dominant emphasis on the role of Unionist consent, but more importantly it showed that the Irish government was more willing to negotiate with the British government than it was with the Nationalist and Republican communities.[39] As a consequence, the Irish were seen to be favorable toward the Unionist communities. The Provisional Army

Council instantly rejected the Downing Street Declaration on the grounds of what it included as well as what had been omitted. At no point did the declaration mention a planned British withdrawal from Northern Ireland. Of equal importance to PIRA was the observation that in their view, it copper-fastened the concept of a "Unionist veto" on Irish unification. The declaration stated: "The British Government agree that it is for the people of the island of Ireland alone, by agreement between the two parts respectively, to exercise their right of self-determination on the basis of consent, freely and concurrently given, North and South, to bring about a united Ireland, if that is their wish."[40]

However, Adams convinced the Army Council not to reveal their rejection immediately and to "play for time." Senior figures within PIRA called for clarification on points within the document, while also touring the island of Ireland to solicit views from their constituencies on their thoughts and aspirations for the movement.[41] This tactic has often proved beneficial for the Republican movement as the grassroots membership could not feel aggrieved for not being consulted on major policy decisions and what might be constituted as compromise of core Republican principles.

In 1994 major inroads were made in the burgeoning peace process. In February of that year Gerry Adams was granted a 48-hour visa to the United States by President Bill Clinton. Similarly the Irish government got rid of the broadcasting ban previously preventing Sinn Féin members from speaking on national media (on the grounds that allowing this would help the actions of terrorists). These steps were all regarded as shows of faith in the possibility of the Sinn Féin leadership bringing about a cessation of violence. From early to mid-1994 the possibility of such a ceasefire was discussed at leadership levels within the Provisional movement. The topic was first broached in discussions about the possibility of a short, exploratory cessation—basically a period to see what might happen, while also allowing PIRA to recover from recent losses in the ferocious tit-for-tat campaign with Loyalist paramilitaries that had dominated 1993.

Although talks collapsed between Republicans and the British they continued between Republicans, the SDLP, and the Irish government, and therefore shifted from targeting British withdrawal to the establishment of a pan-nationalist front.[42] These talks were essentially a blueprint for future Republican strategy and action. However, what the Republican leadership told its membership was different from what they told negotiators.[43] Although negotiations were oftentimes fraught, the Provisional Army Council eventually announced a 4-month ceasefire on 31 August 1994, which was later extended. The announcement came as the acceptance of a 14-point proposal issued by Taoiseach (Irish prime minister) Albert Reynolds.[44] The ceasefire was greeted with celebrations across the whole island of Ireland as well as Britain.[45] For the first time in 25 years, a period of breathing space was allowed for initiatives to develop on all sides that might herald a long-lasting respite from violence. At the very least, it would allow other initiatives to develop in an effort to sustain the cessation.

However, although the broader Republican community greeted the ceasefire with varying degrees of triumph, there was growing unease throughout this period among a number of members within the PIRA and Sinn Féin who believed that the leadership was moving away from the ultimate aim of the movement: Irish unity. There was a developing belief that the Sinn Féin leadership in particular was gaining too much control and that their aims were more focused on the full politicization of the movement rather than the "best" way to achieve a united Ireland. This discontent was evident at the rank-and-file level but more significantly for the Army Council, the PIRA leadership body of seven to eight core figures, it was most prominent in the Army Executive, the body that elects the Army Council. The Executive had largely been excluded from the negotiation process to that date. They felt that little to no progress was being made on behalf of Republicans and this was being held back by the British government's refusal to sit down with Sinn Féin officials while also standing firm on the need for a significant move by the Republicans on the issue of decommissioning. Within the Executive the discontent was led by the quartermaster general Michael McKevitt and another key figure, the PIRA director of engineering "Frank McGuinness" (an alias). These were not the only strong voices. Other high-ranking PIRA figures, including key strategist Brian Keenan, also voiced their disapproval.

In January 1996 the Executive called an extraordinary General Army Convention. It was clear to the Army Council that the intention of the Executive was to bring an end to the ceasefire while also ousting the Adams leadership. In a move to prevent this, the Army Council met in the same month and called an end to the (by then) 15-month-long ceasefire. The end was dramatically marked with a huge car bomb detonated in the Docklands area of London's Canary Wharf on 19 February 1996.[46] Adams' remarks about the difficulties faced by the PIRA during the 1975 ceasefire, some 20 years earlier, proved nothing if not prescient.

When the convention eventually took place in October 1996 the Adams leadership had retained some of the membership's faith due to a number of successful PIRA attacks on British security targets. However, they still faced considerable dissent among certain members of the Executive and other delegates. The majority of the motions at the convention were highly critical of the peace process and sought to weaken the power of the Army Council to call extended ceasefires and decommission weapons.[47] One of the most important votes came with the election of the new Army Council by the new Executive. Although it seemed at first that the newly elected Executive would be able to fill the seven-man council with dissident voices alongside Gerry Adams, their hopes were dampened by a last-minute vote of confidence for the peace process from Executive member Brian Keenan and the inability of Frank McGuinness to attend the Convention.[48] The new Council that was finally elected contained a majority loyal to the Adams–McGuinness leadership and therefore the peace process.[49] The role of Keenan is one that should not be underestimated. The seniority and respect that he held within the PIRA provided him with significant influence in Republican circles. In one of a series of interviews with *An Phoblacht/Republican News* in 2008, Keenan outlined his logic for supporting the continued politicization of the Republican struggle and his opposition to the continuation of paramilitary activity:

> At a time of great change we need to constantly lay out the republican vision. We
> need to constantly remind people we are for "equality, liberty, fraternity." We are

against exploitation and inequality. Those who continue to use armed struggle need to hear that message. They also need to be faced with the consequences of their campaign. There is no revolutionary logic to their activities.[50]

In the aftermath of the 1996 convention the tense atmosphere continued within the leadership and membership of Sinn Féin and the PIRA. This did not stop both Adams and McGuinness from issuing statements in the following months about the possibility of another unequivocal ceasefire and Sinn Féin entering into talks parallel to beginning the process of decommissioning.[51]

One of the most significant breakthroughs for the entire peace process came with a change of government in Britain. On 2 May 1997 the electorate voted Tony Blair's Labour Party into power to replace the Conservative government of John Major. One of Blair's most significant cabinet appointments was that of Marjorie "Mo" Mowlam to the position of secretary of state for Northern Ireland. Within weeks of her appointment Mowlam assured the Republican movement that if they declared a ceasefire they would be admitted to all-party talks. This controversial and risky step removed the obstacle of the PIRA decommissioning its arms as a precondition for the leadership to enter talks, much to the anger and concern of Unionist politicians. One of Mowlam's most impressive achievements at this time was simultaneously convincing the Ulster Unionist Party (UUP) to participate in these talks, the success of which was in no small part due to their new UUP leader, David Trimble.[52]

In July 1997 the Army Council responded by voting for another ceasefire. This move was justified to the Executive on tactical grounds. With the rising electoral popularity of the Sinn Féin party and the combined pressure of the British and Irish governments the British set a firm date of September 15 for the start of talks, which would be concluded in May 1998. Internally, however, disquiet grew. There remained a lingering distrust of the Adams leadership within the Executive, especially from McKevitt, Frank McGuinness, and Belfast-based PIRA commander Brian Gillen. They believed that another ceasefire would only succeed in weakening PIRA. So the ceasefire was called without the full support of the Executive.[53]

Although the issue of cessation strengthened the divide between the Army Council and the Executive, it was the Mitchell Principles[54] that heightened the tension to the point of an actual split. Drafted by U.S. senator George Mitchell, the principles were a framework of six core recommendations that were to be met by both Republican and Loyalist paramilitaries in order for their political wings to be able to take part in the political process. To partake in talks the participants had to commit to the following:

1. To democratic and exclusively peaceful means of resolving political issues;
2. To the total disarmament of all paramilitary organizations;
3. To agree that such disarmament must be verifiable to the satisfaction of an independent commission;
4. To renounce for themselves, and to oppose any effort by others, to use force or threaten to use force, to influence the course of the outcome of all-party negotiations;

5. To agree to abide by the terms of any agreement reached in all-party negotiations and to resort to democratic and exclusively peaceful methods in trying to alter any aspect of that outcome with which they may disagree; and

6. To urge that "punishment" killings and beatings stop and to take effective
steps to prevent such actions.[55]

The Executive's position was unequivocal: signing up to the principles would
denounce the very purpose of the PIRA and would be "unconstitutional." Because
members of the Sinn Féin negotiating team such as Adams, Martin McGuinness, and
Pat Doherty were not only members of the political party but were also influential on
the Army Council, they were faced with a critical dilemma. With the Army Council
and Executive in deadlock over whether this was constitutional or not, a General
Army Convention was organized to decide on the matter. The Army Council had
prepared for the Convention and had been assured that they were surrounded by
supporters who agreed with their leadership as well as their stands on the matter of
the Mitchell Principles and the relationship between the Executive and the Council.

In hindsight, the situation was even more precarious than historical accounts
may portray. One of the key factors that swung in their favor was Brian Gillen
changing his affiliation to support Adams' position at the last minute, similar
to the way Brian Keenan had switched his support the previous year. The entire
Convention went in favor of the Adams faction, who were given the support to
enter Stormont talks. The new Executive, still "dissident" to the Adams leadership,
was so by only a margin of two votes. At their first meeting, however, five key
members resigned and left the Provisionals. McKevitt and Frank McGuinness led
the pack. Along with them came the majority of the PIRA's Engineering department and all its Southern Command quartermasters. These breakaways went on
to set up a group they named "Óglaigh na hÉireann" ("Irish Volunteers," a name
with immense historical and cultural significance, and the official name in Gaelic
of the legitimate army of the Irish republic), but who are more commonly referred
to as the Real IRA (a title they quickly adopted to distinguish themselves from the
Provisionals). The official reason for the split was given as the PIRA's acceptance
of the Mitchell Principles.[56] This rejection of the Mitchell Principles is described in
32CSM's description of their support for the Real IRA and its principles:

> Acceptance of the Mitchell principles flew in the face of the very spirit of the Army
> constitution and when an Army convention held in Co. Donegal failed to satisfy
> the concerns of the "Republican camp," a small but significant section of the Army
> leadership withdrew to re-organise Óglaigh na hÉireann along traditional Republican
> lines, in the spirit of the Constitution and outside of the Provisionals' remit.[57]

In a television interview in 2003 representatives of the leadership explained
their continuation of armed struggle. This was an explanation that can also be
viewed as a rationale for their actions from the very outset of their existence:

> We believe that the so called "peace process" is a misnomer and is grounded on a
> false premise that it is the road to a final settlement. We regard the implementation

of the Belfast Agreement and the full participation of the Provisional movement in that process as a classic example of a successful counter-insurgency strategy practiced on the part of the British and Dublin governments. Remember the words of Seamus Mallon, that the entire process was "an exercise in Sunningdale for slow learners." We believe this assertion to be politically accurate and correct and in fact from a Nationalist perspective the 1998 Agreement was a much weaker package than that offered by the Sunningdale Agreement in 1973.[58]

This is a message that was not just to be passed on to the general public but more importantly was meant as a justification for their activity and existence to the wider Republican community. In the immediate aftermath of the splits in both the PIRA and Sinn Féin the Provisional leadership came out in force attempting to deny any split in either organization. Once again *An Phoblacht/Republican News* was used to convey their intended message of Republican unity. On those occasions when representatives did admit to the exit of members the significance of that exit was downplayed: "Those who are set on promoting division or a split within the IRA will themselves be disappointed to learn that the IRA remains intact, united and committed."[59] Furthermore:

Any impact on the IRA of a small number of resignations should be viewed in the context of years of struggle, an IRA source told *An Phoblacht*. During a sustained period of struggle it is perhaps inevitable that individual personnel will change for a number of reasons at different times. Some people may leave for personal or political reasons and many more have been imprisoned. Hundreds of IRA Volunteers have been captured and jailed by the British without undermining the army's ability to sustain itself. Taken in this context a few resignations are not significant, the source maintained. The IRA as an organisation remains intact.[60]

However, the Provisional leadership and membership attempted to deny the impact of the split in vain. The years that followed would prove that although small in number, the Real IRA would commit the worst single atrocity in the history of Irish terrorism. The armed group aligned themselves with the political dissidents, the then 32 County Sovereignty Committee (32CSC), who were led by Francis Mackey and Bernadette Sands-McKevitt, the wife of Michael McKevitt and the sister of Bobby Sands. This group had formed from dissident members of Sinn Féin in December 1997 in opposition to the signing of the Mitchell Principles and in support of the right for Irish Republicans to use armed struggle in the pursuit of national sovereignty.[61]

32CSC was of the belief that the peace talks were failing to deal with the issue of Irish sovereignty, the right for the island to exist as a united country independent of any British influence or control. Central to this was its belief that the Mitchell Principles and the framework documents were guaranteeing the continued existence and implementation of the "Unionist veto."[62] From its origins the group made this issue of sovereignty the cornerstone of its very existence. It was its stated belief that it must be central to all Republicans, not just members of their organization.

In its opinion the first aim of the organization must be to "Seek to achieve broad unity amongst the Republican family on the single issue of Irish Sovereignty."[63]

32CSC set itself up as a political pressure group, and under the leadership of Mackey and Sands-McKevitt went about drafting a paper to present to the United Nations accusing the British of denying Ireland its right to national sovereignty.[64] Their aim has been to present "the case for Irish self-determination before the international community": "We believe that much of the conflict in Ireland could be resolved if the United Nations were to intervene in upholding Irish Sovereignty."[65]

Although CIRA took approximately 8 years to officially announce its existence in the aftermath of the 1986 split, RIRA waited a little more than 6 months to proclaim its arrival. In May 1998, after several months of preparation and organization, the group declared its existence by stating to the media that "the ceasefire as called by the old leadership [of PIRA] is over and our war machine will once again be directed against the British.... a partitionist statement will not bring peace."[66] In addition, the group called for *all* IRA members and Republicans "to remain unified."[67]

The original estimates of membership size of the new grouping were small, but the seniority, experience, and skill levels of those members led to a severe assessment of their intent and capabilities. The Garda (Irish police) Commissioner at the time, Pat Byrne, intimated to the Irish prime minister Bertie Ahern that this new group was the most significant threat faced by the peace process.[68] This assessment proved tragically accurate. On 15 August 1998, only 4 months after the signing of the Good Friday Agreement, the Real IRA detonated a bomb in the County Tyrone town of Omagh that killed 29 people and two unborn babies, and injured at least 300 others.[69] In a move that was to be echoed throughout their existence, the group's immediate reaction was to deflect all blame from themselves. Claiming the civilian deaths were unintentional, they instead suggested that their logic in targeting Omagh was essentially economic in nature: "It was a commercial target.... [This was] part of an ongoing war against the Brits.... We offer apologies to the civilians."[70]

Public outrage, both national and international, was unprecedented, and the pressure felt by the RIRA was palpable. In the immediate aftermath of this deflection of responsibility the group declared a cessation of activity, citing the political and public appeals for a ceasefire: "As a direct result of the Omagh tragedy and also in response to the appeals of Bertie Ahern [Irish prime minister] and others we are currently embarking on a process of consultation on our future direction. In the meantime all military operations have been suspended from 12 midnight."[71]

The RIRA would eventually continue its campaign in the years after Omagh, following a short-lived ceasefire and leadership upheaval. But a resurgent RIRA found it difficult to sustain itself. The movement was decimated with arrests, departures, and infiltration at the highest level, and found it close to impossible to recruit new members. Among the most high-profile arrests were those of McKevitt, Liam Campbell (the RIRA's director of operations), and Colm Murphy, who was arrested for conspiring to cause the Omagh bombing. In October 2002 McKevitt and other imprisoned members of the Real IRA issued a statement calling on the organization to discontinue activity. However, far from heralding the end of the

Real IRA, McKevitt's proclamation was merely the catalyst for yet another division within Irish Republicanism.

■ ÓGLAIGH NA HÉIREANN (RIRA)

Like the CIRA, the RIRA has faced a fractionalization of its own, with the development of the splinter group Óglaigh na hÉireann.[72] This group is believed to be strongest in Belfast, South Armagh, and Louth.[73] At least in public, not as much is known about its origins compared to other VDR groups. However, the split that took place within the RIRA after the Omagh bombing is believed to have had two main causes. First, there was a leadership struggle between Michael McKevitt and Liam Campbell, heralded by a call from McKevitt in 2002 for the RIRA to cease all armed activity. In a statement thought to have been released by McKevitt and his followers, he argued that the time for armed struggle was over and that those outside prison who claimed to be the inheritors of the leadership were essentially corrupt:

> We will not demean our struggle or provide succour to our enemies by revealing the comprehensive catalogue of evidence which has exposed this leadership. However, we do feel duty-bound to state that this Army leadership's financial motivations far outweigh their political commitment to our struggle at this time.

> IRA prisoners find this morally and politically unacceptable. We believe that the current Army leadership has forfeited all moral authority to lead the [Real] IRA. To date, the leadership has failed to respond to our demand. Thus we feel we are left with no option but to withdraw our allegiance from this Army leadership.

> We would like to take this opportunity to reaffirm our commitment to Republican principles and reiterate our steadfast opposition to the Belfast Agreement and British rule in Ireland. Furthermore, in order to dispel recent, mischievous leaks to the media, we would like to state that no IRA prisoners' representative has entered negotiations with any government regarding the early release of political prisoners.
>
> —IRA unit, Portlaoise.[74]

Although the statement claimed to speak on behalf of the [R]IRA unit within Portlaoise, it and its allegations were strongly rejected soon after its publication. Those within the movement who distanced themselves firmly from McKevitt's position publicized contradictory sentiments. This strong rejection of the McKevitt faction was detailed in the 2003 television interview with representatives of the leadership of the RIRA:

> The statement from Portlaoise should be viewed as absolute treachery.... In simple terms the motivation behind the statement was an attempt to force a ceasefire on this Movement by two individuals. They have manipulated a situation for their own selfish agenda. The days of the Republican Movement following false icons are over and we will be guided by our principles and the views of all our Volunteers. Our Volunteers' position is not reflected in the statement from Portlaoise.[75]

This intraorganizational conflict unsurprisingly led to yet another split, this time within the ranks of the Real IRA. After the separation, the new group ONH remained loyal to McKevitt even though he was no longer a significant military actor because of his imprisonment.[76] At the same time there was disquiet among a number of senior members of the Provisional IRA about who had been given the Sinn Féin leadership. They were no longer convinced that the political process would culminate in the ultimate goal of the organization, namely a united Ireland. The disquiet within the PIRA at this stage focused particularly on the issue of full decommissioning of Provisional weapons.

Around the time of the decommissioning, these individuals met with the dissident RIRA members loyal to McKevitt, as well as with dissident members of another splinter group, the Irish National Liberation Army (INLA). The PIRA members defected and formed Óglaigh na hÉireann (ONH) in 2005–2006. The reason they did not join up with another, already existing VDR group was their perception that these groups were disorganized, ineffective, and heavily infiltrated. This was recognized in one of the initial stated aims of the newly forming group: to design an organization that did not lend itself to easy infiltration.[77] Although the group was ostensibly formed in 2005, it is not until 2009 that it became active. The Independent Monitoring Commission (IMC) reports have treated it as an element within the RIRA. However, it is probably more accurate, and mirrors the assertions of ONH representatives themselves, to treat the two groups as separate entities.[78]

The name Óglaigh na hÉireann has proven to be confusing for media, analysts, policy makers, and security forces alike.[79] Meaning *Volunteers of Ireland*, it has been adopted by every group declaring themselves to be the Irish Republican Army but has taken specific prominence in recent times. As noted earlier, this is the name used by the Real IRA itself in 1997, and also that used by the Strabane splinter group when it left the Continuity IRA. However, it is the splinter group created from a schism within the RIRA that has, according to the IMC, proven to be the most dangerous and active of all the VDR groups in recent times.[80]

Unlike the CIRA and the RIRA before them, the formation of ONH was not accompanied by a split in the political wing, 32CSM. Until recently it was believed that ONH had no political wing of any kind. However, at their 2011 Ard Fheis the "political pressure group" Republican Network for Unity (RNU) sent "comradely greetings to Óglaigh na hÉireann." It is widely believed that these greetings were directed toward ONH.

ONH remains a mysterious group, but it contains some important features. It is apparent from the sophistication of the devices the ONH use in its activities that a number of their members are operationally experienced in both the planting of and development of explosive devices. This might suggest the involvement of senior former members of the Provisional IRA, or at least people with paramilitary experience. Prominent examples of this malevolent expertise can be seen in the undercar bomb that seriously injured Catholic PSNI officer Peadar Heffron in January 2010 and the car bomb attack on Palace Barracks in April of that same year. In a 2010 interview with the *Belfast Telegraph,* an ONH representative suggested that the group was using skill-based recruitment. At the formation of the organization, he said, "the vast, vast majority of people who were recruited were deliberately selected for their skills, experience and know-how."[81]

As stated earlier, in conjunction with their high-level attacks ONH has also partaken in a number of punishment attacks and other forms of vigilante "justice." This strategy has been employed by groups and individuals throughout the history of Irish Republicanism, in particular to gain the trust and support of the communities in which they are operating and based. In so doing the groups have aimed to question the credibility and effectiveness of the police service. This is especially important across VDR groups, as one of their central objectives is to discredit the role of the PSNI within Nationalist communities. If they are able to do this successfully, and deter significant numbers of young Catholics from joining the PSNI, they will attempt to claim credit for the PSNI being an "unrepresentative" police force no different from its predecessor, the Royal Ulster Constabulary (RUC).

■ . . . AND THE OTHERS?

CIRA, RIRA, and ONH pose the most significant and consistent threats to peace in Northern Ireland since the Provisional IRA's ceasefire of August 1994. They have proven capable of posing a sustained threat to the security of the region. However, they are not alone. There have been other VDR groups that have been shorter lived and have posed a less sustained threat. Among these are Saor Uladh, The Irish Republican Liberation Army (IRLA), Saoirse na hEireann, and The Republican Defence Army. These groups' short lifespans and the continuous emergence of other new groups often result in confusion among analysts as to their true nature. Short-lived groups often act as fronts for larger paramilitary organizations that do not wish to have their names associated with a particular action (or when the perception of there being more than one group benefits the strategic objectives of a leadership that values the appearance of multiple dissident fronts). This is similar to the mid-1970s, at the birth of the Irish Republican Socialist movement, when the Irish National Liberation Army (INLA) was originally called the People's Liberation Army (PLA) as the leadership of the new group did not wish to have their official name associated with the mistakes of a new organization. Alternatively, some of these groups may be operational for only a small period of time due to their lack of support, preparation, or skilled members.

In 2011 there was the emergence of what at least on the surface appears to be another VDR group. On April 2, 25-year-old Catholic PSNI officer Ronan Kerr was murdered in Omagh when a mercury tilt switch car bomb detonated under his car. The attack was claimed close to 3 weeks later by a new paramilitary organization simply calling itself "the IRA." Although the Omagh murder was the first known action of the group, its existence had been suspected for several months before the attack.[82] However, and consistent with the findings of Martyn Frampton, there are indications that this group may have existed since 2008. Although the group is often referred to as being based in Tyrone, the early indications are that although strong in Tyrone, Lurgan, and south Armagh, it is actually led from Belfast.[83] In a Republican community with an ever-growing number of dissident paramilitary groups, group members emphasize that they are a separate entity from each of the other existing groups, and intend to stay so.

In a statement to media, the group claimed responsibility for the attack on PSNI officer Peadar Heffron as well as the bombing of the Police Board head-quarters, both previously claimed by ONH, as well as the RIRA-claimed attack at Massereene Barracks. This raises the question as to whether the group is in reality aligned with ONH and the RIRA, and possibly is acting as a front group to claim specific attacks. Like all the other groups, its stated aim is to bring about the end of "British occupation" through the use of violence. The group members claim that the imperative for their actions is to ensure that they do not "pass the 'armed struggle' onto a future generation and are determined to end the conflict and achieve Republican goals in their own lifetime."[84]

The true nature and capabilities of this apparent new group at present remain unclear. Early reports (mostly interviews given to trusted journal-ists) suggest that the group consists of a number of former senior members of the Provisional IRA who have become disgruntled with the peace process and Sinn Féin's continued involvement in the political institutions of Northern Ireland. Members state that they left mainstream Republicanism to reengage in paramilitary violence as they have seen "scores of broken promises" made to Republicans, which have not brought a united Ireland any closer and have not created "an Ireland of equals" as Sinn Féin promised at the outset of the pro-cess.[85] In their opinion certain problems brought through from the Troubles have been further exacerbated. They believe that this is particularly true with respect to security laws, as in their opinion tougher laws with respect to "stop and search, arrest and detention" have been introduced recently. Although the murder of Ronan Kerr has been their only claimed attack to date, the group has stated its intent to bring its "struggle to a successful conclusion through military operations."[86]

This emergence of yet another VDR group further emphasizes the faction-alized nature of modern-day dissident Irish Republicanism and the danger the groups pose individually and collectively to the people of Ireland and Great Britain.

■ RAAD AND VIGILANTE REPUBLICANISM

This chapter has so far focused on the traditional paramilitary-style groups. Individually, and at times together, these groups engage in paramilitary activ-ity to promote their ultimate goal of a united Ireland by "defeating the British occupying forces." Their strategies vary from high-level attacks on the PSNI, MI5, and the British army, to the disruptive tactic of an ongoing series of hoax devices and security alerts across Northern Ireland. Chapter 3 explores these activities in greater detail. But although these groups partake in vigilante attacks as a part of their overall strategy, there are violent dissident Republican groups whose sole tactic appears to be the use of vigilante punishment beatings and attacks on known and suspected drug dealers, sex offenders, and other criminals within their communities. The purpose of these attacks is identical to that of the main VDR groups. They want to discredit the PSNI within their communities and promote themselves as the legitimate guardians of the peace, in the hope that they will gain the support of elements of the local population while simultaneously taking control of others through the fear of retribution.

This is not a new phenomenon within Irish Republicanism. In the mid-1990s, for example, the Provisional IRA, operating under the cover name Direct Action Against Drugs (DAAD), shot and killed a number of known and suspected drug dealers across Belfast.[87] Although the three main VDR groups are based and operate across Ireland, and at times in Britain, these "single-issue" vigilante groups are generally based within more localized communities. The most active recently has been Republican Action Against Drugs (RAAD), which operates in the city of Derry and across the border in the Inishowen peninsula in County Donegal. RAAD's membership is largely made up of former members of the Provisional IRA and other Republican groups.[88] The group originated in Derry in 2008 and has since been involved in the continuous targeting of both suspected and known drug dealers within the community. Its stated aims, as detailed in a 2009 interview with a RAAD representative, are to rid the areas of drug dealers: "Our objectives are very simple. We are determined to rid the local community of these individuals. We view them as career criminals whose activities have ruined the lives of so many young people in the past and we're not prepared to tolerate that any longer."[89]

Unlike the other VDR groups, RAAD appears to have consistently claimed all of its violent actions by issuing statements to the *Derry Journal*, and its activity appears to have increased in 2010 and 2011. Although it may benefit the three main VDR groups to create confusion within the media and security services about the attribution of specific attacks,[90] a similar strategy would defeat the purpose of a group such as RAAD, which can successfully discredit the police and gain popular support as a vigilante force[91] if the community knows about its actions. Its strategy does not focus only on direct violence against those involved in the drugs trade; members have also issued a number of threats to drug dealers in which targeted individuals have been ordered to leave the area: "We have been involved in several operations, with active service units punishing those we know are involved in dealing drugs to vulnerable members of the community in Derry. Other dealers have been told to leave the city and never return—or suffer the consequences."[92]

In its threats and attacks, RAAD constantly attempts to convince the community that RAAD is a viable, more effective alternative to the PSNI in the area. The group also highlights the cessation of similar action on the part of the Provisional movement, positioning itself as the only group that can protect the communities the Provisionals have "forgotten":

> These thugs and criminals are under the misguided belief that, because the Provisional movement has forgotten its roots, they [the "thugs and criminals"] now have a free hand to beat and intimidate at will....RAAD will be ferocious in its defence of the republican and Nationalist community. We will target anyone who involves themselves in these activities.[93]

Although RAAD is the most active of the dissident vigilante groups, it is not the only one. Across Ireland, but mainly in Northern Ireland, there are other dissident Republican groups that operate in a similar way. Among them are the Ardoyne-based Concerned Families Against Drugs (CFAD) and a group based in Co. Carlow in the Republic of Ireland that has vowed to "avenge" a crime wave in the town, which the group attributes to Eastern European gangs.[94] Similar to RAAD, CFAD has reportedly participated in attacks on known and suspected drug dealers across North Belfast, some of which have included the use of pipe bombs. However, the group, led by prominent Republican Martin Óg Meehan, has denied these allegations, originally put forward by the IMC.[95] Although the CFAD denies its use of violent tactics in its action against drugs it is apparent that its links to violent dissident Republicanism are significant. Each of these groups has identified a particular social problem in their community and vowed to tackle it through the threat and use of vigilante violence in order to gain the support, respect, and at times fear of elements of the community, while simultaneously discrediting the legitimate police force.

■ NONVIOLENT POLITICAL GROUPS

Not all dissident Republicans engage in illegal or even subversive activities; there are those who express their dissidence through legal and peaceful political action and protest. This can come in the form of protests, demonstrations, meetings, marches, journalistic articles, and statements. The existence of such individuals and groups and their actions demonstrate the ability of disillusioned Republicans to express their discontent with, and their alternative strategy from, Sinn Féin in a peaceful manner. The existence of an alternative voice to Sinn Féin within the Republican community allows the members of that community to have a more open debate and a wider choice of representatives. As we shall see in the concluding chapter, the role of nonviolent dissident groups may be especially significant in quelling the rise of the VDR groups.

Of those nonviolent dissident groups, arguably the most dominant has been Éirígí. Éirígí (Gaelic for "rise up") was established in April 2006 as a political campaign group. However, at their first Ard Fheis in 2007, its membership unanimously voted to become a full political party. Since then it has contested mainly local elections both north and south of the border, with only moderate success. At present, only two Éirígí members had been elected across Ireland.

Like many dissidents before them, Éirígí emerged due to the perceived failings of Sinn Féin. The group came into being at a time when Sinn Féin was performing poorly at the polls south of the border. However, its birth was not solely tied to these electoral failings. It was also linked to the peace process and the view among those forming the new group that Sinn Féin was failing the Republican cause. Leading figure Brian Leeson alluded to this in an interview with Martyn Frampton:

> The IRA was fought to a standstill on the battlefield—or certainly the leadership believed it was fought to a standstill—and they moved the battlefield into the

negotiating arena. There they were defeated. And off the back of that defeat you are now in a period of post-defeat—a historic defeat I would say, with parallels to the post-1921 period. And if you study what happened in 1921 to 1931, republicanism went through the same somersaults, demoralisation, fragmentation, splintering, ever-decreasing circles of frustration.... [96]

The group's policies and strategies have developed beyond this in recent years, while still maintaining its disdain for the strategy of the Sinn Féin leadership. Frampton summarizes Éirígí's narrative as "centred on the inadequacies of the Provisional movement's leadership."[97] The struggle for Irish unity is central to the group. However, this is coupled with a radical economic and social agenda. Therefore traditionally Republican campaigns such as "Campaign for British Withdrawal," "Imperialists Out," and "No British Royal Visits!" sit alongside radical social and economic campaigns such as the environmental campaign to protect Ireland's natural resources "We Only Want the Earth!" and the campaign for wealth equality "The 1% Network." These campaigns have seen Éirígí members operate alongside others from the dissident Republican community as well as partners from the wider national and international socialist family.

The description of Éirígí as a "nonviolent political group" does not necessarily imply that some of its members have not been involved in paramilitary activity. A number of them are former members of the Provisional IRA and other groups. There are also accusations that some of the group's membership is still involved in paramilitary Republicanism. These accusations have largely (but not exclusively) centered on Colin Duffy, a former PIRA prisoner who was charged with the murder of two British soldiers at the Massereene Barracks in March 2009. At least north of the border, Duffy had acted as a spokesman for Éirígí in the time leading up to his arrest. Afterward, Éirígí members, although not showing support for armed action, stopped far short of condemning it. In an interview with *The Irish News,* leading Éirígí member Breandan Mac Cionnaith stated the following:

Éirígí is an open, independent, democratic political party which is not aligned to, or supportive of, any armed organisation. While supporting the right of any people to defend themselves from imperial aggression, Éirígí does not believe that the conditions exist at this time for a successful armed struggle against the British occupation. As can be seen from the recent attacks on Britain's armed forces it is clear that not all republicans agree on how the British occupation should be resisted at this time. Those who carried out those attacks are best placed to explain their own rationale.[98]

To date Éirígí has retained a principal focus on nonviolent protest and campaigning, coupled with electoral participation as its main strategy of achieving a socially equal united Ireland. As with all the dissent groups it is relatively small in number. However, its ability to campaign alongside like-minded groups has provided the group with a louder voice in its campaigns. Although Éirígí is not the only purely political dissident group, it is the most prominent.

■ CONCLUSIONS

The goal of this chapter has been to introduce the relevant VDR groups and their origins. As complex as the individual group histories are, a comprehensive account of each group probably merits a book-length treatise on its own. As it is, along with Chapter 1, we now have the context for a closer analysis of what the dissidents do, and who specifically does it. From the descriptions presented in this chapter, the story behind the origins of each of the paramilitary dissident groups reveals some common threads. Central to their origins has been the issue of politicization or demilitarization of the parent grouping. From the CIRA right up to "the IRA," this issue has remained a predictable catalyst for the formation of new dissident organizations. Invariably one group wishes to maintain or expand political involvement to the perceived detriment of paramilitary activity, whereas the other views a continuation, expansion, or return to armed struggle as a fundamental necessity if it is to achieve its overall goal of a united Ireland.

However, closer examination suggests that strategic, goal-oriented, or organizational issues are often barely as important, and at times less important, than overriding personality figures and prevailing social issues. Understanding at least the contours of the origins of these groups allows us to better understand the strategic positions associated with each group. This, in turn, equips us with the tools to understand the significance of the nature and extent of the group's armed action.

What follows in Chapter 3 is an analysis of the event data in the VDR database. This analysis focuses on VDR activity, across all the relevant groups, from 1997 to 2011. Although some of these events may have been mentioned in the present and previous chapter they should by no means be seen as a comprehensive list of VDR events. Rather they have been used to illustrate the kinds of activities in which each group engages. Each of the chapters to follow focuses mainly on the paramilitary and vigilante groups, but the nonviolent groups and their members are also addressed (if briefly) in order to provide a fuller picture of contemporary dissident Republicanism.

■ NOTES

1. This is how Irish Republicans refer to Northern Ireland.

2. Representative of the Continuity IRA Belfast Brigade speaking on RTE's *Prime Time,* 19 April 2011.

3. The split of 1969–1970 resulted in the formation of the Provisional IRA.

4. 1986 and 1997 splits combined have proven to be major stepping stones in the politicization of the Provisional Republican movement. See Morrison, J. F. 2010. *"The Affirmation of Behan?": An Understanding of the Politicisation Process of the Provisional Irish Republican Movement Through an Organisational Analysis of Splits from 1969 to 1997.* Ph.D. dissertation, University of St. Andrews.

5. For a more extensive list and description of the existing dissident groupings, as well as other relevant organizations, see Frampton, M. 2010. *The Return of the Militants: Violent Dissident Republicanism.* London: The International Center for the Study of Radicalisation and Political Violence. Pp. 4–5.

6. The phrase "microgroups" is one that has been adopted by Sinn Féin in their description, dismissal, and condemnation of the continued action of the VDR groups. See, for example, "Martin McGuinness Distances Himself From Gerry Adams by Issuing a Fuller Condemnation of N Ireland Shootings." *The Telegraph,* 17 March, 2009. www.telegraph. co.uk/news/worldnews/europe/ireland/5008395/Martin-McGuinness-distances-hims elf-from-Gerry-Adams-by-issuing-fuller-condemnation-of-N-Ireland-shootings.html. Accessed May 18, 2011.

7. The IRA was restructured in this fashion in the late 1970s.

8. This strategy of a long war was articulated by Jimmy Drumm in Bodenstown in June 1977.

9. Frampton, M. 2009. *The Long March: The Political Strategy of Sinn Féin, 1981–2007.* London: Palgrave Macmillan. Pp. 10–11.

10. In 1978 Gerry Adams took over from Daithi O'Conaill as joint secretary of Sinn Féin.

11. Clarke, L. 1987. *Broadening the Battlefield: The H-Blocks and the Rise of Sinn Féin.* Dublin: Gill and Macmillan. P. 29.

12. Taylor, P. 1998. *Provos: The IRA and Sinn Féin.* London: Bloomsbury. Pp. 281–282.

13. O'Rawe, R. 2005. *Blanketmen: An Untold Story of the H-Block Hunger Strike.* Dublin: New Island Books; O'Rawe, R. 2010. *Afterlives: The Secret Offer and the Fate of the Hunger Strikers.* Dublin: Lilliput Press.

14. Feeney, B. 2002. *Sinn Fein: A Hundred Turbulent Years.* Dublin: O'Brien. Pp. 320–321.

15. This was required as it was a proposed constitutional change.

16. White, R. 2010. "Structural Identity Theory and the Post-Recruitment Activism of Irish Republicans: Persistence, Splits, and Dissidents in Social Movement Organizations." *Social Problems, 57*(3), 341–370.

17. Frampton, M. 2011. *Legion of the Rearguard: Dissident Irish Republicanism.* Dublin: Irish Academic Press.

18. See Murray, G., & Tonge, J. 2005. *Sinn Féin and the SDLP: From Alienation to Participation.* Dublin: O'Brien. Pp. 136–152.

19. They believed that they were still the legitimate Sinn Féin and therefore the meeting that followed in their eyes was a continuation of the Ard Fheis and those who stayed with the Adams leadership could no longer be regarded as Sinn Féin and therefore were the dissidents.

20. Members of Republican Sinn Féin do not regard this as a new party and believe that they are a continuation of Sinn Féin and that the Adams led Sinn Féin are the ones who have deviated.

21. However, this statement was not publicized until 1996. Ó Brádaigh, R. 1997. *Dilseacht: The Story of Comdt. General Tom Maguire and the Second (All Ireland) Dail.* Dublin: Elo Press.

22. Maguire had similarly declared the Provisionals to be the legitimate IRA in 1969.

23. To this day Republican Sinn Féin declares no official affiliation with the Continuity IRA but it is broadly acknowledged that the link does exist.

24. See Twenty Second Report of the Independent Monitoring Committee, November 4 2009. Paragraphs 2.2–2.9.

25. Frampton, M. 2009. *The Long March: The political Strategy of Sinn Fein, 1981–2007.* London: Palgrave Macmillan.

26. Mooney, J. 2009. "Real IRA May Be the Winners of the Continuity's Big Split." *The Sunday Times,* 4 October.

27. *Prime Time,* 19 April 2011.

28. "RSF Will Not Yield to Threats." *Saoirse,* June 2010, p. 1.

29. See, for example, *Late Liam Kenny Was a True Republican,* June 9, 2011. www.sinnfeinpoblachtach.com/pressreleases.htm.

30. Frampton, 2011, p. 244.

31. Frampton, M. 2010. *The Return of the Militants: Violent Dissident Republicanism.* London: International Centre for the Study of Radicalisation. Pp. 2–3.

32. IMC Report 18, paragraph 2.3.

33. Frampton, 2009, p. 59.

34. Moloney, E. 2003. *A Secret History of the IRA.* London: W.W. Norton.

35. Frampton, 2009, p. 91.

36. Mallie, E., & McKittrick, D. 1996. *The Fight for Peace: The Secret Story Behind the Irish Peace Process.* London: William Heinemann (see especially pp. 189–212 and 270–275).

37. The two national premiers at the time.

38. English, R. 2006. *Irish Freedom: The History of Nationalism in Ireland.* London: Pan Books. Pp. 403–407.

39. Frampton, 2009, pp. 91–92.

40. The Joint Declaration of 15 December 1993 (Downing St. Declaration). Paragraph 4.

41. Moloney, 2003, pp. 417–418.

42. Ibid., pp. 418–422.

43. The membership was being told that the option of the armed struggle was still there although the constitutional nationalists were informed that the leadership wished to move forward with purely political strategies. This is best illustrated through the use and manipulation of the TUAS document. Ibid. p. 423 and Bean, K. 2007. *The New Politics of Sinn Féin.* Liverpool: Liverpool University Press. Pp. 118–120.

44. Moloney, 2003, pp. 424–425.

45. McDonald, H. 2008. *Gunsmoke and Mirrors: How Sinn Féin Dressed Up Defeat as Victory.* Dublin: Gill and Macmillan. Pp. 149–151.

46. Moloney, 2003, pp. 433–441.

47. An issue that was significantly on the agenda with the introduction of Senator George Mitchell to the Peace Process. Mitchell issued six principles of nonviolence that would govern political talks. De Breadun, D. 2008. *The Far Side of Revenge: Making Peace in Northern Ireland.* Cork: The Collins Press. Pp. 15–16

48. McGuinness missed one of his connecting pick-ups to the Convention; similar to both 1986 and 1969 this is treated as suspicious by the dissidents and they believe that it was purposively organized by Adams loyalists.

49. Moloney, 2003, pp. 445–454 and also Mooney, J., & O'Toole, M. 2003. *Black Operations: The Secret War Against the Real IRA.* Meath: Maverick House. Pp. 22–23

50. Keenan, B. 2008. "The Brian Keenan Interview: Revolutionaries have to be pragmatic—wish lists are for Christmas." *An Phoblacht/Republican News.* April 10, p. 11.

51. Moloney, 2003, pp. 454–457.

52. Taylor, 1998, p. 354.

53. Moloney, 2003, pp. 464–473.

54. A set of principles put forward by Senator George Mitchell, in addition to his report on decommissioning, which essentially required any paramilitary groups entering into talks to commit to the use of exclusively peaceful means in the pursuit of their political objectives. Guelke, A. 1999. "Political Violence and Paramilitaries." In P. Mitchell & R. Wilford (Eds.), *Politics in Northern Ireland* (pp. 29–53; also see pp. 44–45). Oxford: Westview Press.

55. Coogan, T. P. 2002. The IRA, p. 694.

56. Moloney, 2003, pp. 468–479; Taylor, 1988, pp. 355–363.

57. Background and Objectives." *32CSM,* www.32csm.info/aboutus.html. Accessed, July 14, 2011.

58. RIRA Televised Interview, February 2003, irelandsown.net/rira3.html. Accessed July 13, 2011.

59. "Split Stories Slammed: IRA Talks to An Phoblacht." *An Phoblacht/Republican News,* November 13, 1997.

60. "Media Reports 'Greatly Exaggerated' —IRA". *An Phoblacht/Republican News,* November 13 1997.

61. Taylor, 1988, pp. 358–359.

62. "Background and Objectives." *32CSM,* www.32csm.info/aboutus.html. Accessed July 14, 2011.

63. Ibid.

64. Mooney & O'Toole, 2003, pp. 47–49.

65. "Background and Objectives." *32CSM,* www.32csm.info/aboutus.html. Accessed July 14, 2011.

66. Breen, S. 1998. "Military Attacks to Resume say IRA Dissidents." *Irish Times,* May 9.

67. Ibid.

68. Brady, T. 1998. "Dissident Provos Declare New 'War.'" *Irish Independent,* May 9.

69. De Breadun, 2008, pp. 168–172.

70. "First Statement issued by the 'real' IRA, 18 August 1998," *Cain,* cain.ulst.ac.uk/events/peace/docs/rira18898a.htm. Accessed July 13, 2011.

71. "Second Statement issued by the 'real' IRA, 18 August 1998," *Cain,* cain.ulst.ac.uk/events/peace/docs/rira18898b.htm. Accessed July 13, 2011.

72. Breen, S. 2009. "Unshakeable Believers in the Power of the Bullet." *Sunday Tribune,* 15 March.

73. Brady, T. 2010. "Óglaigh na hÉireann Is Now the Main Threat." *The Belfast Telegraph,* 2 December. Also see BBC News Online. 2010. "Who Are The Dissidents?" 23 August. www.bbc.co.uk/news/uk-northern-ireland-10732264. Accessed July 28, 2011.

74. *Irish Independent.* 2001. "Republican Prisoners Statement Portlaoise." 20 October.

75. RIRA Televised Interview, February 2003 irelandsown.net/rira3.html. Accessed July 13, 2011.

76. Brady, T. 2010. "Óglaigh na hÉireann Is Now the Main Threat." *The Belfast Telegraph,* 2 December.

77. Rowan, B. 2010. "Dissidents: Interview with Terror Splinter Group." *The Belfast Telegraph,* 2 December

78. Ibid.

79. See IMC Report 25, footnote 12.

80. IMC Report 25, paragraph 2.28.

81. Rowan, 2010.

82. Belfast Newsletter. 2011. "Freed Republicans 'May Be Sent Back to Prison.'" 7 February. www.newsletter.co.uk/news/local/freed_republicans_may_be_sent_back_to_prison_1_2387860. Accessed July 12, 2011.

83. Breen, S. 2011. "Former Provos Claim Kerr Murder and Vow More Attacks." *Belfast Telegraph,* 22 April. www.belfasttelegraph.co.uk/news/local-national/northern-ireland/former-provos-claim-kerr-murder-and-vow-more-attacks-15146426.html#ixzz1SFCIlO00. Accessed July 12, 2011.

84. Ibid.

85. Ibid.

86. Ibid.

87. Moloney, 2003, p. 437.

88. *Londondery Sentinel*. 2010. "RAAD Has Dissident Links." 3 June. www.londonder-rysentinel.co.uk/news/local/raad_has_dissident_links_1_2102164.

89. *Derry Journal*. 2009. "Only Way to Eradicate Drugs Scourge Is to Remove the Dealers." 18 August. www.derryjournal.com/news/local/only_way_to_Eradicate_drugs_scourge_is_to_remove_the_dealers_1_2139827. Accessed July 13.

90. See Rowan, 2010.

91. For a detailed interview with a representative from RAAD about the origins and stated aims of the group see *Derry Journal*. 2009. "Only Way to Eradicate Drugs Scourge Is to Remove the Dealers." 18 August.

92. Ibid.

93. *Derry Journal*. 2011. "'We Will Defend Our Community': RAAD." 13 July. www.der-ryjournal.com/news/local/we_will_defend_our_community_raad_1_2856060. Accessed 12 July 2011.

94. *The Nationalist*. 2011. "Gang War," June. www.carlow-nationalist.ie/tabId/369/itemId/10397/Gang-war.aspx.

95. BBC News Online. 2009. "Concerned Families Against Drugs Meets IMC." 9 December. news.bbc.co.uk/2/hi/uk_news/northern_ireland/8403069.stm. Accessed August 2, 2011.

96. Frampton, 2011, p. 230.

97. Frampton, 2011, p. 231.

98. *Irish News*. 2009. "Eirigi Is Not Aligned to or Supportive of Any Armed Organisation, Spokesman Says." 13 March. saoirse32.blogsome.com/2009/03/14/eirigi-is-not-aligned-to-or-supportive-of-any-armed-organisation-spokesman-says/. Accessed July 14, 2011.

3 The Rise of Dissident Activity[1]

■ INTRODUCTION

Now that we have established the context in which the dissidents operate, we can examine more closely precisely what they do. This chapter focuses on Violent Dissident Republican (VDR) activity from 31 August 1994 to 8 July 2011. The analysis presented here considers some overall emerging trends in VDR activity while dissecting specific aspects of it. Violent dissident activity is characterized by bombings (both successful and attempted), hoaxes, threats, and shootings. There are discernible temporal and geographic patterns in it, as well as patterns in victimization and targeting behaviors. The data also suggest that we can consider VDR activity as having taken place in three distinct waves thus far.

Event Databases

Since 2001, the academic and counterterrorism communities have increasingly relied on the development of data-driven research, both to inform an awareness of changes and trends in terrorist activity and to provide a context for decisions made both in military and political policy. In general, the function of these databases is to provide comprehensive, systematically collected (and verified) data on terrorist events. This in turn can help inform analysis by helping to detect any underlying patterns, generate estimates of future activity, and, as suggested by Schmid,[2] contextualize the success of counterterrorism strategies.

In their 2011 overview of 20 such databases, Bowie and Schmid[3] observe that the majority of these focus on documenting terrorist events. Perhaps the best known of these are the START Global Terrorism Database (GTD). Notably absent from unclassified database efforts, however, has been a repository for data on those responsible for this activity—the terrorists themselves. Although some exceptional initiatives (e.g., Smith and Damphousse's *American Terrorism Study*[4]) have focused on specific geographic regions, most databases that include data on actors tend to do so at the group or organizational level. There is far less systematic, data-driven knowledge at the unclassified level about those who engage in terrorist activity as well as precisely what they do. This is despite the fact that it has never been easier in a practical sense to collect and collate, from open sources, information on who has engaged in terrorism. Furthermore, those actor-level databases that are well known to researchers in the field (e.g., Marc Sageman's[5] database on al-Qaeda militants) tend to be privately held and unavailable to the broader research community. Others, often available on a commercial basis, lack both transparency and rigor in their inclusion criteria and are constructed without any meaningful front-end input from eventual end-users.

Bowie and Schmid list seven shortcomings of current database efforts:

1. One-sidedness
2. Underreporting of failed and foiled attacks and threats
3. Political violence other than terrorism is not reported, or is underreported
4. Nonreporting of nonviolent and not violent activities of terrorists
5. Absence of monitoring of nonpolitical, criminal intimidation
6. Absence of parallel systematic monitoring of terrorist communications
7. Inadequate coverage of state or regime terrorism[6]

The purpose of the events database of the International Center for the Study of Terrorism (ICST) VDR project is to answer the following question: *What does VDR activity look like and how has it developed over time?* The wording and specific focus of this question directly deal with a number of the issues raised by Bowie and Schmid. Within the question there is no mention of *terrorism*, and therefore the definitional debate has not affected the nature of the data gathered; as the aim is to gain an overall understanding of what VDR activity looks like, the data are not just restricted to what can be defined as *terrorist* activity. VDR activity goes beyond terrorism, and those who engage even in violent dissident activity are not necessarily solely engaged in violent activity. Among other actions the VDR events database also includes data on involvement in organized crime and vigilantism. It also catalogues failed and foiled attacks and threats, nonviolent and nonpolitical violence attributed to the relevant actors, and nonpolitical, criminal intimidation.

Bowie and Schmid's shortcoming number 6, "absence of parallel systematic monitoring of terrorist communications," is also addressed. As we will see in Chapter 5, part of the focus of the research that led to this book is to consider how VDR groups portray and justify their actions as well as attempting to place their activity within a strategic context. This includes an analysis of the primary documents and statements produced by the paramilitary groups as well as by their nonviolent wings. Although Bowie and Schmid's shortcoming number 1, "one-sidedness," is not directly addressed in the database, throughout the research there has been a continued examination of the public actions and statements of those who counter the VDR threat. Without this understanding it is possible that the data would have been misinterpreted through a failure to contextualize the results within the overall situation in Ireland and Britain. The final issue raised by Bowie and Schmid is that of state or regime terrorism. If this were a database aiming to understand all forms of terrorism, it would be vital to include state or regime terrorism. However, due to the specific VDR focus, this issue is not relevant here.

In the design process of the database, we analyzed the structures of existing databases and identified not only their shortcomings but also their strengths. This provided a framework on which to base the design of the codebook and the overall database itself. Similar to the ITERATE database, and others, each entry contains both quantitative and qualitative information on each event including basic information on location, group responsibility, and the number of deaths and injuries.[7] It also contains detailed qualitative information on the consequences of each event. The database is divided into six sections, each containing a number of individual elements[8]:

1. Timing
2. Location
3. Responsibility
4. Event Type
5. Direct Victims
6. Summary and Sources[9]

For the purpose of event identification the suggestions of the Criteria Committee of the START Global Terrorism Database (GTD) provided insight into how best to gather data. Similar to the GTD, the ICST VDR project relies on the utility of exclusively open-source data. To overcome the bias present in the reporting, we took into account the suggestion of their Criteria Committee and made it a requirement of the database, where possible, to provide at least two independent sources of information.[10] These sources include media reports, both at national and local levels; official reports; and statements and publications attributed to the VDR groups themselves. This has strengthened both the reliability and validity of the data. What follows is a detailed analysis of the events data collected, with a focus on events between 31 August 1994 and 8 July 2011.

▪ THE "BIG PICTURE"

Low-level terrorist activity by Irish Republican splinter groups has escalated and has recently reached its highest level in 10 years. For the 17-year period under analysis the events database has records on a total of 1244 primary events; 899 of these were violent, 194 were nonviolent, and 151 were labeled as threats of violence.[11] There has been a steady stream of violent events since 1997, with 2010 seeing a dramatic increase. This pattern is consistent with increased activity in both 2008 and 2009. In 2010, 238 violent events were recorded. Prior to 2010 the highest annual rates were 118 in 2009, 56 in 2001, and 39 in 1998, the year of the Omagh bombing. However, 149 VDR events were recorded by 8 July 2011, already making it the second most violent year in our database; by the same date in 2010, only 109 violent events had been recorded.

Figure 3.1 presents an overview of violent dissident Republican activity from 1994 to the present day.

An immediate pattern is unclear, though a dramatic rise in dissident activity from 2009 is unequivocal. However, it is only when these data are analyzed at a microlevel that the evolution of VDR activity becomes more apparent. The data indicate that there have been, to date, three separate waves of VDR activity.

- **Wave 1:** 31 August 1994–15 August 1998
- **Wave 2:** 16 August 1998–27 January 2007
- **Wave 3:** 28 January 2007–the present day

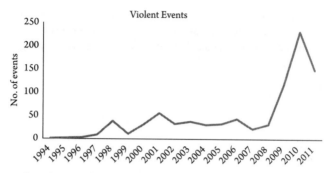

Figure 3.1. Violent dissident Republican activity 31 August 1994—8 July 2011.

The Omagh bombing of 1998 killed more people, 29, than any other single attack.[12] Since then, two people have been killed by VDR bombings: David Caldwell in August 2002 (the civilian building contractor killed by a booby-trapped bomb) and PSNI officer Ronan Kerr in April 2011. As displayed in Tables 3.1 and 3.2, the more discriminate tactics have proven to be the most lethal in Waves 2 and 3. Both of these men died as a result of victim-activated devices. The data show that the more lethal tactic employed by the groups in Waves 2 and 3 involves shootings: 10 people were killed in VDR shootings in Wave 2 and 18 in Wave 3.

A similar but not identical pattern is observed when injuries are analyzed. As with the number of deaths, the figure of 270+ injuries from bombings in Wave 1 is largely the result of the Omagh tragedy. Similar injury levels have not been reached in either of the other two waves, with 42 people being injured from bombings in Wave 2 and 20 in Wave 3. The most prevalent reasons for injuries in these later waves are riots and shootings/punishment attacks. Riot-related injuries tend to be less severe than those sustained by any of the other tactics and it is at times difficult to determine from the open sources whether all the injuries were purposefully inflicted by members of VDR groups, even when the groups acknowledged responsibility for the riots.

Although the riot figures do not provide clear indications of intentionality, the 109 people injured due to VDR shootings clearly signal group intentions. Included in the shooting statistics are all VDR shootings, encompassing shootings with broader (national) political motives *and* narrower (local) vigilante motives. The majority of these shootings relate to vigilantism. Consecutive IRAs have used this tactic over time in their respective efforts to assert control in their communities, acting as self-proclaimed judges, juries, and executioners.

TABLE 3.1. *Violent Dissident Republican Deaths*

	Wave 1	Wave 2	Wave 3	Total
Bomb	29	1	1	31
Shooting	0	10	18	28
Total	29	11	19	59

TABLE 3.2. *Violent Dissident Republican Injuries*

	Wave 1	Wave 2	Wave 3	Total
Bomb	270+	42	20	332
Shooting/punishment attacks	0	14	95	109
Assault	0	3	16	19
Riots	14	130+	110+	254+
Total	284+	189+	241+	714+

N = 233.

▪ WAVE 1: 31 AUGUST 1994–15 AUGUST 1998

Even though the first of the VDR groups, the Continuity IRA (CIRA), was established as early as 1986, the first true wave of VDR activity did not begin until after the first Provisional IRA (PIRA) ceasefire of 1994. Before the ceasefire, the CIRA focused its efforts on preparations for an armed campaign. It had neither large numbers of personnel nor weaponry and consequently was not able to have an immediate paramilitary impact.[13] However, even at the beginning of this initial wave of activity, the onset of VDR activity was slow and gradual in nature. As Figure 3.2 illustrates, the initial period of this first wave showed very little VDR activity. However, the last 2 years of the wave, 1997 and 1998, are noted for a significant spike in activity, with violent events rising from 9 in 1997 to 39 in 1998.

The first 4 years of Wave 1 are characterized by the gradual rise of CIRA activity. However, it was not until the emergence of the Real IRA (RIRA) in the aftermath of the 1997 split with the PIRA that there was a significant spike in activity. In 1998 there were 24 violent events attributed to the RIRA or the RIRA/CIRA. These attacks alone surpassed the activity of any other previous year. Events classed as "RIRA/CIRA" are those attributed to, or claimed by, both groups by at least two

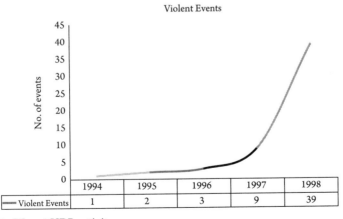

Violent Events					
	1994	1995	1996	1997	1998
Violent Events	1	2	3	9	39

Figure 3.2. Wave 1 VDR activity.

different sources. Although this may at times be due to an attribution error by one or more of the sources, the multiple group events recorded for this year and others may also demonstrate the potential for coalition. There is no predominant policy of collaboration between any of the VDR groups. However, there have been examples of this on occasion, notably the Omagh bombing of 1998. This was a combined action by the CIRA and RIRA with a crossover of operatives involved in planting the bomb and calling in the inaccurate warning.[14]

As expected, the majority of the violence in this wave, as well as in the subsequent two waves, was based in Northern Ireland; only nine of the 54 violent acts took place outside of Northern Ireland, all but one in the Republic of Ireland. The exception involved the interception of a number of RIRA bombs in London in the summer of 1998; the bombs were intended to target a variety of locations across the city. Three men—Anthony Hyland, Liam Grogan, and Darren Mulholland—were all convicted of conspiring to cause explosions in London. The RIRA returned to the strategy of targeting major cities in England in Wave 2.[15] All but one of the nine acts in total that took place in the Republic of Ireland served the purpose of either funding or strengthening the resurgent campaign in the North; they included two robberies and six bombs that were intercepted and defused. It is believed that all of these bombs were destined for planned attacks in Northern Ireland.

■ WAVE 2: 16 AUGUST 1998–27 JANUARY 2007

If the trajectory of violence in Wave 1 is defined as consistently upward, Wave 2 is notable for the highly sporadic level of activity. In the immediate aftermath of the Omagh bombing there was a significant decline. Omagh happened in mid-August, and for the remaining four and a half months of 1998 there were only two clearly registered violent acts, a CIRA-claimed gun attack on police[16] between Moy and Portadown in County Armagh and a mortar equipment test that took place between Crossmaglen and Forkhill, also in Armagh. In the following year, 1999, there were only 12 known violent events.

The dip is easy to explain—it was caused by the ceasefire announced by the RIRA in the aftermath of the Omagh bombing and the various counterdissident initiatives taken by police on both sides of the border in the aftermath of the attack. These included the arrest and incarceration of a number of suspected leading members of the RIRA, including Mickey McKevitt, Liam Campbell, Seamus McKenna, Seamus Daly, and Colm Murphy. With these leading members and others in prison and thus "out of action," the RIRA was significantly debilitated. However, the leadership regrouped in 1999 and relaunched its campaign of violence with a partially exploded bomb at the Shackleton barracks in Derry.[17]

With the reorganization and return to violence, VDR activity rose in intensity once more, reaching a new high of 56 violent events in 2001 alone. Although this was the highest level attained within this wave, the annual figure never dropped below 31 events for the next 5 years.

The group attribution data for this wave reveal the inconsistent nature of both RIRA and CIRA activity. Both groups showed little or no recorded activity in 1999.

However, the RIRA was particularly resurgent in 2000 due to the reorganization. Within this wave both groups regularly revived their activities by first replenishing lost members. Recruitment and training of new members took considerable effort during this time. This training, often not revealed until cases came to court of dissidents arrested for training and "membership" offenses a year or two later, often took place in remote rural parts of the Republic of Ireland. It involved a number of new recruits partaking in paramilitary drills and weapons training from older more experienced members. Between 1999 and 2003 several members attending such training camps were arrested in Meath, Tipperary, and twice in Kildare, and subsequently convicted. This continuous disruption of VDR training and the discovery of a number of significant arms finds were key factors in the groups' failure to mount sustained campaigns of violence.

Yet despite the arrests, the dissidents proved nothing if not resourceful. Within this wave the two groups targeted both army barracks and police stations; the RIRA also launched a bombing campaign in mainland Britain that included audacious and highly symbolic attacks on the headquarters of both the BBC and MI6 in London.[18] However, as with Omagh, a number of successful arrests and consequent convictions by the British police further weakened the organization. The attacks may have been dramatic and high profile, but the RIRA was paying a high price for its efforts. This wave culminated with attacks that focused on the targeting of economic targets, as well as members, both past and present, of the District Policing Partnership in Northern Ireland.[19] By this time, the dissidents' attack pattern was beginning to emerge. In each wave, activity takes place in condensed periods of time, with similar target types attacked within a short space of time.

An example of this can be seen in April 2006 where within a week, two members (one former) of the District Policing Board and a former PSNI officer were targeted within the Sion Mills area of Strabane, County Tyrone. All three were targeted with pipe bombs because of their affiliation with the police. These attacks were all carried out by the newly emerging ONH (CIRA), which was cultivating a strategy of targeting the police. They took place against a backdrop of contentious political debate within mainstream Republicanism about the potential acceptance of the PSNI by Sinn Féin.

Across all three waves of VDR activity there are a number of event clusters that suggest at least a short-term focused strategic plan. There are examples of condensed, sustained levels of activity focusing on one specific type of target in order to emphasize a specific message. Within Wave 2 these targets were largely, but not exclusively, policing structures and personnel as well as some economic targets.

Others have commented on the nature of the activity, and the broader context in which it both emerged and faded. Frampton notes that this wave of activity came to an end as the political wings of the main VDR groups, Republican Sinn Féin and 32CSM, were less capable than ever before of having any effect on the political agenda of Northern Ireland, and at a time when both the CIRA and the RIRA had endured a number of setbacks that weakened their operational capacity.[20] The result was a near cessation of activity until 2007.

There is no question that toward the end of this period, both the CIRA and the RIRA were suffering from significant organizational setbacks. Internal feuding was rife, and probably not helped by the successes the police were having in continuing to disrupt dissident activity on the whole. Furthermore, Sinn Féin was by that point deeply committed to the ongoing politicization process, consistently drawing support from the Republican and Nationalist electorate across Northern Ireland. VDR groups and their political wings were becoming less relevant to the people they claimed to represent.[21] But eventually, as we shall see in Chapter 6, the groups began to use the pressure, which many felt would lead to their ultimate decline, as a mobilizing force and a source of psychological strength.

The path to peace for Sinn Féin in particular was far from smooth, and in hindsight it may be easy to forget the crisis-driven nature of how that process was choreographed and allowed to unfold. There were a number of occasions when the Stormont Assembly had to be suspended for sustained periods due to perceived irreconcilable differences. Frampton notes the irony that these stumblings did not represent, or at least were not taken as, opportunities for the dissidents to strengthen their own influence and support. In these periods they did not mount any form of credible challenge to Sinn Féin within the Republican community. Although Sinn Féin lacked results the dissidents still lacked credibility and strength within Republicanism: "… an implicit assumption … has been that the [Good Friday] Agreement and its institutions represent the best antidote to the challenge of violent dissident republicanism. Yet, in reality, the period in which the Agreement was almost wholly in abeyance also marked the nadir of violent dissident republicanism."[22]

One of the most significant elements toward the end of Wave 2 was the proliferation of splits within the Republican movement, which led to the emergence of a number of new VDR groups. The most significant of these proved to be the two ONHs, ONH (CIRA) and ONH (RIRA). This multiplication of VDR groups further emphasized the complete disarray within dissident Republicanism at this time.

As with each of the waves, the geographic focus of violent and illegal activity was Northern Ireland, where 237 of the 283 events took place. However, as at the end of Wave 1, the turn of the twenty-first century saw the RIRA partake in a short-lived bombing campaign in Britain. This and two significant arms finds in Strathclyde, Scotland, and Lancashire, England account for the 12 events in Great Britain during this period. The analysis of bombings and shootings includes a more localized focus on the geographic hubs of activity. Table 3.3 displays a percentage

TABLE 3.3. *Wave 2 Northern Irish County-Based Activity*

	RIRA	CIRA	RIRA/CIRA	Other	Unknown	Total %
Antrim	14.1%	10.73%	1.72%	0%	15.02%	41.57%
Armagh	5.15%	5.58%	0%	0%	4.3%	15.03%
Derry	10.3%	0.86%	0.43%	0%	3.86%	15.45%
Down	7.73%	2.58%	0%	0.43%	2.58%	13.32%
Fermanagh	0.43%	4.3%	0%	0.43%	0.86%	6.02%
Tyrone	3.43%	2.58%	0%	0.43%	2.15%	8.59%
Total %	41.14%	26.63%	2.15%	1.29%	28.77%	100%

$N = 263$.
RIRA, Real IRA; CIRA, Continuity IRA.

TABLE 3.4. *Wave 2 Violent Dissident Republican Activity by Population Size*

	RIRA	CIRA	RIRA/CIRA	Other	Unknown	Total %
Under 2,000	8.37%	3.8%	0%	0%	2.28%	14.45%
2,000–10,000	3.8%	3.8%	0.38%	0.76%	0.76%	9.5%
10,001–50,000	12.55%	6.84%	0.76%	0%	8.37%	28.52%
50,001–100,000	5.32%	0.38%	0.38%	0%	3.8%	9.88%
Over 100,000	13.31%	12.54%	2.28%	0%	11.41%	39.54%
Total %	43.35%	27.36%	3.8%	0.76%	26.62%	100%

RIRA, Real IRA; CIRA, Continuity IRA.

breakdown of activity location and group attribution over the course of the wave at a Northern Irish county level.

The most striking observation from this county-level activity data is the predominance of Antrim-based activity. This is because, during Wave 2, a large proportion of VDR activity took place in Belfast, where both the RIRA and the CIRA focused their efforts. If the large amount of unattributed activity is taken into consideration, it is likely that the CIRA and RIRA activity in this county is even higher than the data initially suggest. Although the RIRA had significant levels of activity in the city of Derry (10.3%), the CIRA had close to no activity in the county (0.86%), in spite of the fact that it was the second largest county for VDR activity. One possible explanation for this is that there may have been a strong RIRA unit operating in the county during Wave 2, with little to no CIRA presence. This is reversed on a smaller scale when Fermanagh is assessed. Even though this county had the lowest level of activity in Northern Ireland, it did host the third highest level of CIRA activity (4.3%) and the lowest level of RIRA activity (0.43%).

An assessment of the population size of the areas targeted by attacks, presented in Table 3.4, suggests that the majority of attacks (77.94%) took place in urban areas populated by more than 10,000 people. However, 14.45% took place in rural villages with less than 2000 residents. This significant amount of rural activity could be due to the restructuring of the RIRA. It is possible that these areas, with a minimal number of residents, provided training sites for new members and testing sites for new equipment and explosives. Such sparsely populated areas, some with no more than 200 residents, provide more space than urban environments for devices to be tested and young members to be trained with less fear of arrest.

At the very least, we can say that the overall sporadic nature of activity observed within Wave 2 illustrates the groups' inability to mount sustained, focused campaigns of violence. The groups themselves admit that this was partially due to organizational infiltration,[23] an observation that in turn led to restructuring. RIRA leadership figures intimated that leaders focused on recruiting new members as well as expelling those who they felt they could no longer trust, while also disbanding a number of units in order to "tighten up the organisation."[24]

▪ WAVE 3: 28 JANUARY 2007–THE PRESENT DAY

In July 2005 the leadership of the PIRA issued a statement saying that they "formally ordered an end to the armed campaign," that "all IRA units had been ordered to dump arms" and "all volunteers (had) been instructed to assist the development of purely political and democratic programmes through exclusively peaceful means."[25] This was quickly followed by the decommissioning of the PIRA's weapons, verified by the Independent International Commission on Decommissioning (IICD).[26] On 28 January 2007, what many believed to be the final obstacle to a successful peace process was crossed: the Sinn Féin Ard Fheis voted by more than the requisite two-thirds majority to support the Police Service of Northern Ireland (PSNI), the reformed successor to the Royal Ulster Constabulary (RUC). This was an historic vote on what has been described as a "touchstone" issue in Republicanism.

Up to that point, Frampton[27] notes that the opinion of the wider Republican community was that policing reform had never gone far enough. The party's acceptance of the new police force, and its encouragement of young Catholics to join the force, greatly strengthened the normalization process in Northern Ireland. Although the dissidents attempted to portray this as an act that had isolated Sinn Féin's Republican base, Tonge and Evans[28] found that in the elections immediately following Sinn Féin's acceptance of the PSNI, dissident candidates managed to achieve only 3% of the Nationalist vote.[29]

Yet in spite of their electoral failure, the dissidents were not dead. Sinn Féin's compromises—its historic acceptance of peaceful politics and support for a "British police force" the PIRA had spent 30 years mercilessly targeting—transformed it into a barely recognizable shadow of its former self, but one that had still not delivered a united Ireland. The dissidents could now focus their efforts. They persisted in emphasizing Sinn Féin's actions as "treachery," but also as an opportunity for rebuilding Irish Republicanism independently of the Provisionals and for launching a new paramilitary campaign:

> Republicanism has been dealt a grave blow in the last decade and more. Its revolutionary character has been drowned in sea of reformism, separatist politics has given way to constitutional nationalism. This is a situation that all Republicans have a duty and responsibility to reverse.... Óglaigh na hÉireann [RIRA] call for a realignment of the Republican forces around the defence of the Republican position. For too long we have allowed ourselves to be fragmented, marginalized and isolated.... The scale of treachery that would encourage Irish Republicans to support a British police force has cut through the ambiguous double speak and no amount of spin can conceal what Republicans are being asked to endorse.[30]

The steps taken by Sinn Féin led to discontent within mainstream as well as dissident Republicanism. A small number of individuals believed the Provisional leadership had "sold out" the movement and was moving closer to accepting the "British occupation" of the six counties. Throughout Wave 3 the VDR groups consistently targeted members of the police force as well as their facilities and families. There had been particular emphasis on Catholic members of the force. It was this sustained targeting that led to the murder by the CIRA of Constable Stephen Carroll in Craigavon in March 2009, the severe injuries endured by Constable

Peadar Heffron as a result of an ONH (RIRA) bomb in January 2010, and "the IRA" murder of Constable Ronan Kerr in April 2011.

The trajectory of violent activity in this wave (see Figure 3.3) is very similar to that of Wave 1. The initial year (2007) saw a relatively small level of activity, but from that point on there was a consistent annual rise. As of 8 July 2011 the three most recent years are the most active across any of the waves. This is the most intensive period of VDR activity on record. That said, VDR activity during the period is significantly less intensive than PIRA activity at the height of the Troubles, a point reiterated in the Independent Monitoring Commission (IMC) final report.[31] The VDR groups have acknowledged that a sustained campaign similar to that of the Provisionals is not viable and have been explicit about that comparison.[32]

The significant increase for 2009–2010 aside, we are still faced with a steady overall increase in activity since 2007. This is why security forces on both sides of the border have increased the threat level posed by VDR groups and focused more strongly on dissident activity. However, attempting to unravel this phenomenon further has given rise to significant challenges. When we consider group responsibility, a frustratingly unclear picture emerges. Of the 239 acts of violence committed in 2010 and attributed broadly to Republican dissidents, for instance, 122 were committed by unknown perpetrators (that is to say, they cannot be attributed to a *specific* dissident grouping); the comparable figure for 2011 reached 122. The challenge of event attribution is a very common one that faces the entire spectrum of analysts, not only those exclusively using open-source data. In their final report the IMC emphasized a similar obstacle in their work: "... particularly when it was not fully clear how far members of paramilitary groups were acting on their own initiative and how far with the sanction or on the orders of the leadership, local or central."[33] Although the data may indicate a decrease of RIRA activity for 2010, it is not possible to determine if this represented a true decrease in overall activity by the group. Since 2007 RIRA activity has increased every year, and there is a strong possibility that if and when the unattributed attacks are claimed by or attached to a specific group, the data will show that RIRA activity has continued to rise.

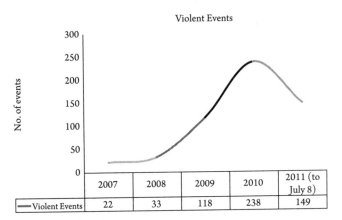

Figure 3.3. Wave 3 VDR activity.

This possibly also explains the less dramatic stagnation in CIRA activity recorded for 2010. On other issues, we can be more certain, however. A signal of how dramatic 2010 had been is that even if we were to completely disregard the "unknown" event data, it would still have the second highest amount of violent activity by both groups, surpassed in both cases only by 2009.

An event-based analysis of these unattributed events provides a better understanding of the situation. Table 3.5 shows that three types of violent activity account for 77.62% of all unattributed violent events within Wave 3. These are hoax incidents (34.97%), defused bombs (22.72%), and shootings/punishment attacks (19.93%).

The main purpose of hoax bombings and warnings is to disrupt the normalization of daily life in Northern Ireland. This goal is central to the strategies of all of the VDR groups and was emphasized in a 2010 issue of *The Sovereign Nation,* the newspaper of 32CSM. This paper, similar to *Saoirse* for the CIRA, regularly hosts statements by the RIRA and reports of their activity:

> Militarily, the [R]IRA and others are at the forefront of an insurgency that is engaging normalisation head on. The actions of these organisations are having a significant effect on Britain's normalisation policy in Ireland. Images of dead British crown force members, bombings and shootings are certainly not representative of the "New Northern Ireland" that the establishment wishes to present. The last thing the British needs is the global media recognising the efficiency of the [R]IRA. There cannot be a peace process without peace.[34]

Although hoaxes and their subsequent security alerts cause significant levels of disruption on their own, the absence of claims of responsibility adds to this. As for defused bombs, it may prove counterproductive for the groups to claim all their defused bombs and explosives, which do not help maintain or strengthen their support or membership. But by examining attempted, failed, and foiled attacks, we approach a more complete picture of the scale of dissident activity. The number of defused bombs exceeds those successfully detonated across the wave. Claiming

TABLE 3.5. *A Percentage Breakdown of Currently Unattributed Violent Dissident Republican Activity in Wave 3*

Type of VDR Activity	Percentage of the "Unknown"
Hoax incidents	34.97%
Bomb (defused)	22.72%
Shooting/punishment attacks	19.93%
Petrol bombs	9.44%
Bomb (detonation)	6.3%
Arson	3.49%
Assault	2.74%
Hijacking	1.75%
Riot	1.75%
Vandalism	1.75%
Robbery	1.4%

$N = 507$.
VDR, Violent Dissident Republican.

all these "failures" may well have a significant detrimental effect on an individual group's desire to depict itself as a capable paramilitary force.

Although there are a significant number of shootings and punishment attacks claimed by individual organizations in Wave 3, the dominance of this tactic and its local nature have resulted in its high percentage within the overall unattributed statistics. These attacks are meant to have local, not national, influence, so the groups do not always feel it necessary to claim each attack. Therefore it is important for the attribution of these attacks to be known only within the local communities, and the attribution may not always be known or reported within the media and other open sources.

When we consider acts that *can* be attributed to a group some interesting patterns emerge. There was a significant increase in RIRA activity in 2007–2009. In fact, the RIRA has consistently been the most active of all the groups across each of the three waves. However, the group's activity showed a sudden decline in 2010. There are several hypotheses to consider here. It may be that the RIRA was responsible for some of the aforementioned unattributed attacks—certainly this is consistent with previous patterns of a failure to immediately claim responsibility for events. An example of this is the death of Denis Donaldson, a leading member of Sinn Féin who was executed in April 2006 after it was revealed that he had been an informer for Northern Irish police and British intelligence. However, it was not until the Real IRA's Easter address of April 2009, 3 years after the event, that it claimed responsibility for Donaldson's murder. This claim came right after the RIRA murders of British soldiers Mark Quinsey and Patrick Azimkar at Massereene Barracks in March 2009, and Martin McGuinness' subsequent dismissal of the dissidents as "traitors to the island of Ireland."[35]

In claiming responsibility for the Donaldson murder at this time the RIRA members were intentionally positioning themselves as the group to maintain the Irish Republican struggle in the vacuum left by the politicization of Sinn Féin and the Provisional IRA:

Denis Donaldson was a traitor and the leadership of the Provisional movement, under the guidance of the British government, made provision for Donaldson to escape Republican justice…. It fell to the volunteers of Óglaigh na hÉireann to carry out the sentence and punishment demanded in our army orders and by the wider republican family.[36]

This illustrates the importance of timing, not just of an event itself but also of the subsequent claim of responsibility. Groups do not always think that taking credit for an event will provide them with the best advantage *immediately*. They may wait until they believe circumstances are beneficial to claim specific attacks. This is especially the case when the group, and the wider dissident movement, is perceived negatively within Republicanism, internally as well as externally.

A major development for 2010 was the emergence of Republican Action Against Drugs (RAAD). The 2010 data suggest that RAAD was the most active VDR group in this year. However, when all the unattributed events are eventually accounted for, this may no longer be the case, because of all the VDR groups, RAAD was the group quickest to claim responsibility for its actions, most regularly through the *Derry Journal*. It is therefore less likely that the group was responsible for the many unattributed attacks of 2010, and more likely that groups such as the RIRA, ONH (RIRA), or the CIRA were.

There is no doubt, however, that Wave 3 has seen a proliferation of VDR groups. Joining the consistently dominant RIRA and CIRA are numerous others claiming to be independent Republican paramilitary groups. However, the RIRA, CIRA, and the relatively new ONH (RIRA) have been responsible for the deadliest activity since 1998 and have done more to assert their identities than any of the other, smaller coalitions, which have largely centered around a tiny group or people or a specific geographic location. This multiplying of VDR groups has now become confusing to the point of exasperation. In an article on the *Forthwrite* website the former Republican prisoner Richard O'Rawe bemoaned the complexity of the current situation:

"... the Real Continuity IRA, which recently broke away from the main Continuity IRA, has split into three different factions. That's four CIRA Army Councils. Then there's the Army Councils of the Real IRA, Óglaigh na hÉireann, the Provisional IRA, and the Official IRA. That makes eight IRA Army Councils at the last count...."[37]

Another suspected contributing factor here is the confusion within the media about the emergence of ONH (RIRA) and other dissident groups. Since the formation of that group along with a number of others, several events may have been wrongfully attributed to one group over the other. In 2008 the database recorded only one violent event confirmed as ONH (RIRA). This increased to five confirmed events in 2009, 12 in 2010, and six in 2011 (up to July). However, when the "unknown" events are factored in it is highly likely that for all 4 years ONH (RIRA) activity will be higher. There are also 15 attacks that have been attributed to both the RIRA and ONH (RIRA) in 2010. This may demonstrate the confusion within the media about the two groups; there have been instances in which both groups made claims and counterclaims for the same events, most notably in the aftermath of the April car-bomb attack on Palace Barracks in Belfast. Initially the RIRA claimed responsibility for this attack before a representative of the Belfast branch of ONH (RIRA) contacted *The Belfast Telegraph* with a counterclaim, which was authenticated through the use of a recognized code word.[38] Similarly, in June 2008 both the CIRA and RIRA claimed responsibility for a landmine attack on members of the PSNI. The RIRA clearly disgruntled the CIRA when it produced another statement showing its disquiet: "those making spurious claims of responsibility would be better employed in their own acts of resistance rather than seeking to confuse Republicans."[39] In the absence of a verified claim of responsibility, it is common for attacks to be described in the media simply as "dissident activity."

VDR activity in Wave 3 shows a continued focus on Northern Ireland. Of the 562 violent events in this wave to date, 512 took place in Northern Ireland, 45 in the Republic of Ireland, and only two in Britain. Therefore, although the threat levels of a VDR attack in Britain have been raised, violent events there have actually decreased. This, however, should not be construed as a reason to lower the threat level, as it is possible that future British attacks and/or campaigns are being

TABLE 3.6. *Wave 3 Northern Ireland County-Based Activity*

	RIRA	CIRA	RIRA/ONH (RIRA)	Other	Unknown	Total %
Antrim	4.93%	4.14%	2.17%	4.34%	30.18%	45.76%
Armagh	3.55%	4.93%	0.2%	0.79%	6.51%	15.98%
Derry	4.14%	0.2%	0.39%	8.28%	8.88%	21.9%
Down	0.99%	0.79%	0.39%	0.39%	2.96%	5.52%
Fermanagh	0.39%	0.99%	0%	0%	1.58%	2.96%
Tyrone	2.56%	0.2%	0.2%	1.78%	3.16%	7.9%
Total %	16.56%	11.25%	3.35%	15.58%	53.27%	100%

N = 546.
RIRA, Real IRA; CIRA, Continuity IRA; ONH, Óglaigh na hÉireann.

planned. As will be illustrated toward the end of this chapter, most of the events in the Republic of Ireland are connected to VDR involvement in organized crime and vigilante justice.

Similar to Wave 2, the three most dominant counties for activity in Wave 3 have been Antrim (45.76%), Derry (21.9%), and Armagh (15.98%) (Table 3.6). The data show a drop from 13.32% to 5.52% in County Down. This further supports the claim that VDR activity is becoming more focused on specific locations as well as specific forms of activity within these locations. The continued dominance of these three counties in terms of activity can be attributed to the types of targets within them.

When the location of events is analyzed by population size it is clear that violence in Wave 3 has been focused on urban rather than rural communities (Table 3.7). Although this was also true in Wave 2, the earlier period included a significant minority of violent events in small rural villages, which may be connected to the training of new members and the testing of new devices and weapons. However, in Wave 3 the VDR groups have focused their activity almost entirely on urban areas. In total, 95.02% of all violent activity has taken place in areas with a population of over 10,000 people; only 12.98% has taken place in areas with 10,000 or less residents (these percentages are more than 100% combined because some events are deemed to take place in more than one location, and therefore could be in areas of different population size; while they are analyzed as one event, both locations would need to be acknowledged in a geographic analysis of attack behaviors).

RIRA, Real IRA; CIRA, Continuity IRA; ONH, Óglaigh na hÉireann. A combination of the tactics of disruption of normalization and the targeting of criminals and antisocial offenders within communities has resulted in this urban focus of

TABLE 3.7. *Wave 3 Overall Violent Dissident Republican Activity Based on Population Size*

	RIRA	CIRA	RIRA/ONH (RIRA)	Other	Unknown	Total %
Under 2,000	2.56%	1.28%	0.18%	0.36%	0.55%	4.93%
2,000–10,000	2.93%	0.36%	0.18%	1.28%	3.3%	8.05%
10,001–50,000	4.39%	4.76%	7.33%	4.03%	18.86%	39.37%
50,001–100,000	3.84%	0.36%	0.18%	6.96%	8.24%	19.58%
Over 100,000	4.39%	4.21%	1.83%	3.85%	21.79%	36.07%
Total %	18.11%	10.97%	9.7%	16.48%	52.74%	100%

RIRA, Real IRA; CIRA, Continuity IRA; ONH, Óglaigh na hÉireann.

activity. The most disruption is caused during security alerts and attacks within urban areas. This results in the closure of transportation infrastructure and the evacuation of large numbers of residences and businesses. It is through this wide-spread disruption that the groups have their largest impact, the levels of which are not obtained through the targeting of less populated areas. The majority of the punishment attacks and shootings target drug dealers and other criminal and antisocial offenders, individuals who operate largely within densely populated areas.[40]

Bombing Incidents

The Omagh bombing of August 1998 still epitomizes the very nature of VDR activity and its personnel. This attack, which killed 29 people and injured more than 200 others, demonstrated the lethal capabilities and intent of the newly emerging RIRA and CIRA. It came at a time of great hope for Northern Ireland. The Good Friday Agreement had been signed the previous year and the peace process was receiving both national and international recognition as a success.

A "detonated" bomb indicates a device exploded in an attack, and not destroyed in a controlled explosion by the security forces. The bombs referred to here *do not* include petrol bombs or other similar incendiary devices. It includes all other explosive devices including pipe bombs, mortars, grenades, improvised explosive devices (IEDs), and rocket-propelled grenades (RPGs). The "defused" devices are those that were made safe, disabled, or destroyed in a controlled manner by the security forces. This includes bombs that were defused after the explosive was planted as well as those that were intercepted and defused or abandoned and defused. Whereas detonations cause both physical and psychological damage, defused bombs can and do result in sustained fear and anxiety:

> The pipe bomb doesn't have to explode to have an effect. You put a device outside somebody's door, they know that the person who has placed that device has some link in with an organization that can do you harm or with a group of individuals that can do you harm. So just putting it there can have the same effect as the device exploding.[41]

There were many incidents in which more than one explosive was present. The data presented here do not aggregate the number of devices but refer to the number of bombing *incidents*.

As shown in Figure 3.4, the extent of VDR bombings, both detonated and defused, has significantly increased in recent years. However, as with all forms of VDR activity, this is still far short of the extent of bombings experienced during the height of the PIRA. Ryder reports that at the end of 1971, the year that internment was introduced, the number of bombings had reached an annual level of over 1000.[42]

Patterns of bombing activity across the three waves are similar to the overall evolution of VDR activity. The data show that the threat of bombings posed by VDR groups is more constant in Wave 3 than in the previous two waves, even though more casualties resulted from bombings in both Waves 1 and 2. The most

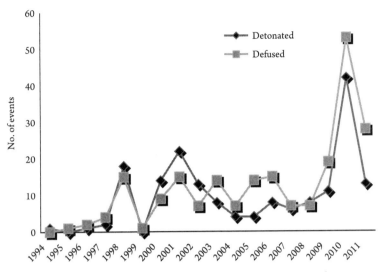

Figure 3.4. Annual detonated and defused bombings across entire period.

active year to date for VDR bombings was 2010. In that year there were 42 deto-nated and 53 defused devices. This is a significant increase from the previous high of 22 detonations and 15 defused in 2001.

As with the overall pattern of VDR activity, in Wave 1 the bombing activity, both detonated and defused, showed a spike in activity in 1998, the year after the formation of the RIRA (Figure 3.5). In the final year of the wave there were 18 detonations and 15 bombs defused. Although the first wave of activity is defined by the Omagh bombing, a number of other attacks by both the RIRA and the CIRA resulted in casualties across Northern Ireland. Among these were the CIRA

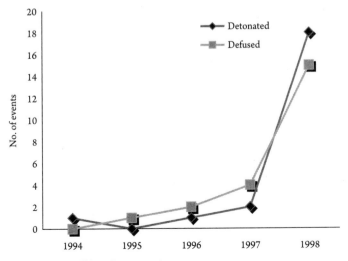

Figure 3.5. Wave 1 overall bombing activity.

attacks on the Killyhevlin Hotel in 1996 and Moira RUC station in February 1998. The most notable attack prior to Omagh came only 2 weeks earlier, when the RIRA planted a bomb in Banbridge. Each of these three attacks brought about a number of casualties, but luckily no one was killed. The only deaths in Wave 1 were the result of the Omagh bomb.

The aftermath of the Omagh bomb brought a close to Wave 1 and saw the gradual emergence of Wave 2. The data on the one hand indicate the immediate success of the counterdissident strategy post-Omagh—it *appears* that no bombings were even attempted by dissident groupings in all of 1999. However, in 2000 there were 14 detonated and 9 defused bombing incidents, followed by 22 detonated and 15 defused incidents in 2001 (Figure 3.6). For each year into Wave 3, from 2003 to 2010 (excluding 2008), the number of *defused* bombs surpassed the number detonated. By 2001 the data show that the RIRA in particular was growing in its capabilities. This was its most "successful" year with respect to bombings in Wave 2, though it would not reach that level of proliferation again until Wave 3. Frampton[43] emphasizes decimation through arrests as a major factor in the group's operational decline. Arrests in 2001 alone included skilled bomb-makers Kenneth and Alan Patterson for possession of explosives, John Maloney and former Irish Army soldier Richard Whyte for running an RIRA training camp, and leading members for attempting to buy weapons in eastern Europe. The end of the year also saw the sentencing of RIRA leader Liam Campbell to 5 years for "membership of an illegal organization."[44] The consistently higher level of defused bombs from 2003 onward, and the steady decline in "successful" attacks from 2001 on, may indicate skill depletion within the organization.

Frampton[45] suggests that the continuing lack of success from the RIRA caused significant internal tensions, both inside and outside of the prisons. As detailed in Chapter 2, this led to a split in the group and the subsequent formation of Óglaigh na hÉireann. As with all Irish Republican splits the issue of the continuation and intensity of the "armed struggle" was central to this debate. Although

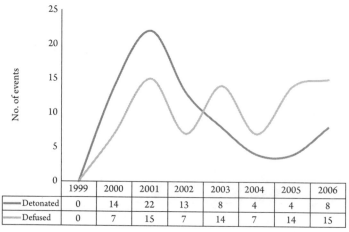

	1999	2000	2001	2002	2003	2004	2005	2006
Detonated	0	14	22	13	8	4	4	8
Defused	0	7	15	7	14	7	14	15

Figure 3.6. Wave 2 VDR bombing activity.

those who formed ONH temporarily ceased activity at this point the Republicans who remained under the banner of the RIRA vowed to continue their armed campaign. However, toward the end of the wave, due to the "mistakes made" by members who "weren't up to scratch," the RIRA entered into a "three year period of restructuring."[46] The group blames this "period of restructuring" for its decline in activity at the end of the wave.

By 8 July there had already been 41 bombing incidents in 2011: 13 detonations and 28 bombs defused (Figure 3.7). By the same time in 2010 there had been five detonations and 10 defused bombs. As with the overall violent event data this suggests that 2011 activity was consistent with an annual rise in VDR activity. This increase in attacks from 2007 to 2010 is echoed specifically through VDR bombs, both those detonated and those that were defused. In 2010 alone there was a total of 95 dissident bombing incidents—53 defused and 42 detonated—compared to 30 (19 defused and 11 detonated) in 2009. Though nowhere near the lethality of the Omagh bomb, this increase in higher-level activity (the highest year on record since the formation of the dissidents) supports the assumption that in 2010 there was a growing sophistication in tactics, technology, and determination on the part of the dissidents. It may also signal the presence of new, or newly trained, bomb-makers within the groups.

Wave 3 shows a more focused targeting approach by all of the groups, both old and new. The RIRA leadership explains their rationale in a 2008 interview: "With more attacks on the RUC/PSNI we believe the stage will be reached where British soldiers are brought back onto the streets to bolster the cops. This will shatter the façade that the British presence has gone and normality reigns. People will once again be made visibly aware that we remain occupied."[47]

For decades Irish Republicans had been fighting for the removal of British soldiers from the streets of Northern Ireland. When this was successfully achieved in 2005, with troop withdrawal and the dismantling of army posts, there was a

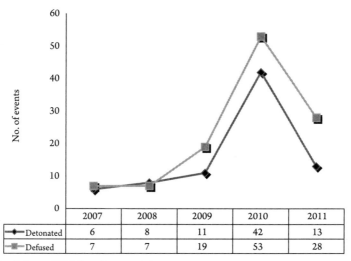

	2007	2008	2009	2010	2011
Detonated	6	8	11	42	13
Defused	7	7	19	53	28

Figure 3.7. Wave 3 VDR bombing activity.

definite decline in the perceived justification for a continued armed Republican campaign. This led the leadership of the RIRA and the other dissident groups to realize that without a visible British presence in Northern Ireland, support and sympathy for their fight would decline significantly. This in turn resulted in their strategy of targeting police and soldiers in order to bring back the very troops they had been fighting to get rid of for so many years.

Geography

Across the three waves, 77.04% of bombing incidents, both detonated and defused, took place within three different population sizes (Table 3.8):

1. Population over 100,000 (25.6%)
2. Population from 10,0001 to 50,000 (31.95%)
3. Population under 2000 (19.49%)

Whereas the predominance of cities with a population size of over 100,000 (e.g., Belfast and London) can be easily explained by the high profile of the targets, the high level of attacks in small rural villages with a population under 2000 may at first seem more confusing. However, when this is analyzed across the three waves, there is a clear regression in this tactic; it fell from a high of 28.57% in Wave 1 to a low of 12.23% in Wave 3. There are various possible explanations for this. To move from their point of inception in Wave 1 to the high levels of activity in Wave 3, the groups have had to train new members while also developing their attack capabilities. This required the training and testing of new recruits. As already detailed, these rural, less populated locations provided ideal locations for this. However, as the groups have built up their arsenals and developed more experienced memberships, they may have less need for these sites as Wave 3 continues.

The prevalence of attacks on mid-sized towns across the three waves also requires consideration. Although the rural locations provide the best training and testing sites, more populated areas provide ideal targets for the dissidents to cause the most disruption. Whereas the groups consistently target heavily populated areas with populations of 50,000 or more, there are also more security risks for them in these locations. A higher police presence increases the risk of arrest and the interception of bombs. Such towns may therefore be regarded as compromise targets for the dissidents—targets that do not have as much impact as attacks on larger cities, but at the same time cause significantly more disruption than rural targets.

TABLE 3.8. *Violent Dissident Republican Bombings Incidents*

	Wave 1 (N = 42)	Wave 2 (N = 147)	Wave 3 (N = 188)	Total (N = 377)
Under 2,000	28.57%	17.68%	12.23%	19.49%
2,000–10,000	7.14%	10.88%	11.17%	9.73%
10,001–50,000	35.71%	24.49%	35.64%	31.95%
50,001–100,000	11.9%	8.16%	18.62%	12.89%
Over 100,000	16.67%	37.78%	22.34%	25.6%

Hoax Incidents

The dissidents' desire to disrupt the normalization of Northern Ireland is nowhere more apparent than via one particular tactic: hoaxes. Some researchers are wary of collecting data on hoaxes (let alone attempting to offer explanations or interpretations of what they might mean) and threats due to the fact that this kind of activity can be perpetrated by anybody, with little to no clear confirmation of responsibility. Yet the sheer scale of hoax events in Northern Ireland, which is increasing in parallel with other VDR activity, warrants attention (Figure 3.8). The dissidents have been responsible for planting classic "hoax" devices (i.e., nonviable devices) and issuing hoax warnings (e.g., a warning of a bomb when none is present in a specific or general area). Hoax devices can be quite elaborate (i.e., purposefully designed to look like an explosive device) or as simple as a suspicious device (an abandoned bag). The nonelaborate "suspicious" devices are unattended objects left in situations and places in which they are perceived to be out of the ordinary and are thus treated as suspicious. Unlike the elaborate hoaxes, these are not designed specifically to look like explosive devices. However, their very presence can potentially cause a major security alert.

A major challenge of the analysis of hoax devices involves attribution. For Wave 3, 81.5% of hoax incidents cannot be attributed to an individual or group. Although there are cases in which individuals not connected to VDR activity are responsible for hoax events, we do not include these. The example of William

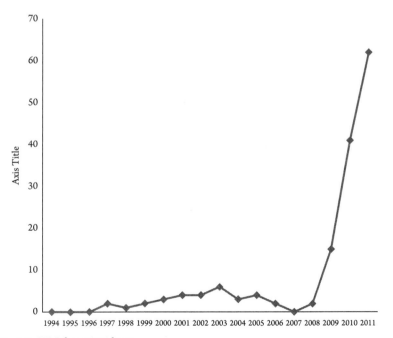

Figure 3.8. VDR hoax incidents.

O'Connor, a convicted sex offender with no dissident affiliations, emphasizes this need for caution. In May 2011 O'Connor pleaded guilty for causing two bomb alerts in Derry.[48]

The two most common objectives of a hoax are to cause disruption or to create a situation in which the security services are susceptible to attack: "A hoax device may on occasion be intended only to cause disruption, but it may also be designed to lure police officers into a situation where they are vulnerable to attack; this mode of attack has been used on a number of occasions in the recent past."[49] The increase of hoax devices and warnings, from 15 in 2009 to 41 in 2010, indicates that it has been a deliberate tactic of VDR groups (a view supported by the IMC). Hoaxes not only disrupt Northern Irish life but also overextend the security service response units and explosive ordnance disposal (EOD) teams. A major target has been the transport infrastructure of Northern Ireland through the placement of hoax devices on motorways and railway tracks.

In addition to causing general disruption and spreading the resources of the security forces, the dissidents sometimes engage in hoaxes to make a more specific point. This is often followed by a claim of responsibility. An example of this is the July 2004 hoax alerts across Belfast claimed by the Real IRA. These operations targeted the transport infrastructure of Belfast, both road and rail, and were conducted to protest perceived mistreatment of Republican prisoners in Maghaberry jail.[50]

Although hoaxes have been used as a tactic throughout the history of Republicanism, at no period from 1997 to the present have they been used as prominently as they were in 2010. Prior to 2009, the highest recorded rate of hoax incidents in the database was six in 2003. In fact, it is likely that these events are underreported; because of the nonlethal nature of the devices not all hoax attacks will be reported in the media. In 2011, 62 separate hoax devices and warnings were reported in Northern Ireland.[51] By 8 July, the number of hoax incidents in 2011 (62) outnumbered detonated and defused bombs combined (41).

Shootings and Punishment Attacks

Shooting still represents the most lethal form of VDR activity. Although the bombing data indicate a wide range of locations targeted by VDR groups, the locations at which shootings take place are more defined. Most of these have taken place in urban areas with populations of 10,000 and above. Invariably the targets are known and suspected drug dealers, sex offenders, and other criminals as well as those accused of repeated social order offenses. The largest group targeted involves drug dealers accused of operating within urban Republican communities. The cities of Belfast, Derry, and Dublin have sustained the largest number of punishment attacks. The focus on the urban drug problem specifically is further emphasized when the local dissident newssheets are examined. The urban editions of 32CSM's regional newssheet *Beir Bua* ("Triumph Over") places a strong emphasis on the problems of crime, particularly drugs. This can be seen in headlines both north and south of the border, such as "Derry Cocaine Epidemic"[52] and "Sick of the Scourge of Drugs in Your Area?"[53] This emphasis on local crime problems as opposed to attempts to proselytize the need to reclaim Republicanism (more prominent within the rural newssheets) represents a distinct focus of the dissidents to gain support in urban areas. However, there is more to this tactic than simply shooting drug dealers to win hearts and minds. Brian Rowan explains: "In a much wider frame it's about attacking [Gerry] Adams and [Martin] McGuinness and it's about that question of authority and right within the republican community."[54]

This significant upsurge in Wave 3 is the result of one major factor. Even though Sinn Féin was engaged in the political process in Northern Ireland for all of Wave 2, PIRA was still involved in punishment attacks. Their reluctance to disengage from this tactic proved a stumbling block in the final stages of the negotiation processes surrounding both elections[55] and Sinn Féin taking its seat on the PSNI policing board. But since then, according to the IMC and other bodies, the PIRA refrained from punishment attacks or any other forms of violence. This has left a vacuum within Republican communities, one the dissidents have been quick to occupy.[56]

The rise in punishment attacks is nowhere better illustrated than through the recent emergence of the Derry-based group Republican Action Against Drugs (RAAD). RAAD represents the latest incarnation of Republican vigilante antidrug groups. The database recorded 31 confirmed violent actions by this group in 2010 and eight in 2009, all of which constituted punishment attacks and pipe bombs targeting known or suspected drug dealers in Republican areas of Derry and surrounding regions. By 8 July, RAAD had been responsible for eight separate attacks since the beginning of 2011. They do this under the guise of protecting the communities and of doing the job they claim the PSNI is not. As Knox states, they use these actions to illustrate that they are "acting on the communities' behalf."[57] They target and intimidate convicted and suspected drug dealers, often continuously targeting specific individuals over a long period of time.

In 2010, for example, the group targeted Gavin Nixon, a convicted drug dealer from Hazelbank, Derry. Nixon's home was first targeted with a pipe bomb in June and he was then kidnapped in September. He was subsequently released, issuing a statement detailing his abduction and calling an end to his involvement in the drug trade. In this statement he also warned all other drug dealers in the area of the potential for similar targeting of them, by RAAD, if they did not cease activity.[58] However, it is not only drug dealers who are targeted by such attacks. An example of this was the kneecapping of a 48-year-old convicted sex offender in the Carnhill[59] area of Derry city in October 2010. This punishment attack was claimed by RIRA,[60] again reinforcing its determination to be portrayed as providing police protection to Republican areas in place of the PSNI. In a time when the issue of victimhood is being debated across Northern Ireland, the victims of punishment attacks are often viewed in a light different from other victims of the Troubles and subsequent stages of paramilitary violence. Even though they are one of the largest groups of victims, due to the reasoning for their targeting—their suspected links to crime—the culpability of their attackers can at times be decreased or abated in the opinions of many observers.[61]

Shootings are also carried out against a group's own members for a variety of reasons, including suspicion of informing or otherwise bringing public disrepute upon the group. An example of the latter is what led to the murder of RIRA member Kieran Doherty in February 2010. Doherty, a prominent member of the RIRA in Derry, was tortured and killed after being publicly connected to a drug seizure in Donegal. To defend its reputation as an organization purportedly asserting a consistent stance against the scourge of drugs, RIRA murdered him. Whether this was the real, or only, reason for Doherty's murder by RIRA is uncertain, but the action alone sends a message to other members and to a wider public, both Republican and otherwise, about the importance with which the leadership views its public image. This is emphasized by Derry civil rights activist Eamon McCann:

> The Real IRA were saying something to their own supporters and perhaps their own members about discipline, about loyalty, about the fact that you don't step out of line, the fact that you don't, as they would say, besmirch the organization. The way that this killing was done and the way that the body was left, it tells us something about the way that the Real IRA sees itself. The Real IRA is not just a bunch of kill-crazy hooligans as they've been represented in some coverage. They are people who have got a sense of themselves as the likes of the last men standing as far as traditional republicanism is concerned.[62]

In addition to conducting punishment attacks to solicit passive and active support, VDR groups are also suspected of using this method as a means of testing the commitment of new recruits. Because the victims of these punishment attacks often have criminal records and fear reprisals, they rarely report the attacks to the police.[63] Consequently, senior figures within the dissident groups see a valuable opportunity to initiate new members with little risk of getting caught.

■ CONCLUSIONS

The threat of VDR activity is more constant now than it has ever been. Although there has not been an atrocity on the scale of Omagh, the intentions of the active groups are clear. They are committed to activity that effectively helps disrupt the normalization of Northern Irish society through a variety of violent tactics ranging from bombings and shootings to hoaxes and statements threatening violence. The data reveal discernible patterns of violent activity across three distinct waves of activity. These are as follows:

- **Wave 1:** A steady rise in violent activity from 1994 to the culmination in 1998. Although this wave never reached the frequency or lethality (until Omagh) of the second or third waves, it demonstrated the potential and intentions of the newly emerging dissident groups, most notably the RIRA. The final surge in activity was a reaction to the Provisionals' acceptance of the Mitchell Principles and their support for the Good Friday Agreement.
- **Wave 2:** The aftermath of Wave 1, specifically the Omagh bombing, resulted in an upsurge in counterdissident activity both north and south of the border. This weakened all active groups. When the RIRA revoked its ceasefire and

the CIRA restarted its armed campaign they were never able to reach a sustained level of activity due to a number of factors, most notably a lack of support and personnel, infiltration, arrests, and arms finds. Even though the peace process was visibly faltering during this time, they were unable to take advantage of the situation and remained isolated within Republicanism. There was a continuous lack of focus in their activities in terms of geographic location, target selection, and tactics. The unstable nature of VDR activity at this time is best emphasized by the proliferation of further splits toward the end of the wave.

- **Wave 3:** The current wave is similar in trajectory to Wave 1 in that there has been a consistent steady rise in VDR activity annually since 2007. Compared to Wave 1, however, the activity is significantly more frequent. Since the Omagh bombing, 2009, 2010, and 2011 have been the three most violent years so far. The respective groups have each made detectible changes in strategy and personnel. There appears to be a more focused and discriminate strategy to their activities now than in either of the other two stages. We have seen the very deliberate and focused targeting of PSNI officers, soldiers, and criminals. A significant strategic objective here is to help gain (and maintain) a firmer footing within Republican communities. The dissidents are learning from what the PIRA did in the past, and are exploiting the control vacuum they have left behind. Wave 3 has also seen the dissident groups temper expectations of those that would otherwise assess their strength by comparing them with the PIRA. The groups understand that a high frequency of operations is not sustainable, and this in turn helps in understanding the move toward a more tactical and surgical targeting strategy.

The most important observation from the data is that the threat posed by the dissidents is on the rise. Furthermore, it is diversifying and slowly becoming more lethal. Dissident activity is no longer attributable only to the CIRA and the RIRA. New groups have emerged, which has created increased confusion and difficulty surrounding accurate attribution of responsibility for a significant amount of violent dissident Republican activity. Significantly, this confusion is acknowledged both by the security forces and by mainstream Republican commentators.

The data also suggest that although bomb-related events tend to be the most high profile, shootings remain (at least currently) the most lethal and consistent form of VDR attack. This has been especially true since the PIRA called a permanent cessation to violence. Although the main stated aims of the dissident groups are predominantly political in nature, their most lethal attacks best serve a vigilantism strategy. These attacks specifically targeting offenders seemed to be disruptive to community cohesion. The dissidents may have national-level aspirations, yet their day-to-day operations suggest an immediate focus on asserting power and dominance in their local communities. Despite considerable effort by researchers into collating these data, we have no hesitation in acknowledging that the data have limitations and, if anything, underrepresent the true extent and nature of VDR activities. We should be mindful of the involvement of dissident actors in activities that tend to remain underreported if not completely absent from main-stream open-source reports. On 29 June 2011, *The Belfast Telegraph* reported that the Police Federation of Northern Ireland claimed that in the 18 months lead-ing up to June, over 30 PSNI officers were forced to move home over "fears of dissident ... murder bids."[64]

The ICST VDR data are in no way likely to have captured all violent dissident activity. The dissidents engage in a broad range of tactics that do not always result in verifiable, attributable, recordable events. They struggle daily to assert control over the communities they claim to serve. They exert informal justice for criminals, while at the same time taking steps to stifle dissent by those who would oppose them. They can be seen to be engaging in sporadic shows of strength, while also maintain-ing grooming, recruitment, and training activities. As we shall see in Chapter 5, in addition to articulating strategic objectives, they have also begun to forge useful alli-ances in urban and border areas with organized criminal entities that have, in some cases, led to opportunities to explore international dimensions. Though recruitment continues north and south, a spate of arrests in 2011 likely dampened this activity, at least for now. In part because of the fluid and seemingly erratic nature of the dis-sidents' activities, their dynamics appear as fluid and organic as they are unstable.

The reality of all of this is impossible to capture in a database that relies on the ability to count events but cannot record whether there may be opportunistic political factors (if not genuine operational reasons) that contribute to underre-porting of certain kinds of dissident activity altogether, particularly for nonfatal incidents. In the next chapter, we take a closer look at who precisely engages in dissident activity, where they come from, what they do, and what similarities or differences they share.

■ NOTES

1. Some of the information presented in this chapter has previously appeared in Horgan, J., & Morrison, J. F. 2011. "Here to Stay? The Rising Threat of Violent Dissident Republicanism in Northern Ireland." *Terrorism and Political Violence, 23*(4), 642–669; and Horgan, J., & Gill, P. 2011. "Who Are the Dissidents? An Introduction to the ICST Violent Dissident Republican Project." In P. M. Currie & M. Taylor (Eds.), *Dissident Irish Republicanism* (pp. 43–63). London: Continuum.

2. Schmid, A. P. 2004. "Statistics on Terrorism: The Challenge of Measuring Trends in Global Terrorism." In A. P. Schmid (Ed.), *Forum on Crime and Society* [Vol. 4 (1 and 2), pp. 71–92]. New York: United Nations.

3. Bowie, N., & Schmid, A. P. 2011. "Databases on Terrorism." In A. P. Schmid (Ed.), *The Routledge Handbook of Terrorism Research* (pp. 294–340). London: Routledge.

4. Smith, B. L., & Damphousse, K. R. 2002. *American Terrorism Study: Patterns of Behavior, Investigation and Prosecution of American Terrorists: Final Report.* U.S. Department of Justice.

5. Sageman, M. 2008. *Leaderless Jihad.* Philadelphia: University of Pennsylvania Press.

6. Bowie & Schmid, 2011, pp. 338–339.

7. LaFree, G., & Dugan, L. 2007. "Introducing the Global Terrorism Database." *Terrorism and Political Violence, 19*, 181–204.

8. See Appendix A for a full outline of each of the sections.

9. See Appendix B for the events database codebook.

10. LaFree & Dugan, 2007, p. 188.

11. These data are correct up to and including July 8, 2011.

12. For a detailed examination of the victims of the Omagh bombing and the campaigns of their families for justice after the attack see Edwards, R. D. 2009. *Aftermath: The Omagh Bombing and the Families' Pursuit of Justice*. London: Vintage.

13. Morrison, J. F. 2010. *"The Affirmation of Behan?": An Understanding of the Politicisation Process of the Provisional Irish Republican Movement Through an Organisational Analysis of Splits from 1969 to 1997*. Ph.D. dissertation, University of St. Andrews, p. 220.

14. *The Independent*. 2009. "Omagh Bomb Legal Victory: The Men Behind Worst Atrocity of the Troubles." 9 June. http://www.independent.co.uk/news/uk/crime/omagh-bomb-legal-victory-the-men-behind-worst-atrocity-of-the-troubles-1700547.html. Accessed March 20, 2011.

15. BBC News Online. 1999. "Real IRA Members" Jailed. 21 May. http://news.bbc.co.uk/2/hi/uk_news/349554.stm. Accessed July 10, 2011.

16. Even though the CIRA claims responsibility for this shooting the police claim no knowledge of the event ever taking place.

17. Frampton, M. 2010. *The Return of the Militants: Violent Dissident Republicanism*. London: International Centre for the Study of Radicalisation and Political Violence.

18. Ibid., p. 14

19. Tonge, J. 2006. *Northern Ireland*. Cambridge: Polity Press. P. 135.

20. Frampton, M. 2011. *Legion of the Rearguard: Dissident Irish Republicanism*. Dublin: Irish Academic Press. P. 285

21. Ibid., p. 285.

22. Ibid., p. 192.

23. Rowan, B. 2010. "Dissidents: Interview with Terror Splinter Group." *Belfast Telegraph*, 2 December.

24. Breen, S. 2009. "Exclusive: Real IRA 'We Will Take Campaign to Britain.'" *Sunday Tribune*, 12 April.

25. O'Neill, P. 2006. Text of Irish Republican Army (IRA) Statement on the Ending of the Armed Campaign. 29 July. Available at CAIN. http://cain.ulst.ac.uk/othelem/organ/ira/ira280705.htm. Accessed July 10, 2011.

26. "IRA 'Has Destroyed All Its Arms,'" BBC (September 26, 2005). http://news.bbc.co.uk/2/hi/uk_news/northern_ireland/4283444.stm. Accessed July 10, 2011.

27. Frampton, M. 2009. *The Long March: The Political Strategy of Sinn Fein, 1981–2007*. London: Palgrave Macmillan. P. 128.

28. Tonge, J., & Evans, J. 2010. "Northern Ireland: Unionism Loses More Leaders." *Parliamentary Affairs, 63*(4), 742–759.

29. Ibid.

30. *The Sovereign Nation*. 2007. "Oglaigh na hEireann New Years Statement." January/February, p. 5.

31. Independent Monitoring Commission (IMC). 2011. *Twenty-Sixth and Final Report of the Independent Monitoring Commission: 2004–2011 Changes, Impact and Lessons*. London: The Stationery Office, Paragraph 5.6.

32. Bates, D. 2009. "Real IRA Threatens New Attacks on Mainland Britain in Easter Message of Hate." *The Daily Mail*, 15 April. http://www.dailymail.co.uk/news/article-1169828/Real-IRA-threatens-new-attacks-mainland-Britain-Easter-message-hate.html. Accessed July 20, 2011.

33. IMC report, 2011, Paragraph 8.7.

34. *The Sovereign Nation*. 2010. "Continuing the Resistance—The Republican Strategy." October/November, p. 5. http://32csm.info/oct10.pdf. Accessed July 15, 2011.

35. Tonge & Evans, 2010, p. 756.

36. Clancy, P. 2009. "Real IRA Claim Donaldson Murder." *Irish Central*, 15 April. http://www.irishcentral.com/news/Real-IRA-Claim-Donaldson-Murder-43048822.html. Accessed July 20, 2011.

37. O'Rawe, R. 2011. "How Many Do We Need?" *Fouthwrite*, 4 July. http://www.fourth write.ie/?p=162. Accessed July 10, 2011.

38. *Belfast Telegraph*. 2011. "Claim and Counter-claim Over Northern Ireland Bomb Attack." *Belfast Telegraph*, 14 April. http://www.belfasttelegraph.co.uk/news/local-national/claim-and-counterclaim-over-northern-ireland-bomb-attack-14766405.html.   Accessed April 18, 2011.

39. Saoirse. 2008. "CIRA Landmine Attack on Brits." July, p. 1.

40. IMC 23.

41. BBC. 2010. *Spotlight: Blood Summons*.

42. Ryder, C. 2006. *A Special Kind of Courage: 321 EOD Squadron-Battling the Bombers*. London: Metheun. P. 51.

43. Frampton, 2011, p. 144.

44. Ibid.

45. Frampton, 2011, p. 145.

46. Breen, S. 2008. "War Back On—Real IRA." *Sunday Tribune*, 3 February. http://www.nuzhound.com/articles/Sunday_Tribune/arts2008/feb3_RIRA_interview__SBreen.php. Accessed, July 22, 2011.

47. Ireland's Own. 2008. "Oglaigh na hEireann." 3 February. http://irelandsown.net/RIRA13.html. Accessed September 14, 2011.

48. *Belfast Telegraph*. 2011. "Sex Offender Guilty of Two Bomb Hoax Calls." 12 May. http://www.belfasttelegraph.co.uk/news/local-national/northern-ireland/sex-offender-guilty-of-two-bomb-hoax-calls-15154733.html. Accessed July 20, 2011.

49. IMC 21.

50. *The Sovereign Nation*. 2004. "Weapons of Mass Disruption: IRA Cause Gridlock in Support of Republican Prisoners." August/September, p. 3.

51. For a discussion of the problems caused by both hoax devices and genuine false alarms see Ryder, 2006, pp. 50–56.

52. Beir Bua Derry. 2008. "Derry Cocaine Epidemic." May/June, p. 1.

53. Beir Bua Cork. 2007. "Sick of the Scourge of Drugs in Your Area?" p. 1.

54. BBC. 2010. *Spotlight: Blood Summons*.

55. *Observer-Reporter*. 1997. "IRA Distancing Itself from Sinn Féin over Belfast Talks," p. C10.

56. For a discussion of passive and active support see Cronin, A. K. 2006. "How Al-Qaida Ends: The Decline and Demise of Terrorist Groups." *International Security, 31*(1), 7–48.

57. Knox, C. 2001. "The 'Deserving' Victims of Political Violence: 'Punishment' Attacks in Northern Ireland." *Criminal Justice, 1*(2), 181–199.

58. *Derry Journal*. 2010. "RAAD 'Abduct' Convicted Drug Dealer." 10 September. http://www.derryjournal.com/journal/RAAD-39abduct39-convicted-drug-dealer.6524821.jp. Accessed March 20, 2011.

59. Carnhill was targeted by RAAD twice in the middle of April 2011. The same individual was first shot a week before a viable pipe bomb was placed outside his house, which led to a police evacuation of the whole estate.

60. *Derry Journal.* 2010. "Real IRA Shot Sex Offender." 26 October. http://www.derryjournal.com/journal/Real-IRA-shot-sex-offender.6599213.jp. Accessed March 20, 2011.

61. Maillot, A. 2004. *New Sinn Fein: Irish Republicanism in the 21st Century.* London: Routledge. P. 42.

62. Knox, 2001.

63. BBC. 2010. *Spotlight: Blood Summons.*

64. Hamill, H. 2010. *The Hoods: Crime and Punishment in Belfast.* Princeton, NJ: Princeton University Press. P. 12.

65. *Belfast Telegraph.* 2011. "Police 'Move Out over Terror Fears.'" 29 June.

4
Profiles, Patterns, and Personnel

■ **INTRODUCTION**

The previous chapter examined the extent and nature of violent dissident Republican activity. This chapter considers those responsible for it. To date, little is known about the personnel who make up the dissident groups. There are sporadic reports about suspected leadership figures, unrestrained speculation about shadowy dissident "masterminds," as well as various "leaked" estimates of how many dissident actors there might actually be.[1] This chapter seeks to move the discussion beyond conjecture by providing an analysis up to the present time of who precisely the dissident personnel have been. It seeks to provide an understanding of who engages in dissident activity, to determine where they come from, and to explore whether there are discernible patterns of mobilization, recruitment, and action both within specific Violent Dissident Republican (VDR) groups as well as across them.

■ **UNDERSTANDING THE TERRORIST**

In a 2009 review of social science research on terrorism, LaFree and Ackerman[2] describe how despite a 2006 finding by Lum and colleagues that at least 20,000 articles on terrorism were published from 1971 to 2004, "individual and group-level empirical data on terrorism [remain] in short supply." LaFree and Ackerman further identify the following common themes from research on the psychology of terrorism:

- The inability of psychopathology to explain terrorism;
- The absence of any clear terrorist personality profile;
- Common themes of trauma, injustice, and alienation providing strong motivational "push" factors for involvement in terrorism;
- The allure of personal status and other rewards (e.g., excitement) proved a powerful "pull" factor;
- The development of disinhibition of moral restraints on killing.

Throughout the 1970s and 1980s, a popular view was that those who engaged in terrorism were probably as abnormal and unusual as the activity in which they engaged. Disturbing behavior surely reflected a disturbed individual, or so the logic went. These assumptions began to form the basis of attempts to find an overarching terrorist profile—the further assumption being that not only was the terrorist

likely to be "special," or different from the nonterrorist, but that there were probably certain features shared by people who would want to become involved in that
activity in the first place.

Russell and Miller,[3] in one of the earliest and most cited analyses of the terrorist,
found that among 350 terrorist leaders and followers spread across 18 movements
(active between 1966 and 1976), those convicted of terrorist offenses tended to be
male, young, single, from upper-middle class families, and university educated. In
fact, many of them were recruited while at a university. Other studies also challenge
many of the popular stereotypes of who becomes a terrorist, with several confirm-
ing Russell and Miller's early findings that terrorists tend to be better educated and
generally come from higher socioeconomic classes than their nonterrorist fellow
countrymen and countrywomen.[4]

Gambetta and Hertog[5] recently discovered that graduates from science, medi-
cine, and especially engineering are overrepresented in Islamist movements in the
Muslim world though not in violent Islamic groups operating in Western countries. Engineers are strongly represented among graduates in the latter sample,
however. This compares to their relatively miniscule appearance in right-wing
terrorist groups and total absence in left-wing groups.

For every study that shows this, however, there will almost always be another to
offer an opposing, if not contradictory, viewpoint. Bakker's 2006 exploratory study
of European jihadis revealed no profile of either individual jihadis or the networks
to which they belonged,[6] with echoes of these findings suggested in studies by
Gartenstein-Ross and Grossman[7] and Silber and Bhatt.[8]

The reason no definitive terrorist profile has yet been found may not only be
because academics have not had access to the right data or subjects; perhaps it is
because there is not necessarily one definitive terrorist profile to be found. The
inability to find patterns can prove frustrating if it is assumed that these patterns
are there to be found. This frustration is evident in the works of many detailed
studies, including an analysis of jihadi terrorism in the Netherlands.[9] Researchers
from the Dutch Ministry of Security and Justice gained access to police files from
12 large-scale criminal investigations that were conducted in the Netherlands
from July 2001 to July 2005. Though subject to the usual caveats associated with
such enquiry (i.e., not all jihadi activities come to the knowledge of the police and
the police do not initiate criminal investigations into all jihadi activities that come
to their knowledge), the researchers were nevertheless provided an opportunity to
study reports on "113 different actors ... active on Dutch territory."

The researchers found "people with varying life stories and strongly different
backgrounds and motives." The groups with which these individuals affiliate were
characterized by "extremely fluid and informal cooperations, which are part of a
broader movement by their mutual and transnational interrelatedness as decen-
tralised groups [engaging in] a large variety of activities that are spread over a
large area."

These similarities, however, masked a striking heterogeneity of experience. In
terrorism studies, research activity that is data-driven tends to reveal, more often
than not, a diverse pattern of life histories and experiences. Collectively, these

studies render unhelpful the very idea of a simple profile. In fact, heterogeneity of membership is increasingly the norm in studies of terrorist networks, a finding corroborated by studies including comprehensive reviews of the literature, notably that of Davis and Cragin.[10] If there is a terrorist profile to be found, the best of academic terrorism researchers have yet to discover it.

■ PATHWAYS AND PROCESSES: DATA-DRIVEN ANALYSIS

Mirroring developments in contemporary criminology, assumptions about the utility of explaining terrorist behavior in terms of dispositional qualities (i.e., what people are "like," and how they might be different from others who do not exhibit similar behavior) have given way to a greater analysis of the role of situational factors. We have, in other words, seen a shift from profiles to pathways and processes. The study of terrorism has seen valuable analyses of this type emerge in recent years.

Berko et al.[11] compared incarcerated Arab/Palestinian women who were involved in conventional crime with those involved in security violations or terrorism. Though terrorism is traditionally a male-dominated activity, recent evidence (e.g., Bloom[12] and Hamilton[13]) has drawn attention to the increasing prominence of women in frontline activity and how similar or different their motivational factors are from their male colleagues. Berko and colleagues examined background, motivation, and pathways to lawbreaking of the conventional offenders and security violators, as well as their prison experiences. The "security violators" displayed higher education and were more likely to have had "normal" childhoods within traditional family structures. The criminals in the sample were characterized more by mistreatment by family members and less stable family structures overall. Situational issues also played a more significant role in characterizing women's involvement in terrorism. Although the loss of a "prospective husband" or boyfriend appeared to be factor in some cases, becoming involved in militant activity provided "an outlet for women who were seeking excitement from an otherwise uneventful existence. Some women communicated the desire to 'get out of the house and meet the shabab (guys)' or simply 'do something' as their main reason for volunteering."

In the United States, Smith and Damphousse[14] also compared terrorist offenders with nonterrorist offenders. They found a distinguishable difference in sociodemographic characteristics between those indicted for terrorism-related activities and those who can be categorized as traditional offenders. There is also divergence apparent *within* the terrorist dataset. For example, the average age of indicted left-wing and right-wing terrorists grew over the period studied; those operationalized as "international terrorists," on the other hand, declined in average age. Left-wing terrorists also became less educated and held less privileged occupational statuses on average across time. Disproportionate numbers of right-wing terrorists, particularly the leadership, were employed in the aerospace or aeronautical industry. Left-wing and international terrorists generally tended to come from urban environments compared to their right-wing counterparts who typically were far more rural.

In an analysis of Basque ETA activists, Reinares[15] examined judicial summaries and proceedings from 1977 to 1998 in the Juzgado Central de Instruccion number two of the Audiencia Nacional in Spain. Reinares "segregated the different variables under consideration along three consecutive periods of time." Reinares' interviewees asserted that they considered "alternative, nonviolent possibilities of political engagement," but that "militancy … was perceived … as a much more exciting option than any other form of political involvement." He asserts that a major risk factor for becoming involved is not ideological but "when he or she is available in terms of time and personal responsibilities." The territories from which ETA recruited remained remarkably consistent, with a small number of towns providing the bulk of new recruits across time. Typically these towns displayed fewer Basque traits, such as the number of *euskera* (Basque) speakers. Recruits also diverged in their occupational status. Across time, "student" became the major occupation/status, at the expense of specialized industrial and services workers who had encapsulated half of ETA's cadre between 1970 and 1977. Concurrently, these students tended to be middle class, while members from the working classes declined a considerable amount between phases one and three.

In 2004, Marc Sageman[16] presented his major analysis of 172 members of the global Salafi movement. Drawing primarily on court transcripts, he found little or no relationship between the poverty or religious devotion of individuals and their reasons for joining terrorist networks. His jihadis were typically in their mid-20s, relatively more educated, and came from more privileged backgrounds than average citizens. Sageman illustrates (through social network analysis and case studies) that often the compulsion to join groups evolves through friendship and kinship networks. Would-be jihadis typically are first-generation or second-generation immigrants who struggle to assimilate themselves into their new surroundings. This leads to a sense of alienation and they then seek like-minded groups (typically found in prayer groups or mosques) who gradually radicalize together. After the invasion of Afghanistan, Sageman argued, al-Qaeda's structure changed from a mostly hierarchical organization with a number of core leaders at the summit to a far more linear, loosely connected, cellular-based system. This, he argued, provided the organizational context to understanding the development of these small-group dynamics for recruitment and mobilization.

In 2008, Magouirk,[17] along with Sageman and colleague Scott Atran, presented an analysis of activists involved in Southeast Asian jihadi networks. Using primary source documents, Magouirk et al. were interested in establishing the nature of the ties between different militants in the network. Their study drew a sharp contrast between traditional views of terrorist group structures (usually rigid and hierarchical in nature) with a reality that is "more complicated." Their findings support the idea that "kinship networks are the glue that holds radical networks together in Southeast Asia," adding that their research illustrates the existence of a "vast spectrum of overlapping kin relationships that cut across different groups *within* organizations and even *across* organizations." They concluded that "all jihadists are not the same," adding that the majority of Jemaah Islamiyah members were "significantly less radical" than the leadership.

Methodological Issues

Paying attention to studies of terrorists that are based on data is important. It allows us to build our knowledge of the processes of mobilization and recruitment into groups and to come as close as possible (with open-source data) to knowing what precisely might be going on in such groups. We should, however, not allow the emergent complexity of such portraits to overwhelm us to the point of inaction. It is popular now to qualify almost every study in terrorism as complex and ambiguous, with individuals marked both by heterogeneity and idiosyncrasy. Finding a "diverse" collection of motivations may represent valid outcomes, but it may also be the result of a failure to systematically (and with rigorous methods) use the right questions to guide the enquiry. That complexity should certainly not prevent us from offering tentative patterns, where they are to be found. The studies described above represent only a few of the terrorism studies that have been produced even since 9/11, and although it may be invidious to single out the works of specific scholars, these examples (and there are many more) were chosen as illustrations of strong and robust methodological approaches to the study of the terrorist.

Reinares' study is significant not only for the scope of his effort to characterize the recruitment patterns into the broader Basque militant movement but for other reasons too. Firsthand accounts by ETA members relayed the importance of social ties, culture, age, politicization, and prestige as push and pull factors toward joining the group. Some interviewees also related in their accounts the internal dissent that often took place over the presence of women in the group while some female recruits report instances of sexual harassment by fellow ETA members. This is precisely the kind of data unlikely to emerge from secondary source material (e.g., newspaper accounts) alone.

Similarly, Reinares' analysis derives from a large dataset he built on 614 convicted members of ETA. Although the data are not always close to full density (it approaches only 50% on some variables, notably social class, occupation type, town/province/territory of residence, marital status, and age at moment of recruitment), Reinares' use of triangulated methods by incorporating interview data is an excellent approach to this line of enquiry. Given the nature of what is being collected, this is not surprising. However, it limits the ability to engage in an inferential statistical methodology such as a regression analysis. If the data were denser, Reinares would have been capable of determining the causality of the key variables. This weakness is largely overcome by triangulating the descriptive findings with firsthand interview accounts.

Comparison of such diverse cases, from ETA to al-Qaeda in southeast Asia to Dutch jihadis (described earlier), might on the one hand appear self-defeating, and in the context of attempting to understand Irish militants, it may appear at first glance to be inappropriate if not irrelevant. But comparing different studies in this way is both interesting and valuable. Though it should not necessarily be expected to reveal too many similarities (after all, they represent quite distinct and unique contexts, with different sociopolitical and cultural influences even *within* what appears to be homogeneous threats, e.g., jihadi terrorism), using quantitative data derived from verifiable open-source documentation (as well as access to court transcripts and other open-source material where possible) as a starting point is an important common feature in all of these studies.

Comparison of different cases (e.g., Alonso's study of IRA and ETA militants[18]) illustrates that it is possible to delineate common processes from context-specific issues. Similarly, Khosrokhavar and Macey,[19] in interviews with militants from Iran, Palestine, Lebanon, and Egypt, illustrate the need for comparative approaches even within what might appear to be a single context (in their study, that of Islamist martyrdom).

Collectively, these data-driven studies of terrorist recruitment and mobilization give us valuable starting points and tangible data points for identifying the right kinds of questions, including the following:

1. When do people become involved in terrorist activity?
2. Where do they come from? (e.g., urban, rural areas?)
3. When are they first convicted of terrorist activity (or other illegal acts within the group)?
4. What is their occupation?
5. Are they arrested/convicted alone or with others?
6. What specific activities do they engage in while a member of the group, and how does this change over time?

■ WHO BECOMES A DISSIDENT?

The VDR project has seen the collection of open-source information on 662 individuals involved in dissident activity. Of these, 199 are classified as "convicted,"[20] that is, they are associated with a confirmed conviction for illegal activity in the context of involvement in a dissident Republican movement. This includes those who are currently serving their sentence *and* those who have already served a sentence. Also included in the 199 are 14 individuals who were convicted but given a suspended sentence and one person who was convicted and fined. A further 78 are currently charged with VDR offenses and are awaiting trial and two were charged but died before their court date. These data refer only to those people who have been *named* in open sources (more than two). It does not account for reports of unnamed people (e.g., "a 29-year-old man" of whom no information can be verified) being charged for VDR offenses.

In addition, data have been collected on the cases of 25 individuals who were acquitted and 29 whose charges were dropped before trial. There are additional data on known supporters and "alleged" members of VDR groups and five facilitators. The remaining individuals are nonviolent dissident Republicans, those who have demonstrated their dissidence through political activity and other nonviolent methods. Although these individuals are not directly involved in violent dissident Republicanism they do provide a rare natural comparison to those who choose to enter it. The VDR project identified 283 "political" dissidents. This includes people involved solely with political parties such as Republican Sinn Féin (RSF) and 32 County Sovereignty Movement (32CSM) and not associated with violence through a charge or conviction. A significant number of RSF members were identified due to a thorough analysis of the party's paper *Saoirse*.

Table 4.1 provides a complete breakdown of the individual-level data contained within the database. As well as the overall figures it also provides data on whether people were convicted or charged for violent or nonviolent offenses. "Violent" implies *direct responsibility* for a violent act. A nonviolent charge implies membership of, or occupation of a supportive role within, a paramilitary organization. An example of a supportive nonviolent charge is that of weapons possession. Though at first glance it might appear unusual to categorize this as "nonviolent," a charge such as this implies that the weapons were being stored and were not in the process of being transported to commit a violent attack (i.e., they were static). But if a person is convicted of weapons possession with an intent to commit a violent act, then that is classified as a violent conviction. The distinction is critical, and is discussed further below.

The majority of convictions have been for nonviolent charges. The number of people charged for violent and nonviolent convictions is relatively even: 38 people in the database have violent charges and 43 have nonviolent charges.

Of the currently active groups the two affiliations with the greatest representation in the convicted data are the Real IRA (RIRA) and the Continuity IRA (CIRA) (see Table 4.2). We have accounted for 95 convicted RIRA members and 85 convicted CIRA members; there is one further individual whose affiliation with the CIRA or RIRA is unclear. The majority of convictions for both groups have been for nonviolent activity: 61 RIRA and 54 CIRA members were convicted of nonviolent charges, compared with 35 RIRA and 31 CIRA members convicted of violent activity. The database also includes four Óglaigh na hÉireann (ONH) (RIRA) members and one Republican Action Against Drugs (RAAD) member with convictions. This reflects these groups' recent increased activity as well as the

TABLE 4.1. *Dissident Personnel by Status*

Status of Personnel	Number of Personnel
Political dissident	283
Convicted: nonviolent	127
Convicted: violent	72
Charged: nonviolent	43
Charged: violent	38
Alleged members of VDR group	35
Charges dropped: nonviolent	20
Acquitted: nonviolent	15
Acquitted: violent	10
Charges dropped: violent	9
Facilitators of VDR groups	5
Convicted of non-VDR offense	1
Charged with non-VDR offense	1
Community activist	3

VDR, Violent Dissident Republican.

transfer of allegiance of a number of personnel across groups. There are a further 13 individuals whose affiliation is unknown.

Although the CIRA is the oldest group, established in 1986, the RIRA has been the most consistently active. This increased consistency of activity has been coupled with responsibility for the most fatal and high-profile attacks of all the VDR groups, most notably the 1998 Omagh bombing, the English bombing campaign of the early 2000s, and the 2009 Massereene Barracks attacks. As with all high-profile attacks, there has been the inevitable concentration on bringing those responsible for the attack to justice. The resultant investigations have focused not only on those directly responsible for the attacks themselves but also on those who play a more indirect, supportive role.

The reason there are unknown affiliations, even after conviction, is due to the wording of the charges brought against the convicted. Of the nine "unknowns" with nonviolent convictions, seven were convicted of weapons possession and two of group membership. Both sets of charges refer to the VDR groups generically as "the Irish Republican Army, otherwise Óglaigh na hÉireann, otherwise the IRA." This nonspecific phrase used by the courts, especially in the Republic of Ireland, does not signify any individual group. For the four people convicted of violent activity, no claim was made from any group for their actions. However, the offenses for which they were convicted were referred to in the open sources and the courts as being dissident Irish Republican activity.

The data in Table 4.2 portray all of those who have been convicted of VDR activity at any stage, though it is useful to examine this further by specific waves. In all, 25 separate individuals, 14 RIRA and 11 CIRA members, were convicted of VDR activity committed in Wave 1 (i.e., between 31 August 1994 and 15 August 1998). Of these convictions 18 were for violent activity and seven for nonviolent activity. The convictions were for eight separate events, six violent and two nonviolent. Of the violent convictions 14 were for members of the RIRA, and the remaining four were CIRA.

All of the seven nonviolent convictions were for CIRA members, and all but one conviction was the result of a single arms find. The six people convicted were Josephine Hayden, Martin McGrath, Sean Moore, Richard Wallace, Joe Mounsey, and George Buckley. There were found to be in possession of firearms and ammunition in "suspicious circumstances" in Tallaght in May 1995.[21] Similarly, the four CIRA members convicted of actual violent activity were also convicted for one specific incident. Their charge related to the transportation of explosives with intent. Included within the four was one of the original CIRA leaders, Michael Hegarty, who was also on the Ard Comhairle (national executive council) of

TABLE 4.2. *Group Affiliation of Convicted Violent Dissident Republican Personnel*

	RIRA	CIRA	RIRA/CIRA	ONH (RIRA)	RAAD	Unknown
Convicted: violent	34	31	0	2	0	4
Convicted: nonviolent	61	54	1	2	1	9
Total	95	85	1	4	1	13

RIRA, Real IRA; CIRA, Continuity IRA; ONH, Óglaigh na hÉireann; RAAD, Republican Action Against Drugs.

RSF.[22] Prior to the 1986 split Hegarty had been a member of the Provisional IRA (PIRA).

The 14 RIRA convictions were for six separate events: one bomb detonation, four intercepted bombs, and one violent robbery. The four sets of convictions for intercepted bombs are indicative of two distinct strategies adopted by the RIRA at this stage. Two sets of convictions were for bombs being transported from the border county of Louth to Northern Ireland. This highlights the dominance of this county in the quartermaster and bomb preparation role within the RIRA. The other two were for bombs being transported to locations in England for attack. One bomb was intercepted on the way from Ireland to England and the other set of explosives was already in London, the intended target. This strategy of targeting England is one of the defining features of RIRA activity at the beginning of Wave 2 (1998 to 2007). The attacks on England in Wave 2 can be viewed within an overall dissident "England strategy" that began in Wave 1. All of the RIRA convictions in Wave 1 were for violent activities in 1998. The group's ability to be this violently active within a matter of months of its split from the PIRA indicates an initial strength, though not necessarily in numbers of members; the data suggest that the group was strong with respect to expertise and the equipment to which they had access. This can best be explained by the fact that a significant proportion of the founding members of the RIRA originated from the quartermaster and engineering sections of the PIRA.

There were 136 convictions for VDR offenses committed within Wave 2 (August 16 1998 to January 27 2007). Of these, 95 were convictions for violent offenses and 41 for nonviolent offenses. The most common conviction in this wave was weapons possession. Of the 136 people convicted, 63—including 29 CIRA members and 34 RIRA members—were for this offense. These 63 convictions related to 31 separate arms finds. This significant level of arms finds, across every year of the wave, provides evidence of high levels of intelligence within the security services both north and south of the border in the aftermath of the Omagh bombing.

For a terrorist organization to survive and be active it requires a certain amount of financial capital. The VDR groups raise a small amount of funds within the immediate Republican communities across Ireland, as well as within the Irish diaspora abroad. However, these collections alone would prove to be insufficient to sustain a significant armed offensive. VDRs have become actively involved in organized crime. This is apparent in Wave 2, during which five individuals were convicted for two separate instances of cigarette smuggling and another four were convicted for the illegal treatment and distribution of red diesel. These were all in relation to RIRA activity. Six members of the CIRA alone were convicted of armed robbery within the wave.

The leadership of the RIRA was directly implicated in the group's involvement in organized crime. In October 2003 Michael Campbell and Brian Thomas Hoey were convicted for their roles in an RIRA cigarette smuggling ring between the Netherlands and Ireland.[23] Since his release Campbell, the brother of RIRA leader Liam Campbell, has been accused of retaining his smuggling role for the RIRA. These charges are in relation to his suspected attempts at arms acquisition in

Lithuania in 2008.[24] He is currently standing trial for these charges in the Eastern European country.

The 41 convictions for violent offenses relate to 29 separate offenses across the nine years of the wave. The sporadic bombing campaigns of both the RIRA and CIRA are reflected in these convictions. Six people were convicted of successful bombings (i.e., bombs that detonated at their intended target). The most significant of these convictions are those of five RIRA members convicted of the English bombing campaign that targeted the BBC and Ealing Broadway in London and New Street Station in Birmingham in 2001. Two of the men involved in this bombing campaign, brothers Robert and Aidan Hulme, were also convicted of the aforementioned red diesel treatment and distribution that took place in Chilton, Durham, near Leeds. The twin roles adopted by the Hulme brothers show the interconnected nature of the criminal and terrorist activities of the RIRA.

Of the five people convicted for their roles in the bombing campaigns, three were 24 years old or younger at the time. The youngest, John Hannan, was 17; Robert Hulme was 21 and Aidan Hulme was 24. The two remaining members of the group were in their early 30s at the time of the bombings: Noel Maguire, the alleged leader, was 31 and James McCormack was 32. None of the five men had any previous convictions for paramilitary offenses. This appears to have been an intentional strategy of the RIRA to send a team of operatives that was unknown to security forces. This is a strategy that the group also applied in its unsuccessful attempt to bomb London toward the end of Wave 1 in the summer of 1998. The three men convicted of this—Anthony Hyland, Liam Grogan, and Darren Mulholland—were 25, 21, and 19 years old, respectively.

This strategy of using "fresh skins" is an old PIRA one. Gerry Kelly, Hugh Feeney, and Marian and Dolours Price were all aged between 19 and 22 years when they bombed both the Old Bailey and the Whitehall army recruitment center in 1973. "Fresh skins" are used because their presence together in England will not raise any unwanted suspicion, lowering the risk of being caught while they prepare for and execute the attacks. Although still an advantage, this is not as necessary for those operating within Northern Ireland, where they would obviously not evoke as much suspicion. A more important factor may be that within Northern Ireland the groups have a wider support network in place than in England, so that each individual member must be disciplined and inconspicuous in their activity if they are not to draw attention to themselves or the rest of the group.

Wave 3 (January 28 2007 to the present day) saw a total of 36 convictions. CIRA has had 13 personnel convicted and RIRA has had 11. ONH (RIRA) and RAAD have had three and one member(s) convicted, respectively. These low figures are more illustrative of the groups' recent emergence than their low levels of activity; the growing levels of violence for each group have already been demonstrated in Chapter 3. Even though Wave 3 is the most violent of the three waves these conviction statistics are not surprising. The period of time between charge and conviction for VDR offenses has proven to be quite long in some instances, up to 3 years. This is especially noticeable with respect to cases in which the accused is charged with violent activity. Therefore the upsurge in violence has only recently led to a growing number of convictions.

Although the unambiguous violent cases can take a significant amount of time to come to court, one of the most discernible patterns in recent times is the speed of conviction for those facing nonviolent charges, especially the charge of weapons "possession." This relates both to charges of weapons possession *with* intent to endanger a person's life as well as the stand-alone charge of possession. There are two main factors influencing this: the strength of the evidence against the accused and the willingness of a number of charged personnel to plead guilty. In all, 15 separate individuals have pleaded guilty to VDR charges in Wave 3, 11 for weapons possession charges. Members of four groups pleaded guilty. Across the three waves 84 of those who have been convicted of VDR offenses have pleaded guilty; this represents 42% of all of those convicted. Across the groups 36 CIRA, 38 RIRA, three ONH (RIRA), one RAAD, and six personnel with unknown affiliations have each chosen to plead guilty. In light of the large number of arrests for weapons possession in recent times this willingness to plead guilty may result in another upsurge in convictions.

Even when the charges carry long sentences, if the evidence against them is strong enough those charged regularly plead guilty. An example of this can been seen in the case of three CIRA members, Damien McKenna, Gary Toman, and Sean McConville, charged with possession of a mortar with intent to cause harm. They were each jailed for 15 years in 2009 for the 2007 offense to which they admitted. The three men, all in their mid-20s, were not found to be in possession of the device or the launching tube. However, DNA and fiber evidence linked them to the weapon, which was found a mile away from their car. It had been their intention to use the mortar to murder Police Service of Northern Ireland (PSNI) officers.[25] The scenes at their sentencing demonstrate the heroic stature in which Republican prisoners are held. It was reported that as they were led to their cells "the packed public gallery erupted into cheers and applause with a Tricolour being held aloft."[26] Such scenes have been replicated at a number of sentencings.

One of the most significant outcomes of this most recent wave of violence has been the emergence of a number of new VDR groups. This was illustrated in the analysis of the events data presented in Chapter 3. It is similarly reflected both in the four convictions against ONH (RIRA) and RAAD members as well as in the charges brought against members of ONH (RIRA) and the new Tyrone group "the IRA." These new groups account for nine of the charged individuals awaiting trial. Both groups demonstrated their violent intent in their recent actions, which have predominantly targeted the security forces. The murder of Constable Ronan Kerr in April 2011 was claimed by "the IRA." This group is said to be made up of former Provisional IRA members discontent with the perceived lack of progress made by the politicization of Sinn Féin. In the aftermath of Ronan Kerr's murder three men, Brian Anthony Sheridan, Brian Francis Calvin, and Dominic Edward Dynes, were each charged with "possession of firearms and two counts of possessing articles for use in terrorism."[27] In contrast with the previous discussion of dissident Republicans apparently recognizing the legitimacy of the courts, these three men would not reply in court, and refused to identify themselves.[28] This was a tactic employed by the Provisional IRA during the Troubles.

To date little is known about the membership of "the IRA." However, it is reported that it is made up of former PIRA members ranging in age from their late 30s to 50s, with considerable levels of experience and expertise.[29]

Gender

Recent analysis suggests that the role of women in terrorist groups is changing significantly. This can be seen in the increased frontline violent activity by female members.[30] However, evidence of this trend does not emerge from the conviction data within the VDR database. Males account for 98.5% of all VDR convictions, and 100% of those who have been convicted for violent activity across the three waves have been male. Only 2.44% of those convicted for nonviolent activity are female. This pattern of male dominance is borne out in the charged data. Of all those charged and awaiting trial 95% are male, with the remaining 5% being female. As with those convicted for violent activity, 100% of those charged for violent offenses are male and only 9.3% of those charged for nonviolent offenses are female.

These results suggest that women are not yet *directly* involved in violent dissident activity, but a small number are involved in the preparation and support of violent events. Those women who have been convicted have predominantly been convicted for either membership or weapons possession. The pattern is similar for those women who have been charged. In spite of these low figures there are some women who are known to play pivotal roles within the paramilitary organizations. The clearest evidence for this came in 2003 when an unidentified female member of the RIRA read a statement from the Army Council. This statement outlined the group's interpretation of events that led to the 2002 split and the formation of ONH (RIRA).[31] This is a task that would not have been trusted to a junior member.

The convicted and charged data suggest a minimal role played by women within violent dissident Republicanism. However, throughout Irish Republican history there have been a number of high-profile women active in the IRA and throughout the overall Republican Movement. This continued across the three waves of dissident Republicanism. The highest concentration of women appears to be within the political parties. Of all political dissidents 14.13% are women. The two most dominant dissident political parties, Republican Sinn Féin and the 32 County Sovereignty Movement, both have a number of high-profile women in their leadership, including some who have previously been convicted of violent activity and others who have not. Since its birth in 1986 Republican Sinn Féin has had a number of prominent women within its leadership. Cathleen Knowles McGuirk, who had been a joint secretary of Sinn Féin, stepped down from that leadership in 1982 when the Ard Fheis voted to drop "Éire Nua" as an official policy of the movement. She was among the most high-profile members to leave Sinn Féin in 1986 and form RSF.[32] She maintained a leadership role within the party until her exit in 2010 to form Real Sinn Féin with Des Long.

A number of women play dominant roles within the leadership of RSF, notably vice-president Geraldine Taylor and general secretary Josephine Hayden. As well as her political role Hayden was also convicted for transporting arms and ammunition for the CIRA in the mid-1990s,[33] and alongside Richard Walsh she was the visible face of RSF in the aftermath of the murder of Stephen Carroll by the CIRA in March 2009.

Even though Real Sinn Féin portray RSF as a "band of cronies and old women"[34] they are actively promoting young female members such as Cait Trainor alongside those who are considered to be the old guard. In recent years Trainor, a member of the RSF Ard Comhairle, has become one of the most visible spokespeople for the party and an advocate for the continuation of armed struggle. She has recently been charged, alongside Sean Maloney, of encouraging terrorism. This is a result of her participation in a Channel 4 documentary in which she stated that she supported "the right of every Irish man and woman to participate in armed struggle."[35] Although these and other women may or may not be directly involved in the violent activity of the CIRA, or any other groups, they play a prominent role in the promotion and evolution of the party and its armed wing.

32CSM, akin to RSF, has also had a number of influential women within its leadership. Among those are Bernadette Sands-McKevitt and Marian Price. Not only do these women contribute to the organization through their actions but they also help to legitimize it because of the pivotal roles they and their families have played within the PIRA and Sinn Féin. Sands-McKevitt's brother, Bobby Sands, was the leader of the 1981 hunger strikes and remains one of the most iconic figures of Republicanism. In her attempts both to promote 32CSM's position and also delegitimize the politicization of the Provisional Movement Sands-McKevitt has often invoked the memory of her brother. Hennessy cites one such example in her denouncement of the Good Friday Agreement: "Bobby did not die for cross-border bodies with executive powers. He did not die for nationalists to be equal British citizens within the Northern Ireland state."[36] Sands-McKevitt no longer plays as visible a role in dissident Republicanism; she currently appears to be concentrating her political activities on her campaign for the release of her husband, the founding RIRA leader Michael McKevitt.[37]

One of the most visible people involved in dissident Republicanism today is Marian Price. Jailed in 1973, alongside Hugh Feeney, Gerry Kelly, and her sister Dolours, for her part in the London bombings of that year, her history ensures that her beliefs and actions have the respect of a significant portion of the dissident community, and in turn this provides further legitimacy to 32CSM. She is officially a member of 32CSM and denies any current paramilitary involvement. However, her recent actions suggest that, at the very least, she has a close connection with the RIRA. In May 2011, similar to Cait Trainor, she was charged with encouraging support for a paramilitary organization, namely the RIRA. This charge was brought after she held the written statement for a masked RIRA at the 2011 32CSM Easter commemoration in Derry.[38] More recently she has been charged in connection with the murders of the soldiers at Massereene Barracks in March 2009. Her charge relates to providing property and a mobile phone to those responsible for the murder.[39] If convicted this will provide further evidence for the supportive role played by females in the preparation for violent VDR activity.

Age

There are two distinct age groups active within dissident Republicanism, experienced older Republicans and "a younger generation" active for the first time. For those who have been convicted on more than one occasion, their ages at the time of both convictions are portrayed in analysis. Therefore this is more reflective of an individual's age at the point of illegal activity. There are insufficient data available on the ages of the other categories of dissidents (e.g., political, nonviolent members). In some studies of terrorist recruitment, age at first conviction is offered as a proxy for age of "joining." This is misleading, and there is no attempt here to make the same claim. Members often become involved long before they engage in violent activity, let alone face a conviction. The data are purely reflective of age at the time of violent activity, because the most reliable data—the only information that can be supported by secondary sources—are those provided at the point of conviction. However, even with this stipulation, the data still indicate the extensive range of Republican experience within the dissident groups. The experience levels of older members support the argument that the dissidents possess not simply the intention to maintain a paramilitary campaign but also a heightened capacity to at least plan for one. Of particular relevance here is the issue of recidivism, and the extent to which the older members are former paramilitaries from the PIRA and other groupings. We will consider this question later.

As illustrated in Figure 4.1, the most concentrated age range across the two largest groups, the CIRA and RIRA, is 21–30 and 31–40, with significant levels also found at 51–60 years. The majority of younger dissidents, aged 14–30 years,

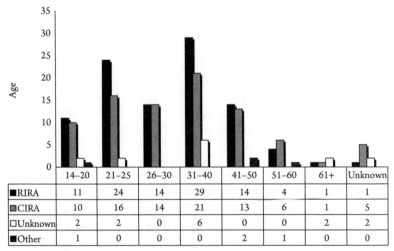

	14–20	21–25	26–30	31–40	41–50	51–60	61+	Unknown
■RIRA	11	24	14	29	14	4	1	1
▩CIRA	10	16	14	21	13	6	1	5
☐Unknown	2	2	0	6	0	0	2	2
■Other	1	0	0	0	2	1	0	0

Figure 4.1. Age range of convicted VDR personnel (at time of illegal activity).

join VDR groups as their first ever experience of Republican activity. The youngest members of the groupings will have had little to no adult experiences of the Troubles, and in some cases have not even been born in Northern Ireland, let alone before the 1994 ceasefires. This issue raises significant questions about motivational factors, with dissident leadership figures and those with previous active service in the Provisional IRA and early CIRA exploiting significant opportunities to glorify active involvement in militant Republicanism.

When the age range of convicted personnel is compared to that of those who have been charged and are awaiting trial, a similar pattern emerges. Within the charged data the most dominant age ranges for both the RIRA and the CIRA are within the younger ranges of 14–20 and 21–30, followed closely by 41–50 years. Though we should be careful not to infer too much from "charged" data, they provide an interesting comparison. However, there is a large proportion of "unknowns" within the 31–40 year range, and it is possible that when their affiliations are known both of the main groups will again show a large active membership within the 31–40 year age range.

The "unknown" members in this age range includes suspected members of "other" groups charged, four arrested in the investigations that followed Ronan Kerr's murder. These people are suspected of being members of the new Tyrone-based "IRA". If these charged data are turned into convictions it would provide some level of support for this hypothesis.

The dominance of younger personnel partaking in violent activity suggests that it is an intentional strategy of the VDR groups to use younger operatives in attacks. Older members are likely to possess greater skill sets for the preparation for attacks (manufacturing bombs, etc.) and the training of new recruits, which come with their more extensive paramilitary experience. However, younger members are also less likely to be recognized by the security forces, which increases the chances of a attack being "successful." These findings are not reflected in the charged data. Within this the largest age range is 31–40, closely followed by 21–30 years. This largest range includes three members of the RIRA, six "others" and three "unknowns." As was mentioned in the discussion of the overall charged data, three of those within the "others" are believed to be from "the IRA"; the other three are suspected of ONH (RIRA) membership.

The three suspected RIRA members within this age range are John Brady (who died before reaching trial), who was charged with assault; Kevin Barry Nolan, charged and awaiting trial for the attempted murder of a PSNI officer; and Brian Shivers, charged for the murder of two British soldiers at Massereene Barracks in March 2009. Shivers is currently charged alongside Colin Duffy, represented in the 41–50 year range.

On convictions for activity other than direct violence, the most represented age ranges are still 31–40 and 21–30 years. There are also 23 individuals in the 41–50 year range. As stated earlier, the most common nonviolent convictions are those of membership and weapons possession.

A new terrorist organization needs financial capital to be able to launch a sustain campaign and the data show that in order to do so the group has partaken in organized crime as well as in violent robberies. One such example was the foiled robbery of a Securicor van in Wicklow in the Republic of Ireland in May 1998. The six robbers, all affiliated with the RIRA, included both new recruits and more experienced members such as Pascal Burke. Ronan McLoughlin was killed during the act and was therefore never convicted. The RIRA was dominated by members from Dublin and County Louth during this initial stage. All six people involved in this robbery were based in Dublin. This leads us to believe it was an action by a local unit of the RIRA in an attempt to finance future activity for the wider national organization.

All of the nonviolent convictions in Wave 1 are representative of CIRA activity. As was stated earlier there was one significant arms find in Tallaght at the beginning of the wave that resulted in six CIRA members being convicted. This group consisted of personnel in their late 30s to mid-50s. As the CIRA had been established in 1986, a number of these members had only ever been involved with the CIRA and RSF. This case further emphasizes the supportive and quartermaster role played by older dissidents, specifically southern-based ones.

The conviction data for Wave 2 (August 16 1998 to January 27 2007) provides the most comprehensive illustration from the three waves of the two dominant age ranges active within dissident Republicanism. Newer recruits convicted in the courts were aged 14–30 years at the time of their arrest; a second group of more experienced Republicans was 31–50 years at the time of their arrest. As this wave has the most convictions to analyze it therefore presents the most reliable data for convictions across the three waves. As with every wave, it is only when these data are broken down into violent and nonviolent convictions that a more comprehensive picture of the significance of age is shown.

The end of this first wave saw the emergence of the RIRA, the most consistently active of all VDR groups. Leading this split was the former quartermaster general of the PIRA, Mickey McKevitt. The aftermath of the Omagh bombing brought the wave to a close. Even though McKevitt's conviction came in the aftermath of investigations into Omagh it is contained within the Wave 2 data because he was convicted for "directing terrorist activity" between 29 August 1999 and 23 October 2000, as well as for belonging to an illegal organization between 29 August 1999 and 28 March 2001.[40] Even though this conviction does not directly relate to a specific violent act, McKevitt was convicted of directing terrorism, so it has been classified as a violent act (an easier distinction to make when compared to weapons *possession*, as in the earlier example).

McKevitt was in his late 40s/early 50s at this time, when he was one of the most experienced members of the RIRA. His knowledge as a former quartermaster for the PIRA and the leadership role he held within the RIRA prior to his conviction had a significant influence on shaping the actual role he and other members of the leadership played within the organization. This marked distinction between the roles of the leadership and the ordinary members is clearly defined within each of the VDR groups, especially the larger RIRA and CIRA.

Younger, inexperienced recruits are given some degree of paramilitary training prior to involvement in violent activity. This training generally happens in remote rural areas, and is usually done with groups of young recruits. There were four such training camps detected in Wave 2, leading to the conviction of 22 individuals: 9 CIRA members and 13 RIRA members. All four camps were located deep within the Republic of Ireland. With respect to age and experience, though, these training camps represent one the most direct examples of the separate roles of the two main age groups. At them the experienced paramilitaries used their knowledge and experience to train the younger recruits. The training invariably consists of weapons training and paramilitary drills, though new recruits are also taught the history, ideology, and purpose of the terrorist organization. This provides the leadership with an isolated opportunity to influence the decisions and beliefs of their new conscripts.

New members can be as young as 14 years, and they tend to be very impressionable. A good illustration of this is the case of the brothers Vincent (14) and Stephen Kelly (18) who were remanded in custody, along with seven others, in 1999 after attending an RIRA lecture and training camp in Stamullen, County Meath. They both received suspended sentences for "unlawful drilling and marching." In 2006 the younger of the brothers, Vincent, then aged 21 years, was sentenced to 5 years in prison for membership of an illegal organization (the RIRA) and weapons possession.[41] Among those convicted alongside the Kellys was Seamus McGreevy, who was running the camp. At the time, McGreevy, who was 45 years old, was a senior member of the RIRA leadership and is reported to have since been heavily involved in the organization and arming of the group.[42]

Although arming is essential, if a VDR group is to partake in a sustained and sophisticated bombing campaign the group requires skilled and experienced bombmakers. This is why the threat posed by the newly formed Tyrone-based "IRA" represents a worrying development. It is believed that the group has an experienced PIRA bombmaker as one of its members.[43] The bombmaker is a very specialized member of any terrorist organization. Although bombmakers are usually not directly involved in the planting of the explosives their skill base determines the success of a bombing operation or an extended campaign. In 2001 two of the most skilled bombmakers in the RIRA, Kenneth and Alan Patterson, were convicted of running bomb factories in Dublin and Louth. It is believed that their bombs were used extensively by the group in a variety of operations, including the London and Birmingham bombings of that year.[44] The Patterson twins were 31 years old at the time of their conviction. However, it was implied after their sentencing that they had possibly been involved in bombmaking for the group for a number of years. Bomb components similar to the ones they had developed were found in Hackballscross in 1998.[45]

Even with a lower conviction rate for Wave 3 activity (28 January 2007 to the present day) the two-group pattern is sustained within the conviction data. The dominant age range is 21–30 years with 13 people convicted. Within this range the 21–25 year subgrouping has the majority of convictions (eight). The data indicate that those aged 41 years and over have the most convictions among the older personnel. Although there are only slightly more people in this range it is still the first time that any of the waves have shown this; the previous two waves showed 31–40 years as significantly the largest older age range, but here the two age ranges are close to equal. The pattern of age data for individuals charged with VDR activity remains the same.

Two explanations are possible for this pattern. First the findings suggest an aging leadership within the two oldest VDR groups, the RIRA and the CIRA. Parallel to this it appears that the groups have been unable to retain a large proportion of their younger recruits who started active service in their 20s, at the dawn of VDR activity. There are many reasons why these people may have left VDR activity behind. From the outside this may seem to suggest the burnout of many younger recruits from the first two waves.[46] Although this may have been an important factor for some recruits, this trend may represent the restructuring processes that took place within the main VDR groups at the end of Wave 2 and the beginning of Wave 3.

In their 2008 interview with journalist Suzanne Breen, the RIRA indicated that a number of members, particularly in Belfast, had been removed:

> We're emerging from a three-year period of reorganizing in preparation for a renewed offensive.... If there was minimal visible military activity in recent years, there was plenty of behind-the-scenes restructuring. Important ground-work has now been completed.... In terms of other internal changes, people have been dismissed from the movement in Belfast and elsewhere. Units that weren't up to scratch have been disbanded. Mistakes were made previously but more rigorous vetting of volunteers is now in place.[47]

When assessed alongside ONH (RIRA)'s interview with journalist Brian Rowan in 2010 it becomes more apparent that this restructuring took place largely due to extensive infiltration. In reference to dissident Republicanism in general the ONH leadership acknowledged high levels of infiltration: "They [the founders of ONH] had watched how the anti-agreement republican military world had the perception of [being] badly organized, ineffective and perceived [as] highly infiltrated, and, in some cases, I suppose they were."[48] The RIRA leadership also admitted to this infiltration, but stated that this makes them no different from any other Republican paramilitaries past or present. With the implementation of "internal rules and regulations" they believe that this is now less likely to occur.[49]

In all analysis it is important not to overemphasize findings based on small figures. With this in mind it is not advisable to draw many conclusions from the age patterns of convictions for violent convictions in Wave 3. With only nine violent convictions to date any perceived patterns at the moment may prove to be misleading. Even though one-third of all convictions in this wave were for people in the 21–25 year age range, this represents only three people, all of whom were convicted for the same offense at the beginning of the wave. Only when more violent convictions are made will we be able to ascertain the relevance of the ages of individuals involved in violent activity. The nonviolent convictions in this final wave followed the pattern, with the largest groups of members being 21–30 and 31–35 years.

Although the RIRA and CIRA still account for the largest number of convictions the data across Wave 3 suggest a shift in the age profile of the two groups. As was suggested at the beginning of this Wave 3 discussion, this may be indicative of an aging leadership failing to retain younger members, who may or may not have been replaced with a new batch of young recruits. The early indications are that even though there are relatively low numbers of convictions in Wave 3 to date, the dominant violent/nonviolent pattern has been retained. The younger members still have the majority of convictions for violent activity, and their older colleagues have more nonviolent convictions. The majority of these nonviolent convictions are once again for weapons possession and "membership."

Employment

To maintain activity the VDR groups must constantly attract, recruit, and train new personnel in the skills required to carry out attacks. As already addressed, experienced personnel are required to continue the training of the young recruits in a variety of roles. This requirement of recruiting personnel with a specific skill base is highlighted when the occupations of the personnel are analyzed. Employment data are not available for the majority of the dissidents (a challenge commonly echoed by other researchers). This is due to significant underreporting of this information. However, we do have employment data on 59 convicted VDR personnel. Although these data provide some interesting results, they must be analyzed with caution due to the low number of personnel.

Of these 59 convicted dissidents, 62.03% were actively employed while simultaneously involved in a VDR group, whereas 25.86% were unemployed at the time of conviction. Of the sample 8.62% were students in higher education whereas 3.49% had been engaged in organized criminal activity.

When the data are analyzed by occupation and employment category they suggest that the organizations may well seek recruits with specialized skillsets beneficial to the pursuit of VDR objectives. Of these, 15.52% were members, or former members, of a legal military organization, dominantly the Irish Defence Forces. These individuals bring with them formal training in the use of a variety of weapons and explosives. Although these skillsets are desirable to the VDR group in a general sense, it is the individual's ability to pass on this training to fellow members and new recruits that is perhaps most beneficial. This is clearly demonstrated in the example of Richard Whyte, a former Irish army sniper who was convicted of training RIRA members in a "sniping training camp" in Kildare in 2001.[50] The bombmaker Kenneth Patterson was also a former soldier.[51]

Beyond the targeted recruitment of those with military experience, there is a longstanding tradition within Irish Republicanism of targeting individuals with specific skill bases to benefit the implementation of organizational tactics. The largest occupational sector among VDR recruits is personnel in the "construction, maintenance, and repair" category. This sector ranges from construction workers to those in the maintenance and repair trades, e.g., electricians, carpenters, and mechanics. Of the VDR personnel 18.97% are within this category and a further

5.17% were previously employed in the sector. These individuals, coupled with the 5.17% from the engineering and technology sectors, may bring with them particular sets of skills for aiding in the manufacturing, development, and maintenance of viable explosives, as well as other weaponry and training devices.[52]

It is possible that skill-based recruitment by VDRs provides them with a greater capacity to develop a longer-term strategy such as the one adopted by their Provisional predecessors. Whether that is a feasible or notional objective remains to be seen. When these data are compared to those of the charged and alleged members of the groups ($n = 32$) the construction, maintenance, and repair sector is once again dominant (29%). Although the charged and alleged membership data are always treated with caution they do provide further verification for the dominance of construction workers within the groups.

Geographic Region

In the previous chapter, we saw that the majority of executed VDR events took place in Northern Ireland. Although a small proportion of violent activity occurred in the Republic of Ireland, this has invariably been in connection with feuds with organized crime gangs and (mostly) is unrelated to the broader political aspirations of the VDR groups. However, the largest proportion of convicted VDR personnel thus far actually resided in the Republic; of convicted RIRA members, 63 were from the Republic and only 20 were from Northern Ireland. Similarly, the majority of convicted CIRA members are from the Republic, with 49 from the South and 28 from the North. There are also four convicted RIRA members who were based in Great Britain.

This disparity between VDR event and personnel origin adds additional challenges for those tasked with countering VDR activity, especially considering that the disparity cannot be understood without a close examination of cross-border differences. The two main county hubs of VDR group membership are Dublin and Louth (with small groupings also emerging in Republic of Ireland counties previously unassociated with PIRA activity during the Troubles), with the majority of VDR events taking place in the six counties of Northern Ireland; in other words, recruitment and initial training take place in one jurisdiction whereas direct action (outside of training) predominantly occurs in another.

Even though the Republic of Ireland has not been the target of significant VDR violence this does not mean that the role of the security services in the South should be solely relegated to countering recruitment and organizational membership. With the data showing a large proportion of the dissident membership living in the Republic of Ireland this, combined with the events data, indicates a strong likelihood that planning and training for actual VDR attacks have largely originated there. Several examples exist of bombs being made in and then transported from the Republic.

An analysis of the geographic origins of nonviolent political dissidents and community activists further emphasizes the dominance of the Republic of Ireland in the dissident community. Of the 141 political and community activists on whom we have gathered geographic origin data 106 are based in the Republic of

Ireland, with 29 from Northern Ireland, four from Great Britain, and two from other countries.

Although the overall convicted, political, and community activist data show that the majority of known dissidents are based in the Republic of Ireland the data on individuals charged and awaiting trial suggest that this pattern may be changing. It shows that 53 of the 81 people charged with dissident offenses are based in Northern Ireland. These charged data indicate that the RIRA in particular has a larger membership base in the North than they did before. This apparent change in geographic base will be proven only if and when these individuals are convicted of VDR offenses.

Although a significant proportion of the convicted VDR personnel were located within the six counties of Northern Ireland, the two main county hubs for the groups across the life of VDR activity have been Dublin and Louth.[53] Although Dublin is the most populous county in Ireland, both North and South, and therefore would be expected to contain many VDR members, Louth has only the twenty-second largest population of the 32 counties, and a smaller population than all but one of the Northern Ireland counties (Fermanagh).[54]

A large majority of convicted members of the RIRA are from these two counties in the Republic. We have recorded 18 convicted RIRA members in the whole of Northern Ireland, compared to 51 from Louth and Dublin combined. CIRA has 28 convicted members in Northern Ireland and 23 in Louth and Dublin. When all the groups are combined there are 57 convicted VDR personnel from across Northern Ireland and 82 from Dublin and Louth combined. Within Northern Ireland the distribution of convicted membership is more evenly spread, rather than focusing on specific "hubs" as in the South. Antrim, Armagh, Fermanagh, and Tyrone have the most sizable VDR populations in the North. Although Tyrone has only nine convicted dissidents the very recent emergence of "the IRA" may well change this in the near future.[55]

Dublin and Louth are critical hubs for VDR personnel. From these two counties 15 of the 25 convictions in the first wave of activity (31 August 1994 to 15 August 1998) originated. Only one person from Northern Ireland was convicted of VDR activity at this stage of the process, and this person was based in Derry. Therefore even though the operational focus was on attacking targets within Northern Ireland and England, the operational planning and organizational leadership was taking place within two county hubs within the Republic of Ireland. Kildare and the border county of Monaghan were the only counties outside of the eight analyzed here that had more than one conviction during this wave; two people were convicted from each. Five other counties across the Republic of Ireland had one conviction each. With this initial wave largely defined by the emergence of the RIRA these county-based data support the belief that the membership of the newly forming group was largely based within the Republic of Ireland, specifically in Dublin and Louth, where the emergent leadership was presumably based.

Wave 2 (16 August 1998 to 27 January 2007) provides the first real indication of a growing dissident membership from Northern Ireland. It specifically sees the emergence of Antrim as a locus of membership. However, the dissident supremacy of Louth and Dublin, especially for the RIRA, was still apparent. As a newly emerging group it can take time to establish a solid membership and support base in areas in which there are influential individuals directly opposed to your activity. As the 1997 split was geographically focused on disaffection from the south (McKevitt and his supporters in Louth), the Provisional membership across Northern Ireland was largely unaffected, at least at the time. This provided a significant challenge for the RIRA.

The CIRA picture is very different. In Antrim alone it had 11 separate members convicted of VDR activity. Similar to the RIRA, the CIRA originally emerged from the 1986 split with the PIRA as a Southern-based organization. However, with the extended duration of their existence the group showed the ability to attract a small number of Northern recruits. Still, the group's membership and support in Northern Ireland and across the Republic remained considerably lower than that of their former colleagues in Sinn Féin and the Provisional IRA.

Across the first two waves there was evidence of two county-based hubs of personnel, and the data collected for Wave 3 (28 January 2007 to the present day) provide further support for the geographic evolution of dissidents. This is specifically relevant with respect to the CIRA, the newly emerging groups, and the "unknowns." However, the RIRA continued to show a Dublin focus, and possibly a failure to sufficiently connect with Northern Republicans. As has been discussed already, however, the lower levels of convictions to date for Wave 3 activity mean that the data from the wave should not be overanalyzed. A significant number of individuals are awaiting trial for Wave 3 activity, and it is only when (or if) more convictions are made that it will become clear if there has been a true shift in the dissidents' base.

A further indicator of this evolution, though one we should interpret with more caution, is contained within the "charged" data. As was shown earlier in this section, the charged data are dominated by people resident in Northern Ireland. There is an indication of four new county hubs of membership emerging: Antrim, Armagh, Derry, and Tyrone. With respect to the RIRA the data suggest that Derry, especially Derry city, may have recently become its strongest base (with Cork and Carlow not far behind). In contrast, the CIRA appears to have developed a base within Armagh, specifically the Lurgan/Craigavon area. This suggestion is consistent with the conviction data from Wave 3. With respect to the overall dissident population Antrim has the most number of people charged; Belfast in particular has provided the majority of these charges. If this is all borne out in convictions we will be provided with evidence of a major shift in the operational makeup of VDR groups, with inevitable implications for the formulation and evolution of responses to counter their activity.[56]

■ CONCLUSIONS

Although the event data indicate that the center of violent activity is still within Northern Ireland and that the tactics of the groups aim to disrupt the normalization of this state, the membership was, previously, primarily from the south.

The existence for specific centers of strength in the Republic of Ireland cannot be explained in the same way as equivalent clusters in Northern Ireland. Although the early conviction data show the dominance of Republic of Ireland personnel, the current "charged" data suggest a shift, with the majority of the membership now based in Northern Ireland. If this proves true it would demonstrate a significant evolution of the VDR groups.

There is evidence for two prominent age ranges present in VDR groups: the younger 14–30 year age group, most of whom are having their first experiences of active Republicanism, and the 31–50 age category continuing on or revisiting Republican activism. This trend deserves close consideration. The rationale for the engagement of the younger generation in dissident Republican activity is qualitatively different from that of their older comrades, and we will explore this in detail in Chapter 6.[57] Although many of the younger generation are experiencing Republican activism for the first time the majority of the older generation have previously been involved in other Republican movements, predominantly the PIRA. They have left to join, or form, these new organizations, due to their disillusionment with the peace process and what they see as the negative consequences of the politicization of the Provisional Republican Movement.

The cornerstone of any organization's survival must be its ability to recruit new members, a point further emphasized by the increase in VDR personnel serving lengthy sentences.[58] The nature of involvement and engagement in terrorism leads to a high turnover of membership for multiple reasons that are well documented.[59] This is perhaps especially pertinent for the VDR groups in their early phase of inception due to competition for membership within a finite community or, in a geographic sense, immediately surrounding a particular leadership figure (certainly the case for the RIRA and ONH).

But for the VDR groups to survive and progress they need to do more than simply recruit new numbers. They must also attract new conscripts with particular skills that will help them in the training and active service of the organization. This is suggested by the emerging data on the occupations of VDR personnel, which may suggest specific targeting of personnel with formal military training as well as others from a construction and "trades" background. These two sectors provide the groups with the requisite skills to continue their development and maintenance of weaponry and explosives as well as the training of new recruits, a first step in the development of a longer-term strategy that the dissidents are not currently viewed as having the ability to formulate, let alone exploit.

In this and the previous chapter, we have examined some critical data points. The next two chapters, on the strategy and psychology of the dissidents, provide the necessary context to understand the nature and direction of dissident activity and its personnel.

■ NOTES

1. McDonald, H. 2011. "Northern Ireland Police Say 650 Republican Terrorists Are at Large." *The Guardian*, 29 June.

2. LaFree, G., & Ackerman, G. 2009. "The Empirical Study of Terrorism: Social and Legal Research." *Annual Review of Law and Social Science, 5,* 347–374.

3. Russell, C. A., & Miller, B. H. 1977. "Profile of a Terrorist." *Terrorism: An International Journal, 1,* 17–34.

4. Sageman, M. 2004. *Understanding Terror Networks.* Philadelphia: University of Pennsylvania Press; Pape, R. 2005. *Dying to Win: The Strategic Logic of Suicide Terrorism.* New York: Random House. Krueger, A. B., & Maleckova, J. 2002. *Education, Poverty and Terrorism: Is There a Causal Connection?* NBER Working Papers 9074, National Bureau of Economic Research, Inc.

5. Gambetta, D., & Hertog, S. 2007. *Engineers of Jihad.* Sociology working paper 2007–10. Department of Sociology, University of Oxford.

6. Bakker, E. 2006. *Jihadi Terrorists in Europe, Their Characteristics and the Circumstances in Which They Joined the Jihad: An Exploratory Study.* Clingendael: Netherlands Institute of International Relations.

7. Gartenstein-Ross, D., & Grossman, L. 2009. *Homegrown Terrorists in the US and the UK: An Empirical Examination of the Radicalization Process.* Washington, DC: FDD Press.

8. Silber, M., & Bhatt, A. 2007. *Radicalization in the West: The Homegrown Threat.* New York City Police Department.

9. Ministry of Security and Justice. 2010. Jihadist Terrorism in the Netherlands. Report of the Wetenschappelijk Onderzoek-en Documentatiecentrum (WODC) Ministry of Security and Justice. Available at http://english.wodc.nl/onderzoeksdatabase/1381a-jihadis t-terrorism-in-the-netherlands-a-description-based-on-closed-criminal-investigations.aspx.

10. Davis, P., & Cragin, K. (Eds.). 2010. *Social Science for Counterterrorism.* Santa Monica, CA: RAND.

11. Berko, A., Erez, E., & Globokar, J. L. 2010. "Gender, Crime and Terrorism: The Case of Arab/Palestinian Women in Israel." *British Journal of Criminology, 50,* 670–689.

12. Bloom, M. 2011. *Bombshell: Women and Terror.* Philadelphia: University of Pennsylvania Press

13. Hamilton, C. 2007. *Women and ETA: The Gender Politics of Radical Basque Nationalism.* Manchester: Manchester University Press.

14. Smith, B., & Damphousse, K. 2002. *American Terrorism Study: Patterns of Behavior, Investigation and Prosecution of American Terrorists.* Washington, DC: U.S. Department of Justice.

15. Fernando, R. 2004. "Who Are the Terrorists? Analyzing Changes in Sociological Profile Among Members of ETA." *Studies in Conflict and Terrorism, 27,* 465–488.

16. Sageman, M. 2004. *Understanding Terror Networks.* Philadelphia: University of Pennsylvania Press

17. Magouirk, J., Atran, S., & Sageman, M. 2008. "Connecting Terrorist Networks." *Studies in Conflict and Terrorism, 31,* 1–16.

18. Alonso, R. 2006. "Individual Motivations for Joining Terrorist Organizations: A Comparative Qualitative Study on Members of ETA and IRA." In J. Victoroff (Ed.), *Social and Psychological Factors in the Genesis of Terrorism* (pp. 187–202). Amsterdam: IOS Press.

19. Khosrokhavar, F., & Macey, D. 2005. *Suicide Bombers: Allah's New Martyrs.* London: Pluto Press.

20. This includes those who have been convicted of both violent as well of those who have been convicted of nonviolent VDR offenses. Of the convicted individuals 70 were

convicted of violent offenses and the remaining 122 were convicted of nonviolent VDR offenses such as group membership. From the total number of convicted individuals 14 were given suspended sentences.

21. *Irish Times.* January 20, 1996. "Six Jailed for Arms Crimes Salute as Supporters Shout 'Up the Republic'." http://www.irishtimes.com/newspaper/ireland/1996/0120/96012000144. html. Accessed July 20, 2011.

22. White, p. 326.

23. *The Mirror.* October 17, 2003. "Real IRA Cig Haul: Man Was 'in Fear'." http://www. thefreelibrary.com/Real+IRA+cig+haul%3A+Man+was+'in+fear'.-a0108946300. Accessed July 19, 2011.

24. McDonald, H. January 24, 2008. "Real IRA Suspect Arrested in Lithuanian Arms Sting." *The Guardian.* http://www.guardian.co.uk/uk/2008/jan/24/northernireland.uknews4. Accessed July 20, 2011.

25. BBC. September 17, 2009. "Dissident Mortar Bomb Gang Jailed." http://news.bbc. co.uk/2/hi/uk_news/northern_ireland/8260859.stm. Accessed July 20, 2011.

26. Ibid.

27 BBC. April 25, 2011. "Three Men Appear in Court Over Armagh Arms Find." http:// www.bbc.co.uk/news/uk-northern-ireland-13187011. Accessed July 21, 2011.

28. Ibid.

29. Breen, S. April 22, 2011. "Former Provos Claim Kerr Murder and Vow More Attacks." *The Belfast Telegraph.* http://www.belfasttelegraph.co.uk/news/local-national/ northern-ireland/former-provos-claim-kerr-murder-and-vow-more-attacks-15146426. html. Accessed July 20, 2011.

30. See Bloom, M. 2010. *Bombshell: The Many Face of Women Terrorists.* Toronto: Viking Canada.

31. Okado-Gough, D. January 28, 2003. "'Real' Irish Republican Army (rIRA) Statement." CAIN, http://cain.ulst.ac.uk/othelem/organ/ira/rira280103.htm. Accessed July 24, 2011.

32. White (2006), pp. 292–293.

33. McDonald, H. August 13, 2000, "I Will Never Surrender to the British." *The Guardian.* http://www.guardian.co.uk/uk/2000/aug/13/northernireland.henrymcdonald. Accessed July 20, 2011.

34. Real Sinn Fein. June 10, 2010. "Press Releases." *Sinn Fein Phoblachtach.*http://www. sinnfeinpoblachtach.com/pressreleases.htm. Accessed June 10, 2010.

35. Breen, S. May 17, 2011. "Heavy Police Presence for Price Court Appearance." *The Belfast Telegraph.* http://www.nuzhound.com/articles/arts2011/may16_Price_in_ court_SBreen__Belfast-Telegraph.php. Accessed July 21, 2011.

36. Hennessey, T. 2000. *The Northern Ireland Peace Process: Ending the Troubles?* Dublin: Gill and Macmillan. P. 112.

37. Breen, S. May 22, 2011. "'My Husband Was Framed' Claims ex-RIRA Chief's Wife." *Sunday World.* http://www.nuzhound.com/articles/arts2011/may22_McKevitt_framed_ says_wife__SBreen_Sunday_World.php. Accessed July 24, 2011.

38. Breen. May 17, 2011.

39. McDonald, H. July 22, 2011. "Old Bailey Bomber Charged Over Murder of British Soldiers." *The Guardian.* http://www.guardian.co.uk/world/2011/jul/22/old-bailey-bomber-marian-price-charged. Accessed July 22, 2011.

40. Cowan, R. March 31, 2001. "Republican Dissident Charged in Dublin." *The Guardian.* http://www.guardian.co.uk/uk/2001/mar/31/northernireland.uksecurity. Accessed July 21, 2011.

41. See McDonald, H. "Boy Soldiers Recruited by the Real IRA." *The Observer,* October 24, 1999.

42. McGuigan, C. March 15, 2009. "Real IRA Suspects Unmasked." *The Belfast Telegraph.* http://www.belfasttelegraph.co.uk/sunday-life/real-ira-suspects-unmasked-14227904. html. Accessed July 22, 2011.

43. "Dissidents Drawing on Provo Expertise." July 27, 2011. *News Letter.* http://www. newsletter.co.uk/news/local/dissidents_drawing_on_provo_Expertise_1_2565304. Accessed July 24, 2011.

44. Sharrock, D. December 12, 2001. "Real IRA Bomb Factory Twins Jailed." *The Telegraph.* http://www.telegraph.co.uk/news/uknews/1365047/Real-IRA-bomb-factory-tw ins-jailed.html. Accessed December 12, 2001.

45. Ibid.

46. See Ross, J. I., & Gurr, T. R. 1989. "Why Terrorism Subsides: A Comparative Study of Canada and the United States." *Comparative Politics, 21*(4), 405–426.

47. Breen, S. February 4, 2008. "War Back On—Real IRA." *Sunday Tribune.* http://www. nuzhound.com/articles/Sunday_Tribune/arts2008/feb3_RIRA_interview__SBreen.php. Accessed July 22, 2011.

48 Rowan, B. November 3, 2010.

49. Breen, S. February 4, 2008.

50. Harding, T. November 2, 2002. "Ex-Soldier Who Ran Sniper Camp Jailed." *The Telegraph.* http://www.telegraph.co.uk/news/worldnews/europe/ireland/1412015/Ex-soldi er-who-ran-sniper-camp-jailed.html. Accessed July 7, 2011.

51. Sharrock, D. December 12, 2001.

52. While it is our opinion that this sector is being specifically targeted for the skill set that they can bring to the groups, it is also conceivable that this is also reflective of Catholic males being traditionally overrepresented in the building and construction sector across the island of Ireland.

53. North Louth, particularly Dundalk, played a significant role throughout the Troubles as a base for members of the Provisional IRA who were on the run; it has had a longstanding role in accommodating violent Republicans. The data indicate that the significance of this county has continued with the activity of the VDR groups. Most notably, Michael McKevitt, the for-mer PIRA quartermaster general and first Real IRA Chief of Staff, was based in the area. For a detailed analysis of the role that the area has played in violent Republicanism see Harnden, T. 1999. *"Bandit Country": The IRA and South Armagh.* London: Hodder and Stoughton.

54. For a breakdown of the population size of each of the counties in the Republic of Ireland visit the Central Statistics Office of Ireland website: http://www.cso.ie/en/statis-tics/population/populationofeachprovincecountyandcity2006/ For a similar breakdown of the population size of each of the counties of Northern Ireland visit the Northern Ireland Statistics and Research Agency website: http://www.nisra.gov.uk/demography/default.asp3. htm. Both Accessed April 12, 2011.

55. "Freed Republicans 'May be Sent Back to Prison.'" *Newsletter* (February 7, 2011): http://www.newsletter.co.uk/news/local/freed_republicans_may_be_sent_back_ to_prison_1_2387860. Accessed March 21, 2011; "Dissident Groups Admits Kerr Murder-Report," *RTE* (April 22, 2011): http://www.rte.ie/news/2011/0422/kerrr.html. Accessed April 22, 2011.

56. It is possible that this apparent geographic shift may also be due to a greater police capacity, and a shift in efforts, of both An Garda Siochana and the PSNI. However, it is the authors' opinion that the data are more indicative of a regional shift in recruitment and VDR membership.

57. Morrison, J. F. 2011."Why Do People Become Dissident Irish Republicans?" In M. Taylor & P. M. Currie (Eds.), *Dissident Irish Republicanism* (pp. 17–42). London: Continuum.

58. See Table 7.1.

59. Ross, J. I., & Gurr, T. R. 1989. "Why Terrorism Subsides: A Comparative Study of Canada and the United States." *Comparative Politics, 12*(2), 206–227.

5 Divided We Stand

"The Provisionals ... are now supporting and lauding a process they rejected for 25 years. In fact Martin McGuiness said of the Sunningdale Agreement in 1973 'we will blow it out of the water'—a quarter of a century later he entered British ministerial office with unashamed zeal and glee and proceeded to administer very bad British rule in the Six Counties. The Provisionals have followed the path of others in abandoning the Republic. They are no longer Republicans."

— *Real IRA leadership, February 2003.*[1]

■ INTRODUCTION

Although the dissidents are enjoying a resurgence of activity, their ability to sustain themselves in the long term remains unclear. Part of the challenge in assessing their capabilities lies in deciphering the nature of the dissident groups themselves. The Violent Dissident Republican (VDR) scene is complex, diverse, ambiguous, amorphous, and highly localized. Sometimes the various groupings appear to overlap in terms of both strategic and tactical objectives; at other times they take steps to assert their individual identities and distinguish themselves from each other. To further complicate matters, they sometimes appear to coalesce while simultaneously competing with each other.

In Chapters 3 and 4, we considered what the dissidents do and what their personnel compositions look like. This chapter, the first of two on strategy and psychology, respectively, provides a broader context to those descriptions. This chapter identifies and examines some key strategic goals of the dissidents and explores the divisive question of whether they appear to have a clear strategic direction. Although they have a vision, it is unclear if that vision can be translated into a plan for action.

■ WHAT THE DISSIDENTS WANT

Although it is important to challenge "the accounts paramilitary groups gave of themselves,"[2] it is equally important to pay attention to the qualities of those accounts, and to the audiences for which they are intended. To understand the dissidents' position, we must recognize how they place unerring historical truths against contemporary events (notably "betrayal" by the ever-compromising Sinn Féin). In a review of his book in the Republican Sinn Féin (RSF) newsletter *Saoirse*,[3] Martyn Frampton was criticized for what the reviewer alleged was a lack of understanding of "*modern-day* Irish Republicanism" (emphasis mine), yet RSF's mantra is that the present day does not really matter. Answers to the current Republican confusion can be answered only with reference to historical precedent.

This example, however, illustrates how, although the ideological framework relies on a core leadership voice to articulate and make relevant today's events, an understanding of that ideology, and an understanding of the interpretive context of that ideology, is often loosely diffused throughout the rank and file of the movement. The dissidents may individually pride themselves on their simplicity, yet even a cursory reading of their policy documentation reveals an overarching, confusing, and frequently (when one looks closely enough) inconsistent litany of positions and aspirations. It is unlikely, and in some cases painfully evident, that many young members even bother reading core documents. Some of the key national-level policy documents of the 32 County Sovereignty Movement (32CSM) and RSF are distantly intellectual in tone, and many refer to seemingly irrelevant historical precedents as inspiration in a way that would confuse anyone without a strong grasp of Republican history. This raises important questions about for whom or what the dissidents' strategies, policies (national and local), and vision are actually relevant.

All of the dissident groups have, with varying effectiveness, exploited the Internet to promote their objectives. RSF and 32CSM in particular have devoted considerable resources to the development of online and print newsletters. These provide detailed insight into the levels of activity (both violent and nonviolent) of the groups. RSF's *Saoirse*, for example, provides details of commemorative ceremonies, public meetings, and other activities throughout Ireland, north and south. During particularly important times for Republicans, such as Easter, it is not difficult to ascertain where the bigger events are likely to be found, but a more thorough spreadsheet of activity can be constructed by looking at those events that take place at other times. The newsletters also provide insight into the ideological frameworks of the respective dissident groups. This, in turn, allows us not only to pinpoint the key similarities and differences between the respective groups, but to identify signature aspects of how respective strategic goals are consistent (or made to appear consistent) with expressions of support in other arenas, whether through statements claimed by the military arms or statements made by members of the groups to media.

We can begin by identifying the core unifying features of the dissident campaign. Dissident Republicans collectively seek the following:

- Rejection of the Good Friday Agreement
- Rejection of the authority of the Sinn Féin leadership
- A withdrawal of British forces
- An end to partition
- The removal of any kind of "British" rule in Ireland
- The formation of a united Ireland[4]

Key tactical steps in working toward those strategic objectives include the following:

- Tactical use of the armed struggle (though only the VDRs advocate this)
- Public rejection of any dialogue until British withdrawal
- Characterization of Sinn Féin as having lost its Republican credentials
- Undermining the authority of the Police Service of Northern Ireland
- Gaining support, both through recruitment as well as community support

It is only when we move beyond this that the dissidents differ both in terms of the tactics they use to pursue these strategic copursuits and, in particular, in terms of what *kind* of Ireland they would like to see.

■ REPUBLICAN SINN FÉIN AND THE CONTINUITY IRA (CIRA)

RSF's document "Towards a Peaceful Ireland"[5] sets out the following objectives in its "Vision":

1. The establishment of a constituent assembly for the 32 counties elected by all the people of Ireland to draft a constitution within a 6-month period. The agreed constitution would then be submitted to the people of Ireland in a referendum.
2. Prior to setting up the assembly, the British government would have to provide a declaration of intent to withdraw all its forces within 12 months of the adoption of a new constitution by the people of Ireland.
3. Finally, an amnesty for all political prisoners and all those on the wanted list. All political prisoners must be released 1 month prior to the election of the constituent assembly.

The acceptance of these proposals, would, in the words of RSF, ensure "no necessity for the continuance of armed struggle and all armed elements should cease action immediately." Until then, however, and in a position originally drafted as a motion proposed in its 1997 Ard Fheis, RSF supports and upholds "the right of the Irish people to use whatever degree of controlled and disciplined force that is required in resisting British aggression and bringing about a British withdrawal from our country."

Details of what RSF envisions with its constituent assembly are described in its document "Éire Nua" (described in Chapter 2), the group's national plan for a "new democracy" in Ireland. Although it has been slightly modernized, the document that Republican Sinn Féin promotes and endorses is essentially the same one written in the early 1970s. In his 2010 doctoral dissertation John Morrison has a quote from Cathleen Knowles McGuirk that emphasizes the extent to which this policy was intrinsically tied to Ruairí Ó Brádaigh especially, and how its removal predisposed him to stand down from the leadership of the Provisional Republican movement: "The major disagreement with the Éire Nua programme was that the Adams crowd knew that if you could outmaneuver Ó Brádaigh on it you could outmaneuver him both strategically and organizationally, and you could undermine him within Sinn Féin."[6]

Éire Nua essentially proposes the formation of a 32-county Ireland, an independent Irish Republic based on the federalization of Ireland's historic four-provinces structure: "... the ideal of an independent Irish republic—the ideal proclaimed by the leaders of the 1916 Rising 80 years ago—still inspires those who continue the struggle for national unity and freedom." Furthermore:

> The Éire Nua programme provides for a strong provincial and local government in a federation of the four provinces, designed to ensure that every citizen can participate in genuinely democratic self-government, and to guarantee that no group can dominate or exploit another. Under this programme all traditions in Ireland can make a valuable contribution to the nation.

RSF describes the partition of Ireland as the root cause of the "nationalist nightmare," and clarifies its position on the Good Friday Agreement:

> The current policy, based on the Belfast Agreement signed at Stormont on April 10, 1998, seeks to make the artificial Six-County State work within the "UK" by an elaborate and convoluted system that has been labelled "power-sharing." Since this agreement did not address the basic problem of English rule in Ireland it was flawed from the start. It was sold to the electorate as a basis for a permanent peace, which it could not deliver. It was dishonest, in that it was sold to unionists as a deal to consolidate the union with England and simultaneously urged on nationalists as something which would weaken the union and lead to a united Ireland. And the unionist veto was endorsed, allowing 18% of the population of Ireland to dictate the political progress of the other 82% and therefore of the nation as a whole. As in the case of the Treaty of Surrender in 1921 this Agreement was put to the people as a question of war or peace. Accordingly it was not a free vote; also, a majority in the Six Counties was stated to be decisive for all Ireland.

RSF sees successive governments in the Republic of Ireland as having "cooperated in the deception of the Belfast Agreement," and as having "thus sought to legitimise foreign rule in Ireland." A "culture of corruption" prevails across Ireland, North and South, "whereby decisions affecting the everyday life of communities are placed in the hands of an elite cadre of politicians and bureaucrats." RSF is equally suspicious of Ireland's membership of the European Union (EU), viewing the EU as a "modern form of imperialism" serving the "interests, above all, of big business and the super-rich."

In an effort to "remedy Ireland's weakened and wasted conditions," Éire Nua outlines a series of structures "designed to embrace and include all the people of Ireland." RSF proposes a new constitution to accompany these new structures. The "New Ireland" would have a new national parliament—the Dáil—currently parliament to the 26-county Republic. "All citizens of the thirty-two counties" are expected to pledge allegiance to this new parliament for all. The new structures evoke a return to Ireland's historic provinces:

> The four traditional provinces—Ulster, Munster, Leinster, and Connacht—have emerged as definite regions within the island of Ireland, with distinctive

characteristics. Irish people in any region will be found to have a natural affinity—in culture, sport and economic interest—with those of their own province and county. Uniting the historic province of Ulster will help eliminate the sectarian divisions of the past and realise the full potential for development of separated counties—especially Donegal, Derry, Tyrone, Fermanagh, Cavan, and Monaghan. The people of the long-neglected province of Connacht will find power to escape from their isolation. The people of the provinces of Leinster and Munster will be able to pursue policies that will secure them a more equitable and balanced form of development.

Since its origins as a Provisional IRA and Sinn Féin document, those advancing Éire Nua actively promoted the federalization of its four provinces as appealing to the Unionist population. Their stated belief was, and is, that this would represent the most attractive form of a united Ireland for the Unionist and Loyalist populations, as the Unionists, if they maintained majority status in the North, would have control in the federal parliament in Ulster, Dáil Uladh. This is a belief that has been echoed by Republicans each time they promote the document, even by Martin McGuinness, Gerry Adams, and others who effectively rejected the policy in 1982.

Éire Nua is nothing if not ambitious in its esoteric vision (a point consistently made by Frampton) and eager in its instructions. It contains deeper structural details of just how various provincial parliaments or "assemblies," as well as regional boards and district councils, will serve and uphold the "interests of the Irish people." The unwavering vision set forth in Éire Nua is unlikely to ever be seriously discussed by anyone on the island of Ireland. Only by looking at more recent statements can we more fully understand the strategic impetus of Republican Sinn Féin and the CIRA. A reading of RSF dogma alone would appear far removed from even a basic appreciation of CIRA activity. On the one hand the relationship between the CIRA and RSF is not difficult to ascertain. The June 2010 issue of Saoirse, under the headline banner "IRA speaks," carries a full statement from the CIRA decrying efforts by dissenters within the CIRA for holding "an unauthorised meeting"—the sole purpose of which, the statement reads, is "to supplant the leadership [and is] without doubt an undermining of the Movement and will not be tolerated."

For most observers, RSF members do not merely enhance their strategic objectives by referring to armed struggle—rather, they are defined by it. A major turning point for the group came in the wake of the March 2009 killings at Massereene and Craigavon. On multiple occasions, RSF spokespersons refused to characterize the killings as murder, describing them instead as "acts of war." Interviewed by reporter Henry McDonald on 1 April 2009, Josephine Hayden, a former CIRA member, described the killings as:

... inevitable, and it was resistance, as far as I'd be concerned. Yes, it was resistance.... They were a foreign army, who were actually training here, in my country, to go to Afghanistan to commit, they would be committing murder out there in Afghanistan.... I don't think we should be a training ground for any British army regiments.

The slain soldiers, Mark Quinsey and Patrick Azimkar, were due to fly to Afghanistan with their regiment.[7]

On 10 March, the "north Armagh battalion" of the CIRA claimed responsibility for Public Service of Northern Ireland (PSNI) officer Stephen Carroll's murder, stating: "As long as there is British involvement in Ireland, these attacks will continue."[8] In a statement carried in *Saoirse*, RSF president Ruari Ó Brádaigh echoed this:

> For more than 20 years Republican Sinn Féin has been warning that the lessons of Irish history have been that as long as the British government and British occupation troops remain in Ireland there will be Irish people to oppose their presence here.... It is only a matter of days since Hugh Orde, the head of the RUC, announced that undercover British troops were being brought back into this country. While everyone regretted loss of life, the hard realities of the situation in Ireland must be faced.

The inevitability of conflict, with the concomitant "regret" about what that conflict brings, is a common theme in RSF's proclamations. The "regret," however, is mostly aimed at the nature of the sacrifice RSF tells its members it will have to endure. The remainder of *Saoirse*'s coverage on the attacks focused on the "hardship" and "intimidation" faced by those arrested in connection with the "shooting of the British colonial policeman": "People were placed under house arrest as they were kept in one room while their homes were searched." The article praised the "remarkable courage" of those who resisted "the British forces of occupation."

The March 2009 attacks proved monumental in other respects. Despite initial delays by Sinn Féin in issuing a response, when it did come it left no doubt as to just how the Sinn Féin leadership had embraced its position in government. Appearing jointly with Democratic Unionist Party (DUP) leader Peter Robinson and PSNI Chief Constable Hugh Orde at a press conference, Martin McGuinness condemned the killings and described the perpetrators in words that would come to have deep significance for both himself and for those on the receiving end. The killers were "traitors to the island of Ireland. They have betrayed the political desires, hopes and aspirations of all of the people who live on this island ... they don't deserve to be supported by anyone."[9]

The dissidents were quick to swoop on their new publicity for their involvement in the attack. Yet this paled in comparison to how they relished the opportunity to respond to McGuinness' "hypocrisy." In a news conference held in West Belfast, under the banner of Republican Sinn Féin, spokesman Richard Walsh charged McGuinness himself with "severe treachery." Hayden then added:

> The bottom line is, the British army are here, you've British rule from Stormont, and you have the likes of Martin McGuinness.... You asked the very same questions of Martin McGuinness 30 years ago like you're asking us now, and I would have liked to say to him ... that it's not inevitable that people turn their coats and put on the armour of the state and then repress the very people that they fought beside, because it doesn't have to be that way.[10]

If the broad RSF membership actually accepts Ó Brádaigh's pseudoreligious vision of Éire Nua (and it is by no means clear that it does), the odds continue to be stacked against them. In June 2011, a survey conducted by Queen's University Belfast and the University of Ulster found that "support for a United Ireland [was] at an all-time low," that only "16% were in favour of unification," and "just 33% of Catholics wanted Irish unity on the long term. More than half of Catholics say they would prefer to stay in the UK, a view shared by 90% of Protestants."[11]

But set against recent "military" actions, RSF's raison d'être is unambiguous in a way that could never be ascertained from their dogma. They have managed to easily position themselves against a steady tide of what they view as compromise, sell-out, and abject failure on the part of Sinn Féin. Their contempt for Sinn Féin deepens with every criticism leveled at them by their former Republican colleagues. RSF's critical limitation, it would seem, is that despite a resurgent CIRA, they enjoy almost no support. For most political groups, this reality would appear to be a serious problem; for RSF, it is a badge of pride. When asked if RSF ultimately has to stand for election to communicate its political message, member Cait Trainor replied, "Certainly not. We have a mandate stretching right back to 1798. We really don't need the public to rubber stamp the republican movement. We've been here for a long, long time."[12] Trainor's response illustrates a key principle of what it means to be a member of RSF—pragmatism continues to be the enemy of the Republican purist. It is this "purity" that is central to RSF's ideology. One of its regularly celebrated martyrs is Charlie Kerins, a former IRA leader from County Kerry. Frampton highlights the views of Ó Brádaigh and other RSF stalwarts of Kerins as the epitome of what it means to be a true Republican: "purity in death, over compromise in life."[13] A refusal to compromise led Ó Brádaigh to walk away from the Provisional movement back in 1986, and this continued refusal sees the RSF dismissing Sinn Féin's role in the current peace process.

Frampton notes, however, that RSF's "vitriolic criticism" of the Provisionals is "from time to time, balanced by RSF attempts to 'reach out' to potentially disaffected Provisional members."[14] Where RSF draw the line is with other Republicans who do not share its core beliefs. However, for a long period these core beliefs were tied to the personality and leadership of Ruairí Ó Brádaigh, more so than any leader within Republicanism. Since stepping down from the movement recently, and though he is still influential, O'Bradaigh's influence is likely to wane. The scene is now set for the new RSF leadership to at least contemplate the revision of its core strategic objectives.

■ 32CSM AND THE REAL IRA (RIRA)

In a 2006 video interview published on their website, 32CSM spokesman Francie Mackey explains the basic origins of 32CSM strategy: "When we were formed in 1997, it was a single issue of national sovereignty to highlight that the issue of national sovereignty was again being usurped by the British government and that Sinn Féin leaders were moving to an internal settlement in the occupied six counties."

32CSM's political vision at a national level is explained in their policy document "Irish Democracy: A Framework for Unity."[15]

- The objective of the 32CSM, the republican separatist objective, is the restoration of Irish sovereignty by the immediate end to the British violation of it. We seek a sovereign Irish democracy for the Irish people.
- Our objective is also our strategy. The politics of Irish freedom must be free from any politics which would subvert it. We seek of others, as we do ourselves, the practicing of the politics of Irish freedom.
- Our objective is the realisation of our Declaration of Independence. Our objective is the objective of Wolfe Tone, of Robert Emmet, of Fintan Lalor, of Charles Kickham, of Padraig Pearse, of Liam Lynch, of Sean McCaughey, of Sean South and of Francis Hughes. Our objective is the historical objective of Irish republicanism.

The 32CSM is not unlike the blind man's elephant. Despite a defining focus on the need to reassert and reclaim Irish sovereignty, the group produced a labyrinthine series of documents, each of which gives a partial view of what it is that strategically distinguishes it from other dissidents. Furthermore, those documents that seek to define local-level policies and strategy are often disconnected, both thematically and in terms of content, from their national-level counterparts. Their followers have made extensive use of the Internet to propagate 32CSM's core values. In a 2008 video entitled "Who We Are," the group provides a "short introduction to the [movement], who we are and our aims and objectives."

32CSM was developed in December 1997, in Dublin, by "likeminded republicans increasingly concerned at the direction the Republican movement was being led." The minutes of the first meeting explains: "those attending the meeting shared a common concern regarding the failure of the current peace talks to tackle the key issue of Irish sovereignty." 32CSM denies it is the political wing of the RIRA, but its members support the use of political violence. It notes that the "founding members were suspended indefinitely from Sinn Féin after being prohibited from addressing the Ard Fheis."

As set out in their video statement (and listed here in the order in which they were originally presented), 32CSM's stated principles include the following:

1. We are not a political party.
2. We hold that the cause of conflict in Ireland is Britain's refusal to recognize the integrity of Irish Sovereignty.
3. We hold that a resolution of the Anglo Irish conflict can be realized only through British withdrawal from our country.
4. The Good Friday Agreement is but an extension of British parliamentary activity in our country and thus cannot be viewed as a meaningful resolution to the conflict.
5. We are committed to presenting the case for Irish self-determination to the international community.
6. We have presented our case before the United Nations as a framework for a true peace process in Ireland.

7. The response of the governments was to push for the U.S. authorities to proscribe our organization, thus denying us the ability to directly pursue our peace strategy.

8. We uphold the right of the Irish people to resort to arms in defense of our national sovereignty.

9. In 2002, we broadened our Constitution in line with the assertion of Pádraig Pearse: "The nation's sovereignty not only extends to all the men and women of the nation, but to all its material possessions; the nation's soil and all its natural resources, all the wealth and the wealth producing processes within the nation."

10. We are an open and democratic movement.

11. We cherish honest debate and move forward on that basis.

At first glance, 32CSM and RSF would appear to share core values. 32CSM pursues a "separatist agenda, rejecting the right or need to any British dimension in Irish politics other than those of mutual interest between two sovereign nations. The policy is predicated on the construction and practice of a new politics, democratically based, people inclusive and sovereign in expression and integrity." The statement continues:

The history of British colonialism in Ireland is one of repression, appeasement and coercion. The objective of British politics in Ireland is to remain in Ireland. The imperial concept of divide and conquer continues to be the principal mechanism by which the British maintains its presence....

We define Irish democracy as an expression of its people's will, inclusive, accountable and unhindered by any external impediment. We reject the notion of it being a statistical headcount or a numerical mechanism by which the violation of its sovereign basis can in someway be legitimised. The British violation of Irish sovereignty is the cause of the Anglo-Irish conflict.

32CSM is primarily concerned with highlighting the argument that Ireland's sovereignty has been compromised. Also, like RSF, the uncompromising nature of its position remains a defining feature: "The flaw in current thinking holds that the resolution to the conflict is to be found in harmonising these diverse political stances rather than holding them to account as they relate to the cause of that conflict." 32CSM, however, recognizes the pragmatic need for dialogue as a means to progress:

The political analysis of the 32CSM is a correct one but will remain impotent unless dialogue is pursued with the other political parties to the conflict. Because we are correct they will not voluntarily come to us but will seek to marginalise and demonise our republican stance. This is part of their failed agenda. The issue of national sovereignty, national self determination and Irish democracy cannot be avoided indefinitely. *Irish Democracy, A Framework for Unity* is a strategy which allows those parties to engage on these fundamental issues with republicans by first and foremost asking them to address the veracity of their own positions.

Like any group striving to assert its identity within a crowded environment, 32CSM needed to justify its independent existence as an Irish Republican organization. It did this through a bold strategy, which it was sure to know would be fruitless. The leadership of the then "32CSC" prepared a document for submission to the United Nations, which it claimed "represent[ed] a challenge to the legal right of a British Government to enact legislation for any section of the Irish people."[16] This framed their arguments, both historical and contemporary, within the framework of United Nations declarations. Though the leadership unsurprisingly gained little to no reaction from the UN, its main audience in this, and all its strategic decisions, was the internal Republican community. By approaching the issue of Irish sovereignty and partition in this way the group was attempting to place itself within Republicanism as a serious and viable alternative to Sinn Féin (in the same way that RSF has used Éire Nua and other policy documents for a similar purpose).

From the outset 32CSC/32CSM has put forward a select number of prominent spokespeople and leaders to speak for the organization. Originally the group was most prominently represented by Francie Mackey and Bernadette Sands-McKevitt; more recently Marian Price and Gary Donnelly have become most visible. In an interview with The Guardian in 2003[17] Price recognizes the fact that 32CSM struggles to gain support and has failed to capture the imagination of the communities it ultimately claims to represent:

> ... the majority of Irish people have never supported the republican cause ... most are not willing to make the sacrifices it requires. But as long as there is a British presence in Ireland there will always be justification. Republicanism will never fade. My principles and ideals will never be crushed.

Not unlike RSF, Price decries Sinn Féin's acceptance of the Good Friday Agreement: "... they'll explain it away to their grassroots as a tactical move, but they'll do it. They conceded the principle in their heads a long time ago."[18]

Just like those of RSF, the statements of 32CSM betray their function. Reading them provides a glimpse into the Republican dream utopia, described with equal doses of vigor and purpose. They read in an almost benign manner. References to armed struggle are sparse across both the documentation of 32CSM and RSF. There is a broader purpose to the grand strategic visions of Mackey, Price, and others in 32CSM, however. They serve, in the words of Frampton, to "prepare the ground ideologically for the Real IRA—to contextualise, explain and legitimise its activity."[19]

To fully appreciate this, it is useful to consider additional statements issued by 32CSM members themselves in the context of how they justify ongoing violence. Britain's Channel 4 news reporter Carl Dinnen met with young 32CSM members in September 2010. One member explained how violence helps to "de-normalize and destabilize" Northern Ireland.[20] When Dinnen raised the example of Omagh and the "risk that innocent people will be killed," 32CSM member Kieran Boyle replied: "as a human being, I'm not comfortable with war ... with bombs or shootings ... but the cause of the conflict remains the same. Britain occupies Ireland." Nathan Hastings, also of 32CSM, asserted the following:

"If you value tranquility more than what you value the contest for freedom, then that's a political choice you make, but I don't consider it 'republican.'" Sinn Féin, by signing up to the GFA and supporting policing, have "brought nothing about. There's been no large milestone toward a united Ireland. There's been nothing."

Tonge[21] cites Marian Price in a further example: "to suggest that a war was fought for what they have today ... diminishes anybody who partook in that war, anybody who died in it and went out there and sacrificed their lives and liberty."[22]

Following the post-2002 split in the RIRA, a resurgent and more focused 32CSM emerged. Articulate spokespeople such as Price and Donnelly became more visible, and the movement began to highlight "violations of Irish sovereignty" such as use of Shannon airport as a stopover facility by the U.S. military. 32CSM launched a new newspaper, *The Sovereign Nation*. It has embraced the Internet such that 32CSM is now a broader entity with *cumainn* (associations) across the land. The national leadership works with regional branches to draw attention to a wide variety of social issues.

In contrast to RSF, 32CSM has tried to build bridges with various dissident factions. Their website presents a discussion video on Republican unity. Explaining that "our enemies are united against us," the video slideshow (entitled "32CSM Republican Unity") places Gerry Adams and Martin McGuinness front and center of the imagery. It goes on: "The British government, Irish government, Unionism, Provisional Sinn Féin and Constitutional nationalism are all arrayed against us. Their opposition is ideological, political and security in nature. They have the full backing of the establishment press." It continues:

Irish republicanism is isolated to the point where our position is not challenged by the establishment parties, but ignored by them. It is not a splendid nor noble isolation, but a strategically damaging one. A marginalized republican movement is detrimental to every republican principle. Only republicans can end this isolation.

This has been a visibly central strategic principle for 32CSM. In an analysis of the various positions of the dissident groups, O'Loan[23] argues that the ultimate strength of 32CSM is "its assessment of the contradictions of others," notably Sinn Féin. Yet 32CSM understands that its potential future membership is largely located within the current membership of Sinn Féin and the Provisional IRA. Price and others portray Sinn Féin and the Republican Movement in general as a broken organization, which should no longer be considered as Republican but as Nationalist. They believe that they themselves follow a "purer" form of Republicanism:

As far as Republicanism goes, I wouldn't consider SF of today being republicans, I see SF as being a nationalist party. And that's by choice. For Republicanism I think we had a setback, I believe that it's fragmented. But I think that if we just stop and take stock, we can rebuild the Republican Movement and probably it will be a stronger movement for this, because the people who will be in the Republican Movement will be republicans, not nationalists or militant Catholics.[24]

32CSM recognizes the need for Republican unity on a strategic level, and its policy documents reveal an acute awareness of the inherent issues:

It is essentially the case that in any political compromise with the British government on the national question Irish republicanism has been the severest casualty. ... The motivations for republicans to compromise are more varied ranging from genuine political efforts in the face of republican inertia, political naivety to outright betrayal. In as much as these varied reasons invariably leave the separatist movement greatly weakened republican reaction to it has also contributed to this weakened state. The principal reason for this lays in the fact that not only does division amongst republicans occur over the very premise of any compromise, between those in favour and those against, but also division occurs amongst those who remain opposed to whatever compromise was formulated. The division becomes twofold and as such republican opposition becomes twice as ineffective. The great irony in all of this is that there exist more reasons to be unified than there does to remain divided.

In a narrative apparent across all strands of dissident Republicanism 32CSM members present themselves as victims of ongoing political and media censorship and vilification due to their opposition to the Good Friday Agreement. Although they probably would not like to admit it this places them in the same bracket as hard-line Unionists such as Jim Allister and his colleagues within the Traditional Unionist Voice (TUV) party.[25] The 32CSM's awareness of their position is expressed in lucid terms:

Political compromises with the British government were always sanitised by making the compromise popular. This popularity insulated those from political scrutiny because the perceived "ending of the conflict" took precedence over the terms agreed for it. Equally those who offered this scrutiny, republicans, were demonised with a vitriol of anti-peace and anti-democratic rhetoric and by consequence the republican objective itself was cast in this light. Invariably recrimination in republican ranks clouded prudent political judgement which allowed the politics of the compromise an almost clear run to take hold, and as such, create a new generation of political thinking to develop amongst the body politic which possessed a virulent anti republican strain.... Disunity amongst republicans is a major contributor to this marginalisation.

Despite a constant assertion that 32CSM is not a political party, and the fact that it runs members such as Gary Donnelly as independents in council elections, the group explicitly recognizes the need to formulate a political agenda, and for Republican unity to be channeled toward that agenda:

> There exists within republicanism an irrational distrust of politics and political activity evidently sourced from the various betrayals and departures that it has suffered. It's irrational because republicanism is about politics and it's irrational because republicanism is confronted by politics. It was the lack of political acumen within republicanism which permitted both the betrayals and ideological departures to take place. The republican objective needs to be expressed politically and republicans need to fully understand it if we wish to both effectively promote and defend it. Defining this expression in a clear and concise manner has proved problematic for republicans.

The group also recognizes the practical barriers to that unity and does not attempt to mask the differences between the factions:

> It is also important to realise that unity amongst republicans is not predicated upon reaching absolute agreement on absolutely everything nor is it about establishing one definitive route upon which all republicans must travel. It is essentially about maximising and prioritising the political effectiveness of our common ground and minimising the political damage caused by whatever differences may exist.

In many ways, this strategy is reminiscent of the "New Ireland Forum" of the early to mid-1980s.[26] With the rise in electoral popularity of Sinn Féin as a result of the 1981 hunger strikes the constitutional nationalist parties and organizations across Ireland came together for a series of meetings to put forward proposals for the future of Ireland and discuss how a united Ireland could be achieved. Essentially what the constitutional nationalists were doing in the 1980s is identical to what 32CSM and other likeminded parties are doing with their strategy. They are trying to present a viable alternative to an increasingly popular Sinn Féin.

32CSM is acutely aware of the divisions that characterize the diversity of the dissident scene. For 32CSM, Republican unity is the key to an effective challenge to Sinn Féin. The group identifies three core areas for unity: protest, publicity, and commemoration, highlighting the "numerous" benefits associated with this approach. Cooperation through publicity offers Republicans "the most potent weapon of all" and they place particular emphasis on this:

> Republicans are no strangers to censorship and a hostile press. It is an essential front on which to engage our struggle, as it is for our enemies to undermine us. Whatever about the extremely limited influence republicans can exert upon media portrayals of the political landscape we can certainly exert a positive influence over the portrayals under our control. Publicity is the ultimate compliment to political activity. … At the heart of both governments' efforts to marginalise the republican position, through publicity starvation and false press, lies a contradiction, which needs their deft management to contain and which republicans need to recognise in order to

exploit. Republicanism is newsworthy. Republicans need to make ourselves more newsworthy.

The group spells out the urgency for such unity: "2016 will mark the centenary of the 1916 Easter Rising. It should be a republican separatist celebration but there is no guarantee of this." 32CSM and the RIRA have also recognized the urgency of an unambiguous set of aims and objectives. In a statement published in *An Phoblacht* on September 12, 2002, the Provisionals claimed that the RIRA could "articulate no coherent strategy":

> We have addressed the activities of these groups on a number of occasions in the past. They are small in number, they have little or no support base. They articulate no coherent strategy. They have no impact on the structures and discipline of Óglaigh na hÉireann. Their attacks are aimed at collapsing the peace process. They need to examine whose interests this serves.[27]

In response, a member of the RIRA Army Council contacted reporter Damien Okado-Gough of the Derry-based Channel 9 Television news and granted him an interview. The interview, widely published in various venues, articulated RIRA's national strategy:

> Our ultimate objective remains the re-establishment of the Republic. The Belfast Agreement has been presented by the Provisional Movement as a transitional mechanism, or stepping stone, to eventual Irish unity and a 32-County Republic. We totally reject this claim and regard this Agreement as a negation of Irish democracy as it was build upon the premise of separate referenda. Remember the Six-County referendum had the power of veto over the 26-County one. We regard this as a copper fastening of partition and an acceptance of the Unionist veto by all participants.

The irony of this statement to observers is that the Good Friday Agreement probably represents the single most democratically inclusive vote there has ever been on the status of Northern Ireland. A cornerstone of the legitimizing narrative of the RIRA has been to put themselves forward as an alternative to the "sectarian" nature of a post-Good Friday Agreement Northern Ireland. Another irony here is that although they are not targeting Protestants in attacks or in their statements they have practiced a different form of sectarianism. As we saw in the previous chapter, they and other VDR groups have purposefully targeted Catholic PSNI officers to dissuade members of this community from joining the new police force. As the definition of sectarianism is the singling out of an individual or a group due to its religious beliefs or ethnic origins, this modern-day VDR tactic can rightfully be regarded as sectarian.

To the RIRA the peace process is

> ... a misnomer and is grounded on a false premise that it is the road to a final settlement. We regard the implementation of the Belfast Agreement and the full

participation of the Provisional Movement in that process as a classic example of a successful counter-insurgency strategy practiced on the part of the British and Dublin governments.

The RIRA spokesman presented a vitriolic characterization of Sinn Féin:

> Just ponder on the sacrifices made by the Provisional movement and its supporters in the periods 1973–94 and 1996–98.... Now we must endure the nauseating spectacle of the Provisional leadership attempting to present the 1998 Agreement as an outstanding political breakthrough and victory. We totally reject this distortion of the truth and the sickening gimmickry and phony pathetic attempts of that leadership to portray themselves as political innovators when in fact they are merely implementing SDLP [Social Democratic and Labour Party] policies which were formulated with the Dublin government as far back as 1972.The war was not fought for seats in Stormont, on Councils nor indeed policing boards.

The Provisional movement has, the RIRA asserts, abandoned the idea of the Republic:

> They are no longer Republicans. Eventually they will become indistinguishable from Fianna Fáil and the SDLP. Our political position and policies are based on ideology and principles. The Provisionals' position is based on an abandonment of principles, political intrigue, ambition, pragmatism and ideological U-turns. A cursory glance at their political track record will confirm this. They have gone from revolutionary Republicanism to constitutionalism nationalism and will eventually take their seats in Westminster.

Whereas the Unionist population in Northern Ireland is described as "a very sizeable minority in Ireland," the RIRA views Unionists as little more than "also the victims of British imperial and colonial history. It has to be borne in mind that they were used by the British in the past, armed and financed by them, to play the role of the colonial garrison." Again, this is similar to RSF's strategy in their promotion of Éire Nua as they attempt to portray an understanding of Unionist suffering at the hands of Britain, an understanding that they suggest will make a united Ireland an attractive alternative to maintenance of the Union.

■ RIRA Military Strategy

In those interviews, conducted in 2003, RIRA members refused to discuss any issue relating to its "future military strategy" because they felt "it would be self-defeating." This would change. In a 2009 interview with reporter Suzanne Breen in which a representative of the RIRA Army Council claimed responsibility for the murder of Sinn Féin's former chief administrator (and self-confessed spy) Denis Donaldson, the representative explained that the RIRA strategy was to "engage in tactical use of armed struggle," adding, "The days of a campaign involving military operations every day or every few days are over. We're looking for high-profile targets, though we'll obviously take advantage when other targets present themselves."[28]

How much the RIRA is willing to say about military activity also appears to depend on what kind of action is involved and whether admitting responsibility for that action serves the broader aims of the group. For example, in October 2010, *The Irish News* received a statement from the RIRA in which the group admitted killing drug dealers on both sides of the border.[29] It confessed to killing five alleged drug dealers in Dublin and Cork (areas in which RIRA and 32CSM have been very active), saying that these individuals were "dealing death" to communities across the country: "To those who believe they can escape the reach of the Republican movement, we have also executed drug dealers on the continent who believed they were safe having fled the country. We have crippled, maimed and exiled numerous others." In the same statement, the RIRA denied it was extorting money from drug dealers, but admitted that "We have in fact relieved them of their firearms and weaponry then closed down their operations."

So far in this chapter the group's *national* strategy has essentially been addressed, but these threats and attacks represent the foundations of the group's *local* strategy. Ironically, the group strives to position itself as the upholder of morality and community stability across Ireland. There is speculation too that the RIRA has also claimed responsibility for murders it may not have committed.[30] On the allegation that the movement is doomed without popular support, the RIRA emphasized that "The men and women of 1916 were outcasts in their time. They were actually spat on by ordinary Dubliners as they were being led away by the British. Being popular doesn't concern us."[31]

On the principle of violence, the RIRA representative asserted: "Armed struggle has always been the right of every Irish person in asserting their independence from a foreign invader. The British continue to claim sovereignty over part of our country and while that is the case armed struggle will always be justified." He adds: "The Republican struggle was never about economic and social change within the Six-County state—it was about destroying that very state and getting the British out of Ireland. We believe that only then can the wider issues of social and economic change take place in a 32-County context. Partition in itself is a controlling factor in holding back change."

Until then, the RIRA promises to continue its operations, including the specific targeting of PSNI officers as part of its military strategy: "Let us be clear so there is no further ambiguity on the matter: any young person fool enough to join the colonial police in the belief that the leadership of the Provisional movement will protect them, or give them cover, is sadly mistaken."[32] However, and while willing to take part in attacks, the group is unwilling to take responsibility for any "innocent" casualties. In their 2011 Easter statement the RIRA attempted to preemptively blame the PSNI for any possible injuries and thereby distance its members from the blame:

[We] repeat our warnings to civilians to stay away from the scenes of IRA attacks or alerts, we have noticed a pattern developing whereby the RUC/PSNI are deliberately putting civilians at risk. These so called modern heroes were brave enough to allow hundreds of non combatants to pass a large bomb in Newry, we do not believe that this was sheer incompetence on their behalf but a calculated action aimed at putting civilians in the danger zone to protect themselves and discredit republicans. With this in mind we ask both the public and all volunteers to be careful and vigilant, with the occupation forces coming under increased pressure from the resistance movement they are more likely to take drastic action out of desperation.[33]

Suzanne Breen suggested that RIRA strategy can be effectively summarized as "an Armalite in one hand and we don't do ballot boxes."[34] In her interviews with the RIRA leadership, she concludes: "There were no mad-cap boasts that the Real IRA would 'free Ireland' in a few years. The organisation has a strategy in the short to medium term: to disrupt the normalisation of Northern Ireland and to draw the security forces back into an openly combative role." For now at least, RIRA operations, not 32CSM aspirations, have come to characterize the movement.

■ ÉIRÍGÍ AND THE REPUBLICAN NETWORK FOR UNITY

The dominant voices within the dissident movement still belong to the Continuity IRA, the Real IRA, and their political partners. At the same time, however, the dissident community is becoming crowded with the arrival of newer groups both political and paramilitary in nature. Two of the most vocal of these have been Éirígí and Republican Network for Unity (RNU). Both groups provide their own independent view on how any Irish Republican organization should strive for the ultimate goal of a united Ireland.

Every Irish Republican group, both dissident and mainstream, pays, at the very least, lip service to the belief that Ireland must not only be united but also socialist. However, the only group that places this at the center of its aspirations is Éirígí. In a strategy reminiscent of the policies proposed by old-school Irish Republicans such as Cathal Goulding, Roy Johnston, Tomas MacGiolla, and others in the 1960s in the lead-up to the 1969–1970 split, Éirígí promotes the centrality of socialism as the core purpose of its political activism:

Éirígí unequivocally asserts that Irish freedom can only be achieved through the establishment of a socialist republic—a republic free from British imperialism and free from capitalist exploitation. Neither British rule nor capitalism can be reformed. In this regard, we are asserting nothing new. However, in doing so, Éirígí is consciously and purposely locating itself firmly within this country's revolutionary political tradition. It is a tradition that acknowledges the working class "as the incorruptible inheritors of the fight for freedom in Ireland." That revolutionary tradition once again appeals directly to this class to join the fight for our collective freedom.[35]

Although they are close in ethos to Goulding and Johnston this is a fact that they, or any other Republican group, is not willing to admit freely due to the historically pejorative implications of being associated with the Marxist-oriented Official IRA. In fact, Éirígí is curiously heterogeneous in its composition. In the

Republic it comprises many disaffected Sinn Féin members, whereas in Northern Ireland its ranks include prominent and authoritative ex-PIRA members. Éirígí place its Republican socialism in line with other historical examples within Irish Republicanism:

> Éirígí identifies exclusively with a revolutionary current that has distinguished itself historically from the predominant conservative nationalist tendency. This current recognizes and accepts the essential and inseparable relationship that exists between the national and social struggles. From the Irish Socialist Republican Party to the Irish Citizen Army, to the Republican Congress and, today, Éirígí, there have been organised bodies of people throughout Irish history that have dedicated themselves to the radical transformation of economic, social and political relations in Ireland.[36]

Drawing on the popular sentiment of anger against Irish politicians (in the Republic) within the general population in recent times, Éirígí places a significant emphasis on portraying the national and international actions of the Irish government as a betrayal of the Irish people, their sovereignty, and their neutrality:

> Those who promote imperialist policies have, unfortunately, no shortage of allies in Ireland. There are many who would bring Ireland into formal military and political alliances with those same countries which for centuries past to the present day treat their fellow human beings as resources to be exploited in pursuit of material gains. We ... believe that the agenda of the Irish apologists for imperialism should be challenged and exposed at every opportunity, be this in relation to the use of Shannon airport by the US military, the British occupation of six Irish counties, membership of the EU rapid reaction forces or the proposed entry of the twenty-six counties into NATO.[37]

All Republican groups place an emphasis on promoting the cause of the Republican prisoners across Ireland, Britain, and Europe. However, the main group that was originally established by former prisoners, and in turn actively promoted their cause, is the RNU. Although the origins of this group can be traced to the issue of "POWs," its central cause in its current form is bringing together a united Republican movement as a viable alternative to Sinn Féin leadership. RNU's argument is that the dissident community is too disparate and fractured to have any significant influence. Not unlike 32CSM, RNU emphasizes the need not to isolate Sinn Féin members:

> In the interests of building Republican unity we should be careful not to fall into the trap of vilifying Sinn Féin supporters; for the most part, it is the Sinn Féin leadership who are the culprits. It is our job to win back the ordinary Republican people and we are confident of doing this by winning the argument and by making our agenda relevant to our community: the working class Irish Republican community.[38]

The main aim of the group is to "reclaim" Republicanism from the Sinn Féin leadership:

> We pledged to continue this political fight to reclaim Republicanism from those who were being used to masquerade a British regime at Stormont. Our means were to present a Republican alternative political analysis and to establish channels of communication or a network of cooperation with other like-minded organizations and individuals.[39]

Like the others, RNU believes that the right for the Northern Irish people to self-determination is in its conception an undemocratic slight to the people of Ireland and amounts to a "Unionist veto." At the very foundations of each Republican group is the belief that the Unionist population is a minority community across Ireland as opposed to a majority community within Northern Ireland. To Republicans this is one of the main injustices against which they see themselves fighting:

> RNU advocate political resistance to the British occupation and imperialism in Ireland. We renounce the Stormont and Leinster House assemblies because they attempt to give partition the veneer of democracy. We also reject the Unionist veto over Irish reunification. The Belfast, St. Andrews and Hillsborough Agreements have not advanced social and economic justice nor freedom in Ireland. We reiterate our commitment to the 32 County Socialist Democratic Republic outlined on Easter Monday 1916. Our network proposes a return to core Republican values and principles. The Irish people have the right to national self-determination and RNU defends that right.[40]

■ ÓGLAIGH NA HÉIREANN (REAL IRA)

RNU is believed in some ways to be linked with Óglaigh na hÉireann (Real IRA). Although RNU will not officially promote the continuation of armed struggle and acknowledges the right of Irish people to "use disciplined resistance to defend the Irish Republic proclaimed in 1916,"[41] an analysis of ONH (RIRA)'s strategy would at this stage only be speculative. They supply few detailed statements and, as of yet, have not actively used RNU or its publications to host their statements. However, we can gain some limited insight into their strategic principles from considering their activity (from Chapter 3) and the few interviews that have been conducted by the group.

ONH (RIRA) has divided its overall strategy into a local and a national strategy. Its national strategy is to emphasize the continued British presence in Northern Ireland by targeting the security forces, be they police, military, or intelligence. This is best illustrated in their targeting of Peadar Heffron, a Catholic police officer, in 2010, and the Palace Barracks in the same year. Although the group denies targeting Heffron or others because of their Catholicism, it is clear that this is an overarching strategic dimension for many of the dissident groups. Their objective appears to be to dissuade young Catholics from joining the PSNI so they can then promote it as a sectarian police force unrepresentative of the significant Catholic minority in Northern Ireland. However, their public message is that these police officers are being targeted not because of their religion but because of their membership in a British police force in Ireland: "We never target an individual in uniform. We target the uniform and what it stands for."[42]

Central to their strategy is that the unification of Ireland cannot be achieved in the short term and therefore they are preparing for the continuation of a "long war." In doing so they have set out to ensure the organization is more secure from infiltration than other VDR groups and that although their members are trustworthy, they are also sufficiently trained to partake in long-term paramilitary activity. The group publicly displays patience in reaching this goal as it does not claim to be capable of actively pursuing a large-scale offensive similar to the PIRA. However, it does state that it is building toward this and that a national level strategy may come in the future:

> Our fundamentals are about securing the organisation, about credible recruitment and carrying out credible, high-grade operations. ... Every time we are not involved in an operation we are recruiting, developing expertise, gathering intelligence and planning the next operation.... I think we would be playing right into the hands of the British [if we went on a full offensive], who, while the Provisional IRA were winding down continued with their war machine in Ireland unabated. To go at it full steam would increase momentum short term, but we believe ultimately would fail within a very short period of time.[43]

Their local strategy is reminiscent of that of their anti-Sinn Féin rejectionist peers. To gain the support, trust, and control of the Republican, mainly working-class communities across Ireland, they continuously target drug dealers and other offenders within those communities. This in turn puts them forward as an alternative not only to Sinn Féin and the PIRA but also to the PSNI: "We also want to offer working class communities, who have been abandoned, protection from criminals and drug dealers."[44]

As illustrated in Chapter 3, the most significant result of this local strategy is that the lethality of highly targeted attacks is most detrimental to those within the communities they claim to represent. The data show that the majority of people killed or injured by these paramilitary organizations are from the Republican and Nationalist communities and are not those who are actively, or even inactively, promoting the retention of the union. Although the dissidents wish to portray themselves as paramilitary Republicans, the reality is that their violent strategies more realistically call for them to be acknowledged as, primarily, vigilante gangs. It is clear, however, that ONH (RIRA) is an emerging force in the anti-Sinn Féin Republican groups, and is taking careful steps to prepare itself for armed action.

■ DIVIDED THEY STAND?

The dissidents are broadly united in their critique of the Provisional movement. As Tonge[45] explains:

> Republican critics adopt a historian's approach in their critique. Sinn Féin's support for the Good Friday Agreement and entry into the Northern Ireland Assembly at

Stormont in 1999 are seen by Republican critics as analogous to the 1926 move of De Valera into Dáil Éireann, the Irish parliament seen by Republican purists as illegal and partitionist. At that time, Fianna Fáil possessed an armed wing, carried most Republicans and protested the evils of partition, yet the quest for power overtook the pursuit of Irish unity as the primary goal of the party.

Frampton[46] also acknowledges this:

Ideologically speaking, there is a corpus of mutually-held propositions, which brings a degree of homogeneity to this otherwise amorphous sphere. Dissident republicans of various hues share certain ways of thinking about the world; they draw on a common political-cultural heritage and use similar modes of expression.

What unites the dissidents is their collective sense of betrayal by the Sinn Féin leadership, the latter defined in their eyes by their "ideological somersaults."[47] Despite their longstanding national-level ideological signatures, at least in a nominal sense, RSF and 32CSM take steps to be seen to be offering the hand of friendship to fellow disaffected Republicans, as well as leaving the door open to potentially disaffected Sinn Féin and PIRA members. They remain acutely aware of the potential to attract support from those currently aligned with the Provisional leadership. A clear indicator of internal unrest in Sinn Féin came through what Frampton describes as a major statement by Martin Ferris' daughter in July 2009. Ferris is a senior Republican, and former PIRA member with unquestionable credentials. She asked: "As a party, what are we at and where are we going?" Frampton explains: "That Toireasa Ferris should have been the one to deliver such a message seemed to confirm the presence of serious unrest inside Sinn Féin."[48]

A significant catalyst both for dissident unity and further dissent within Sinn Féin came in January 2007, when the Sinn Féin party leadership secured 90% support for a motion that effectively "authorised endorsement of the PSNI."[49] The policing issue provided the many disillusioned Republicans with a unifying banner, and dissident voices received a significant boost. Several groups came together to wage debate with, and ultimately offer a challenge to, Sinn Féin. In March 2007, amid the Northern Ireland Assembly elections, candidates standing on the "Concerned Republicans" platform challenged Sinn Féin in three constituencies. A letter published in The Blanket, signed by over 300 prominent Republicans from across Ireland, rejected the proposition of endorsing the PSNI.[50] Despite failing to register much support from the electorate, Frampton says the creation of "Concerned Republicans" "suggested a new readiness, within the extended and disjointed ranks of dissident republicanism, to mobilise and co-operate in efforts to contest the intra-republican supremacy of the Provisionals."[51] Some of the leading figures behind Concerned Republicans went on to form RNU.

Time and time again, the dissidents demonstrate an effectiveness to unite in protest but not in strategy. Operationally, in terms of violent activity, the picture is even more confusing. There have been numerous false hopes of single individuals emerging to unite the dissidents,[52] but this remains haphazard at best. For the most part the development of the broad dissident groupings from the Omagh bombing to the formation of RNU has been characterized by what from the outside seems like a litany of confusing and inconsistent actions: taking responsibility for military operations, denying responsibility for actions, "branding" specific operations such that responsibility was guaranteed, and even actively embracing confusion about responsibility when this suited particular groups. It is little wonder how impossible it is to accurately attribute all dissident activity, whether violent or nonviolent.

The reality of this complex situation illustrates the need to take the public declarations of responsibility from the various groupings with a grain of salt. As illustrated in Chapter 3, false declarations of attribution not only confuse the security forces but also at times anger those who were actually responsible for the action. In response to an apparent false claim of responsibility by the RIRA in 2008 the CIRA issued a statement saying that "those making spurious claims of responsibility would be better employed in their own acts of resistance rather than seeking to confuse Republicans."[53]

Contrary to many post hoc accounts of terrorist activity, it can be very difficult in the immediate aftermath of a terrorist incident, or even later, to reliably determine which group undertook it, and much harder still to deduce the full meaning of the event to a variety of actors and their constituents. Governments and intelligence agencies frequently use both "mimicry" and deceptive tactics to conceal their involvement in acts of violence, especially against other nations. Violent dissident activity offers a case study in the use of deceptive signaling. To this day it remains unclear as to the true nature of responsibility for the Omagh bombing. Despite indicators of RIRA–CIRA crossover, there were several alleged attempts by the RIRA to claim that the CIRA was "more" responsible for Omagh. Frampton argues that in the aftermath of Omagh, which was disastrous for the RIRA's attempt to position itself, McKevitt was convinced that "admissions were counterproductive" and that "it was better to let the press have it and make their story as big as they wanted."[54]

Assertions of identity, in conjunction with efforts to successfully "brand" initiatives and activity, can also be important for any group that attempts to prevent further splitting. The 2002 split in the RIRA leadership (described in Chapter 2) led the emergent faction ONH (RIRA) to pronounce:

Óglaigh na hÉireann attempted to address their so-called grievances but in an unprecedented move within the history of Republicanism these men pre-empted any investigation and ran to the media for highly questionable reasons. In their desperation these men have attacked other Republican prisoners who will not follow their personal agenda. Those Volunteers in Portlaoise loyal to Óglaigh na hÉireann have established new structures and are working harmoniously and constructively with the wider Movement including Republican Prisoners in all other jails.... We would question the motivation of individuals distancing themselves from certain operations and what they hope to gain from such a move. There are mechanisms in place to deal with the relationship between Óglaigh na hÉireann and prisoners. Some individuals in Portlaoise have already been dismissed and further investigations are ongoing.[55]

Thus far, however, we have considered here some of the themes inherent in dissident groups at the national level. Understanding the relationship between local-level policies and activity and the overarching national-level positions is challenging. Like any group, the dissidents engage in activity inherent to their survival, but in some very clear examples, localized activities are difficult to reconcile with any stated policy objectives.

Criminality—Another "Near" Strategy?

As described in Chapter 2, the catalyst for the October 2002 split in the RIRA was a statement issued by Michael McKevitt from his cell in Portlaoise prison. In it, he urged the RIRA leadership to stand down its armed campaign, accusing them of engaging in criminal activity and failing to develop a meaningful strategy for the future.[56] McKevitt's views emerged in the "New Republican Forum" and were promoted as a statement from the [Real] IRA leadership within Portlaoise prison.[57]

Although Frampton argues that McKevitt would never escape the shadow of Omagh, and virtually conceded failure with his statement, successive rejuvenated waves of the RIRA have not escaped the accusation of their involvement with criminality. Furthermore, although Sinn Féin has attracted significant criticism from the dissidents, in several of its statements related to the Real IRA, Continuity IRA, and other dissident Republican groups, it identifies members of those groups as criminals engaged in drug trafficking, thuggery, and extortion. Given the long PIRA history of "ordinary" crime (not least the Northern Bank robbery), the irony of the Provisional movement condemning the dissidents for fraternizing with criminals and engaging in criminal activity is clear, but Sinn Féin is most likely acutely aware of how damaging such allegations can be to the dissidents' efforts to gain the moral high ground within Republican circles. Although this strategy (explored in more detail in Chapter 7) serves to delegitimize these groups (and to champion Sinn Féin by comparison), there is some evidence to suggest that accusations of Real IRA and Continuity IRA involvement with the drug trade are not entirely propagandistic. There have been several clashes between dissident Republicans from the Real IRA and Continuity IRA and established drug traders.

By 2006, the strength and reach of Irish drug gangs had become rampant. It was reported that in that year drug gangs smuggled more weapons into Ireland than the Provisional IRA at the peak of its armed campaign against British forces in the 1980s, and that 22 people had been killed as a result of gang-related shootings.[58] In April 2009, the *Sunday Independent* reported that dissident Republicans were engaged in cross-border trade with criminals in Dublin.[59] According to the report, dissident Republicans were supplying increasing numbers of pipe bombs to drug gangs for as much as €30,000. It was also reported that a large amount of cannabis had been supplied to West Belfast dissidents by a West Dublin drug gang. However, cooperation between dissident Republicans and the drug gangs does not characterize the entirety of their relationship. Association between the two groups is characterized in much greater part by contention and conflict. In 2010, *The Belfast Telegraph* reported that Gardaí had grown concerned that dissident

Republicans had been making attempts to gain "turf" by threatening drug dealers who refused to desist their drug-running and selling operations.[60]

The concerns of the Gardaí are well founded. In recent years there has been an increase in Republican violence against the drug gangs, as several established drug dealers in Ireland and Northern Ireland have been killed or muscled out of their positions. In the Republic, the Gardaí are concerned that the Real IRA has been making "inroads on dealers working for the highly dangerous south inner city gangs."[61] These gangs deal in heroin and cocaine and have extensive links with the European mainland, in particular Spain. Their activities offer a profitable source of extortion money for RIRA.[62]

Through these activities, the dissidents have managed to stake a claim to a portion of the lucrative drug dealing markets of Ireland and Northern Ireland.[63] However, violence has not been completely one-sided. In June 2011 Liam Kenny, a member of the newly formed Real Sinn Féin and reportedly the Real CIRA, was murdered by suspected members of a rival criminal gang involved in the Dublin drug trade. Gardaí initially reported the possibility that he had either been murdered by the RIRA or CIRA. However, Gardaí believe it was non-Republican criminals who killed him.[64]

In a statement to *The Irish News* in October 2010, RIRA admitted responsibility for five killings in the Republic[65]: in addition to Kieran O'Flynn (killed in Cork in 2001), the group took responsibility for the killings of four other alleged drug deal- ers. However, despite this claim, Gardaí are skeptical of RIRA involvement in the murder of O'Flynn. The suspicion is that this may have been vigilante opportun- ism on the part of the group to claim a murder without having to commit it. Much of the violent activity aimed at drug dealers by dissident Republicans, including the activities of RAAD in Derry, has been claimed to "rid working-class communi- ties of drug dealing."[66] However, Gardaí strongly believe that most violent activity perpetrated against drug dealers by dissident Republicans, including RAAD, has been primarily geared toward extorting money from the criminals to fund the groups' political activities rather than for beneficial service to the Republicans' communities.[67]

The dissidents have certainly exploited the drugs issue to its maximum poten- tial. In Cork, where 32CSM members are heavily active, the group has positioned itself as the savior of local communities affected by the drugs scourge. In September 2009 the Cork branch issued a death threat statement "on behalf of Óglaigh na hÉireann,"[68] which a 32CSM spokesman asserted represented an upcoming vote by 32CSM Cork to "publish a name and shame list of drug dealers in Cork." This, he said, was based on the recognition that "it is inevitable that the likes of armed republicans will eventually take action against that part of our society ... borne out of frustration with the Garda Siochána who have failed miserably to tackle this issue."

Unsurprisingly, though most commentators on dissident Republicanism dis- cuss the reality of involvement in organized crime, the groups themselves actively condemn those using the name of Republicanism in the context of crime.[69] Their continued involvement in purging communities of criminals, however, illustrates an ability to successfully tap into public sentiment, both locally and nationally, and to draw the public's attention to their broader objectives in a way that would otherwise prove almost impossible.

■ CONCLUSIONS: THE (F)UTILITY OF ARMED STRUGGLE?

There is no single overarching strategy that unifies the dissident groups. The positions of some groups, notably the more recently active movements (e.g., Eirigi), are likely to fluctuate somewhat until they find a position that satisfies their expectations about their role as an alternative to Sinn Féin. Furthermore, there are undoubtedly far more subtle (but to the dissidents, more significant) strategic and ideological features that both define them as well as distinguish them from one another. At a much finer level than could be allowed in this chapter, these issues are regularly discussed by dissidents and dissenters alike. They are, however, are of limited importance for our purposes here.

Commentary and response from politicians, police, and journalists alike chorus the claim that the dissidents are, in the words of journalist Liam Clarke, strategically "doomed to failure." Most of the criticism leveled at the dissidents (and this will be explored in greater detail in Chapter 7) is predicated on the belief that they lack sufficient popular support. The dissidents, in turn, respond that not only do they not need support from the broader population, but the fact that such support does not exist further strengthens their contention that core Republican ideals have been lost.

In attempting to assess the effectiveness of the dissidents' strategy, then, it may be worthwhile to consider what kinds of factors would result in some degree of success for the dissidents outside of the immediate death and disruption that stem from their tactical operations. In their seminal analysis of how extremist groups attempt to sabotage peace efforts, Kydd and Walter[70] assert that groups "succeed in destroying a peace settlement if they are able to foster mistrust between more moderate groups that must implement the deal; they fail if the moderate groups retain an adequate level of mutual trust in each other's willingness to fulfill the deal."[71] Kydd and Walter's assertion relies on key hypotheses:

- The higher the prior level of trust between opposing sides, the lower the likelihood that extremists will attack in an attempt to disrupt peace agreements.
- The more the government trusts the opposition, the more an attack will convince the government of the opposition's weakness. The less the government trusts the opposition, the less effect an attack will have on the government's beliefs about the moderates' capabilities.

Although these arguments are more easily applied in hindsight to the role of the PIRA leading up to, and beyond, the peace talks that began in 1990, they can be extended to thinking about the challenges facing the currently active Republican groups. The continued condemnation of VDR activity by Martin McGuinness and others in Sinn Féin, as well as their professional approach to power-sharing government, has effectively built significant trust with the DUP, with whom they now enjoy a power-sharing arrangement. The relationship between Sinn Féin and its

Unionist colleagues remains the key factor in understanding why the dissidents' campaign, despite its short-term effects, is unlikely to wreck the power-sharing agreement. The issue of mistrust here is not so much an issue of contention between Sinn Fein and the DUP as the dissidents aim it squarely at the Sinn Féin leadership. The justification for the dissidents' attempts at "spoiling" the peace process is largely directed against the PSNI but also highlights Sinn Féin's acceptance of a British presence and its taking of seats in and running of a British parliament.

Though it will be discussed in detail in a later chapter, it would seem that in order to effectively undermine the dissidents' ability to become an effective spoiler, Sinn Féin's ability to maintain trust with both the DUP and the British government more broadly would seem to be key. Sinn Féin continues to maintain this trust not only through significant statements endorsing the PSNI or openly condemning dissident activity (even using the term "condemn"), but through a litany of every-day examples that may not appear significant in themselves, but effectively signal just how much Sinn Féin has changed from a subversive movement to one that has embraced its new position. These events collectively and effectively signal that Sinn Féin is a party for all segments of Northern Ireland, and is viewed as enormously significant by the communities by which it is targeted. Sinn Féin ministers continue to walk an ideological tightrope by showing that they are supportive of Northern Ireland (again, that Sinn Féin even uses the term "Northern Ireland" over "the Six Counties" is a significant indicator of change) to maintain Unionist trust. Sinn Féin's challenge will be in sustaining that inclusivity while also retaining effective control over its base.

Frampton provides a characteristically insightful summary of the ideological framework shared by the dissidents:

> Central to this ideology is a belief in the fundamental right of an armed minority to act in the interests of the broader Irish nation. That minority is understood to be the embodiment of "the people," irrespective of whether those same people actually furnish their support.... Republicans ... are seen as an enlightened elite, who alone truly understand the situation as it *really* exists in Ireland. They are the guardians of the revealed truth: that the Irish are not free and never can be until British influence is banned from the entire island.[72]

A "colonial interpretation of the Northern Irish conflict"[73] (in the words of Rogelio Alonso) that once served to sustain the Provisionals is now a core part of the dissidents' strategic imperatives. Given this and other issues, the ideological and strategic positioning of the dissidents is easy to understand. The reality, however, is that strategically they are spread thin, and the odds are stacked against them. They have managed to unite across very specific issues, though such issues (especially related to the ongoing protest of prisoner treatment) may be of greater or lesser significance in the future depending on the short-term responses from state actors. Any such unity on these specific issues, however, does not extend to a grand strategic plan to wed operational activity to strategic vision. Additionally, they lack crucial support. Edwards[74] describes how support for the dissidents is concentrated in areas that have traditionally seen much support for the Provisional IRA. Edwards' own explanation for this is that "rejectionist feelings in these places run high and it plays on the disillusionment and discontent of republican youths, who are angry at Sinn Féin's sell-out of fundamental republican objectives."

Yet all of this provides only a partial explanation. The reality for the dissident groups is not always that strategic or linear, and there is a sense that they will take who they can get and run with any issues they can identify as possible stepping stones to greater mobilization and recruitment, whether by appealing to otherwise "recreational" rioters or "flippable" members of sister dissident groups or by forging erstwhile alliances with criminals if this serves their short-term or medium-term future resourcing. Yet the broader Republican population remains, at least for now, a prize that is out of their reach.

Tonge's[75] analysis of support for the dissidents illustrates what can only be seen as an historically inevitable uphill struggle:

> … moves towards peace by the provisional IRA meant that any dissident IRA(s) could not enjoy a significant urban support base. A dissident campaign would have to be launched from border areas, reminiscent of the 1956–62 Operation Harvest Border Campaign, hardly an encouraging precedent for the IRA. That campaign petered out amid recrimination and acrimony, with Republicans claiming that the population had been "deliberately distracted from the supreme issue facing the Irish people—the unity and freedom of Ireland."

Support for Operation Harvest was almost nonexistent. Familiar with their ancestral history, thinkers in the dissident camps attempt to overcome this perception by frequent efforts to tap into public sentiment across a variety of "causes," such as corrupt politicians, the inability to rid inner-city communities of drug dealers, the perceived loss of Irish sovereignty as a result of the International Monetary Fund's actions resulting from Ireland's economic crisis, and so on.

Although the VDR groups are willing to work together on individual attacks and operations, there is no shortage of illustrations of distrust, and at times historical resentment, of their VDR rivals. This is best illustrated by looking at CIRA and ONH, both of which distrust the other groups for their own separate reasons. In their *Belfast Telegraph* interview representatives of ONH emphasized their rationale for not joining any of the other VDR groups, which they claimed were ineffective and, more significantly, heavily infiltrated. In contrast, the traditional leaderships of the CIRA and RSF have refused to engage in "Broad Front" Republicanism due to the historical rejection of the abstentionist policy in 1986, and the continued membership of the Provisional movement by the other VDR groups beyond 1986. This stance led to a significant split within both the armed and political wings of the Continuity Republican Movement.

Given the small base rate of people active in overall VDR activity, as well as in the individual groups, not to mention the even smaller numbers involved in operations for attacks, this sustained separation of groups will more than likely prove to be debilitating to their development and support within their communities. The existence of a variety of groups can hamper the security services in assigning responsibility for specific attacks. However, it is possible that the continued fractionalization will ultimately weaken the already substantial threat posed by these groups. On the other hand, a sustained coalition of VDR groups, combining their membership, intelligence, and arms, could heighten the VDR threat, or leave the sole group more prone to infiltration.

Keeping the Republican "flame" alive, as Frampton traces throughout history, is the overarching concern of Irish Republicans. Although we can gain insight into the importance of this from examining what the dissident leadership advocates in its strategic policy documentation, an analysis of publicly stated strategy merely provides a first glimpse into some of its guiding principles. It provides a context to how the leaders ideologically position themselves (both distinct from other dissident groups, united on some levels, and against Sinn Féin) and how they justify the continued use of armed struggle. The next chapter extends these issues with a particular focus on some of the social and psychological aspects of the dissidents' activities.

■ NOTES

1. Channel 9 News. 2003. "RIRA Televised Interview." Derry. Full text:http://own.net/rira3.html. Accessed September 14, 2011.

2. Independent Monitoring Commission. 2011. *Twenty-Sixth and Final Report of the Independent Monitoring Commission: 2004–2011 Changes, Impact and Lessons.* London: The Stationery Office. P. 45.

3. Reinisch, D. 2011. "Leirmheas: A Lack of Understanding of Modern-Day Irish Republicanism." *Saoirse—*Irish Freedom, May. P. 8.

4. Frampton lists dissident objectives as three-fold: "opposition to the peace process and Good Friday Agreement, a desire to prevent 'normalisation' in Northern Ireland [and] a determination to foment instability" (p. 23). Frampton, M. 2010. *The Return of the Militants: Violent Dissident Republicanism.* London: International Centre for the Study of Radicalisation and Political Violence.

5. Copy in author's possession.

6. Morrison, J. F. 2010. *"The Affirmation of Behan?": An Understanding of the Politicisation Process of the Provisional Irish Republican Movement Through an Organisational Analysis of Splits from 1969 to 1997.* Ph.D. dissertation, University of St. Andrews.

7. McAleese, D. 2009. "Continuity IRA Claiming Responsibility for Killing PSNI Officer." *Belfast Telegraph*, 10 March.

8. Ibid.

9. BBC News. 2009. "McGuinness: 'These People Are Traitors.'" 10 March.

10. Also see Frampton (p. 37) for an account by RSF's Geraldine Taylor speaking about Martin McGuinness in similar tones. Frampton, M. 2010. *The Return of the Militants: Violent Dissident Republicanism.* London: International Centre for the Study of Radicalisation and Political Violence.

11. Clarke, L. 2011. "Survey: Most Northern Ireland Catholics Want to Remain in UK." *Belfast Telegraph*, 17 June.

12. Channel 4 News. 2010. "Terrorism: Dissident Republican Paramilitaries Wage Campaign of Violence in Northern Ireland." 22 September.

13. Frampton, M. 2011. *Legion of the Rearguard: Dissident Irish Republicanism.* Dublin: Irish Academic Press. Frampton, 2011, p. 66.

14. Frampton, 2011, p. 68.

15. Copy in author's possession.

16. 32CSC. 1997. "United Nations Submission." http://www.32csm.info/UNsubmission. html. Accessed July 12, 2011.

17. Cowan, R. 2003. "I Have No Regrets." *The Guardian,* 13 March.

18. Ibid.

19. Frampton, 2011, p. 122.

20. Channel 4 News. 2010. "Terrorism: Dissident Republican Paramilitaries Wage Campaign of Violence in Northern Ireland." 22 September.

21. Tonge, J. 2004. "They Haven't Gone Away, You Know. Irish Republican 'Dissidents' and 'Armed Struggle.'" *Terrorism and Political Violence, 16*(3), 671–693

22. Tonge, 2004, p. 676.

23. O'Loan, D. 2010. "Engaging with Dissident Republicanism." *The Pensive Quill,* 31 August. http://thepensivequill.am/2010/08/engaging-with-dissident-republicanism.html. Accessed September 1, 2011.

24. Price, M. 2002. "The Interview." *The Blanket,* Winter 2002, p. 4.

25. Allister, J. 2009. "No Comment Need." 23 November. http://www.jimallister.org/default.asp?blogID=1779. Accessed July 18, 2011.

26. Coogan, T. P. 2002. *The IRA.* New York: Palgrave. Pp. 507–508; also see Frampton, M. 2009. *The Long March: The Political Strategy of Sinn Féin, 1981–2007.* London: Palgrave Macmillan. Pp. 47–48.

27. *An Phoblacht: Republican News.* 2002. "Exclusive IRA Interview: Army Puts Onus on British," 12 September. http://republican-news.org/archive/2002/September12/12irai.html. Accessed July 12, 2011.

28. Breen, S. 2009. "Exclusive: Real IRA 'We will take campaign to Britain.'" *Sunday Tribune,* 12 April.

29. *Irish Republican News.* 2010. "'Real IRA' Claims Killings," 4 October.

30. Feehan, C. 2010. "Real IRA Claim They Murdered Drug Dealer." *Evening Herald,* 28 January. http://www.herald.ie/national-news/real-ira-claim-they-murdered-drug-dealer-2036295.html. Accessed July 18, 2011.

31. Breen, S. 2009. "Northern Editor's Analysis." *Sunday Tribune,* 12 April.

32. Breen, S. 2009. "Exclusive: Real IRA 'We Will Take Campaign to Britain.'" *Sunday Tribune,* 12 April.

33. RIRA Easter Statement 2011. Copy in author's possession.

34. Breen, S. 2009. "Northern Editor's Analysis." *Sunday Tribune,* 12 April.

35. "Bunreachtai Éirígí." Copy in author's possession.

36. Ibid.

37. Imperialism Ireland and Britain, Éirígí.

38. Republican Network for Unity, Bodenstown Address, June 20, 2007.

39. Republican Network for Unity, Easter Statement 2010.

40. Republican Network for Unity, Easter Statement, 2011.

41. Republican Network for Unity, Ard Fheis, 2011.

42. Rowan, B. 2010. "Dissidents: Interview with Terror Splinter Group." *Belfast Telegraph,* November 3, 2010. http://www.belfasttelegraph.co.uk/news/local-national/northern-ireland/dissidents-interview-with-terror-splinter-group-14993952.html. Accessed July 18, 2011.

43. Ibid.

44. Ibid.

45. Tonge, 2004.

46. Frampton, M. 2010. *The Return of the Militants: Violent Dissident Republicanism.* London: International Centre for the Study of Radicalisation and Political Violence. P. 12.

47. Tonge, 2004, p. 678.

48. Frampton, 2011, p. 228.

49. Frampton, 2011, p. 207.

50. Frampton. 2011, p. 210.

51. Frampton, 2011, p. 211.

52. Clarke, L. 2003. "Revealed: New Terrorist Mastermind." *Sunday Times*, 17 August.

53. *Saoirse*, July 2008, p. 1.

54. Frampton, 2011, p. 115.

55. RIRA Televised Interview, February 2003, irelandsown.net/rira3.html. Accessed July 13, 2011.

56. Frampton, 2011, p. 145.

57. *Irish Independent*. 2001. "Republican Prisoners Statement Portlaoise," 20 October.

58. Cusack, J. 2006. "Feud Killings Are Set to Continue as Gangs Ship in More Guns Than IRA." *The Sunday Independent*, 31 December.

59. *Sunday Independent*. 2009. "Dissident Republicans in Bomb Trade with Gangs." *Sunday Independent*, 19 April.

60. *Belfast Telegraph*. 2010. "Fears Grow of Increased Real IRA Drugs War." *The Belfast Telegraph*, 10 February.

61. Cusack, J. 2010. "Real IRA Turns Screw in Gangland Drug War." *Sunday Independent*, 28 November.

62. Cusack, J. 2010. "Dissident Deal Linked to Kildare Arms Haul." *Sunday Independent*, 16 May. Also see Byrne, C. 2011. "RIRA Chief with Prison Record Has Bouncer Job." *The Herald*, 25 January; Lally, C. 2011. "Real IRA Gang Members Granted Security Work Licenses." *The Irish Times*, 11 April.

63. O'Keeffe, C. 2011. "Man and Wife Held in Real IRA Investigation." *The Irish Examiner*, 9 April.

64 Cusack, J. 2011. "Addicts Become Amateur Assassins to Pay Off Debts." *Irish Independent,* 12 June.

65. *Irish Republican News*. 2010. "'Real IRA' Claims Killings," 4 October.

66. Roche, B. 2011. "Real IRA Targeting Several Cork Drug Dealers." *Irish Times*, 21 January.

67. Ibid.

68. Allen, C. 2010. "Name and Shame." *Cork Independent*, 11 November.

69. Real IRA Easter Statement, 2011.

70. Kydd, A., & Walter, B. 2002. "Sabotaging the Peace: The Politics of Extremist Violence." *International Organization, 56*(2), 263–296.

71. Ibid., p. 289.

72. Frampton, 2011, pp. 38–39.

73. Alonso, R. 2001. "The Modernization in Irish Republican Thinking Toward the Utility of Violence." *Studies in Conflict and Terrorism, 24,* 131–144.

74. Edwards, A. 2011. "When Terrorism as Strategy Fails: Dissident Irish Republicans and the Threat to British Security." *Studies in Conflict and Terrorism, 34*(4), 318–336.

75. Tonge, 2004, p. 674.

6 Ourselves Alone

"I just really do wonder about the kind of guys that go off into splinter groups, because I think most of it is predicated upon inadequacy. They can't handle the bigger organization. I think there is something in that mindset that I think does bring a certain kind of a person...a...strange kind of commitment"

— *Former Provisional IRA member, interviewed September 2008.*[1]

"I call it helping out...throw a couple of missiles...just bricks, bottles, just anything you can get a hold of. Just throw them over."

— *Young rioter, interviewed 12 July 2011.*[2]

■ INTRODUCTION

Dissident personnel are diverse and heterogeneous. Some are former Provisional IRA (PIRA) members (some convicted, others not); others were teenagers or young adults during the peace process and are now in their early 30s. Others again, now in their late teens, are not old enough to remember the 1994 ceasefires. As Hugh Orde remarked: "Some of the individuals were about six at the time of the Troubles—they're just about old enough now to grow a beard."[3] The active mobilization and recruitment of young people are key elements in dissident activity, and are likely to become increasingly important to replace personnel that have been lost through arrest. This mix of new and old is consistent with how Gerry Adams characterized the dissidents, as comprising "adventurers, old-style physical forcers [and] bar-stool revolutionaries."[4]

This diversity, as we saw in Chapter 4, is common in militant actors and their supporters. It is because of this diversity that Frampton cautions against the temptation to overestimate the ideological prowess of dissident personnel. Despite having an uncomplicated view of Irish history, Frampton warns that not every member is "fully cognisant of this background. The average, teenage 'raw recruit' into dissident republican circles is as much (if not more) likely to be motivated by more immediate grievances, common to the working and under classes of any modern state: poverty, chronic unemployment, lack of affordable housing, poor social provision."[5] His point is echoed in additional sentiments by Orde: "in my assessment it's something about belonging, these people are on the fringes of society. If you're disenfranchised, with no job, no education, you use glue or drugs—if they were disenfranchised young kids in London they'd be in a gang—if you're marginalised in Peckham for example, you join a gang—here it'll be CIRA."[6] What distinguishes youth in Northern Ireland from marginalized youth elsewhere, Frampton argues, "is the existence of a republican narrative that offers both explanatory framework and solution."[7]

In this chapter we will consider the contextual factors that impinge upon the dissidents in greater depth. We will examine some of the social and behavioral influences on the dissidents, and how contextual issues other than political ones might affect their activity at multiple levels. If the heterogeneity of the dissidents does not provide us with a distinct strategic profile, efforts to arrive at common, clear psychological themes might appear even more elusive. However, there are some important issues we can explore from a social and behavioral science perspective. These range from understanding how and why individuals become attracted to involvement in dissident activity to why, from a psychological perspective, the violent dissident groups do not necessarily need to engage in militant operations as often as their Provisional predecessors.

■ UNDERSTANDING THE DISSIDENTS

In a thought-provoking analysis of combat motivation in nonstate violent groups, Henriksen and Vinci[8] identify three common problems that permeate analyses of nonstate conflicts. First, most analyses tend to "essentialize" fighter motivation. This gives the onlooker the impression that whatever motivates the militant can essentially be explained via singular causes or reasons. Second, they argue, such analyses fail to recognize the polymorphous nature of conflict, in other words, how the dynamic nature of motivation affects the conflicts. An example of this is how a conflict that emerges from a foundation of strong communitarian motivations (e.g., representing an "oppressed" community) might eventually descend into a criminal enterprise. This can then provide new opportunities to attract people motivated by different kinds of factors than those related to the origins of the conflict. Finally, Henriksen and Vinci caution against confounding "agency" and "structure." The danger here, they argue, is in "fallaciously explaining motivation exclusively with reference to the context, or on the other hand explaining the context exclusively with reference to fighter motivation."[9]

Their analysis serves as an important warning to any efforts to "explain" conflict of any kind, and the biases that might ensue. The dissidents' understanding of what motivates their behavior is likely to be very different from that offered by onlookers or commentators. A frequent challenge in explaining behavior is in falling prone to the fundamental attribution error in which, for example, we may attribute our own behavior to external causes yet attribute the behavior of others to internal or dispositional causes. Of course, the factors that help understand and explain behavior change over time (although, paradoxically, our explanations may not, revealing our own biases). People change, allegiances sway, short-term social and contextual factors vary in their relevance and intensity, and the meaning of the conflict itself changes, thereby affecting those both already involved as well as those who are about to become involved for the first time. Attempting to explain the relevant processes with reference to one factor alone (e.g., a "root cause") is doomed to failure, so gaining a broader sense of the contextual factors that impinge upon behavior is crucial.

Long-time IRA expert Robert White[10] emphasizes the characterization of Irish Republican activism as "complex."[11] This he illustrates with reference to the myriad of factors that impinge upon the Republican activist at whatever stage of his or her involvement we wish to examine: "Once involved, an activist faces a successive series of unavoidable threats to activism, including changes in interpersonal relationships, changes in the activist's relationship with the movement organization, and changes in the activist's relationship with the larger political environment."

Making sense of Irish Republican dissidents represents a major challenge in this respect. Certainly, the dissidents are not typified simply by a raft of disillusioned former PIRA members facing an identity crisis, nor can we explain contemporary mobilization as a function of the ready supply of disaffected and bored teenagers. Not unlike the members of Islamist groups referred to in Chapter 4, dissident membership and affiliation are heterogeneous, not just across the Continuity IRA (CIRA), Real IRA (RIRA), Óglaigh ha hÉireann (ONH), Republican Network for Unity (RNU), Éirígí, and others, but even *within* each group. If anything their individual and group profiles are defined by their heterogeneity. White recognized this quality, and its implications on individual identity, in a longitudinal analysis of Irish Republicans throughout the ages:

> We cannot assume that the expectations and interpretations of an activist identity are homogeneous across persons active in different organizations, whether they are active in the same general movement or in movements that oppose each other. And these activist identities are distinct from the collective identity that may develop across activists (and, for example, the collective identity of Irish Republicans is distinct from the collective identity of loyalist paramilitaries).[12]

Understanding the way in which identity needs are met, and how the allure of involvement is sold to prospective members, is important as part of the process of determining why someone might seek to join the ranks of the dissidents, and might also help us to understand why former PIRA members are not just prevalent in the ranks of the dissidents, but continue to trickle over from the ranks of the now-defunct PIRA. White adds: "All Irish Republicans seek a united Ireland independent of Great Britain. But the salience of different dimensions of Irish Republicanism—to emphasize military or political action, revolutionary politics or constitutional politics, the relative importance of the Irish language and Irish culture, etc.—varies among activists."[13] Deciding to ally with one faction over another can be understood, White says, only with reference to "intra-movement interaction patterns among subgroups of activists that facilitated different internalizations of what is important for Irish Republicanism."[14] He notes that "subgroups of interconnected activists developed shared understandings of what is important for the organization and they acted on these beliefs."[15] Understanding the meaning of affiliation with one particular subgroup will help in understanding its unique, context-specific, and localized attractions.

■ REENGAGEMENT AND REENTRY

White's analysis raises critical questions, not just about why someone who leaves a militant group would want to reengage in militant behavior once more (even in the same group, let alone a different one), but also indirectly cautions us to identify the risk factors that might promote recidivism in paramilitary violence in Northern Ireland. Much of the early political commentary about the recent rise of the dissident militants centered on the question of the extent to which the groups were comprised of former paramilitaries with active experience in PIRA. The broad issue of recidivism has been paramount in Northern Ireland ever since the development of the Early Release Scheme that allowed for the release of political prisoners as part of the Good Friday Agreement (GFA). The release of prisoners has played a prominent role in the management and resolution of conflicts internationally. Releasing prisoners, Dwyer[16] notes, constitutes not only a "confidence-building measure, but...a major factor in securing peace." Shirlow et al.[17] also highlight the significant role that political prisoners have played in reducing the extent and nature of the conflict in Northern Ireland and also describe how critical ex-prisoners have been in maintaining that peace in their communities. However, they also highlight some critical issues. The close relationship between prisoner reintegration programs (often run by former paramilitaries themselves) and "groups that can still deliver physical force when required,"[18] they argue, provides the authority (and muscle) to deter the "possibility of...local 'transgressors.'"[19]

In a study of former terrorist prisoners, Dwyer[20] found that the risk of recidivism was reduced if the former prisoner has strong ties with the terrorist groups. In addition, the role of group leadership in ensuring nonviolence by the group proved critical in ensuring a reduced risk of terrorist reoffending. Comparing nonpolitical prisoners with political prisoners, Dwyer found that although the former revealed a 50% recidivism rate, the latter proved a striking contrast[21]: Of 449 prisoners released since 1999, Dwyer found that only 16 ended up back in prison, with their release licenses revoked.

In a similar vein, Shirlow and his colleagues raise concerns about what might happen when the role of ex-prisoners in community politics and restorative justice programs eventually begins to diminish. In particular, they highlight the practices of some paramilitary groups in drawing attention to the plight of those convicted of terrorist offenses who remain in prison. The fate of "political prisoners," Shirlow et al. describe, continues to be an issue that "evokes suffering and symbolizes effectively the ongoing struggle and objection to partition."[22]

Conducting risk assessment of politically or ideologically motivated offenders is an exceptionally challenging task. The kinds of analysis associated with traditional risk assessment, for instance, are rarely "able to take into consideration the political influences and motivation of the prisoner and how this may change."[23] A key factor in risk assessment of offenders in any task that relates to assessing "dangerousness" is in the assumptions about how past behavior predicts future behavior. Yet in the context of political conflict and terrorism, these issues are complicated. Dwyer distinguishes risk assessment under "normal" penal arrangements and those in

TABLE 6.1. *Recidivist Data by Status*

	Convicted pre-VDR	Charged pre-VDR	Total
Convicted (violent)	5	5	10
Convicted (nonviolent)	4	7	11
Charged (violent)	1	1	2
Charged (nonviolent)	5	0	5
Alleged member	4	0	4
Activist	1	1	2
Political	9	6	15
Acquitted/dropped charges	4	0	4
Total	33	20	53

VDR: Violent Dissident Republicanism.

which risk is assessed on "the individual's affiliation to certain paramilitary organizations."[24] This "collective assessment" appears paradoxical. As Dwyer explains, strong ties to the group during times of conflict constituted high-risk, while strong ties to the group in times of postconflict constituted low-risk.[25]

As with all risk assessment, context is key, and understanding the context in which Violent Dissident Republican (VDR) groups exist (including what they attempt to create for themselves) is critical to understanding how and why greater involvement in any militant group post-GFA might seem like a good idea. We may find some answers to these questions by examining the VDR dataset and looking at the pre-VDR levels of paramilitary involvement of all the personnel in it. To do this we collected data on paramilitary convictions and charges during the Troubles for all members of the database, not just those who have been convicted or charged of VDR involvement. The data show that at least 53 members of our database had either been previously convicted or charged of paramilitary activity. Of these nine can be considered as "true" recidivists (i.e., convicted for both VDR activity *and* previous paramilitary activity). A further 12 of the convicted VDR personnel were charged with paramilitary involvement in the Troubles. The reoffenders were mostly former members of the PIRA.

Table 6.1 presents a breakdown of the recidivist data by personnel status. This provides a starting point into considering the influence that former Provisionals have across dissident Republicanism, not just among those charged or convicted. The single biggest representation of pre-VDR convictions is among political dissidents; there are nine political dissidents—eight members of Republican Sinn Féin and one member of the 32 County Sovereignty Movement—who had previously been convicted of PIRA activity before their current affiliation. When pre-VDR convicted *and* charged data are combined the three largest groups are the political, the convicted (violent), and the convicted (nonviolent).

The data presented in Table 6.2 suggest that the three groups with the highest levels of former paramilitaries are the RIRA, the Republican Sinn Féin (RSF), and the CIRA. Due to the interconnected nature of RSF and the CIRA it is feasible to combine both groups to show the overall recidivist population in the Continuity Republican Movement. Similarly, the RIRA and 32 County

TABLE 6.2. *Recidivist Data by Group*

	Convicted pre-VDR	Charged pre-VDR	Total
RIRA	9	10	19
CIRA	6	2	8
RSF	8	6	14
ONH (RIRA)	2	1	3
32CSM	1	0	1
NIFC	1	0	1
RNU	1	0	1
Concerned Republicans	1	0	1
Unknown	4	1	5
Total	33	20	42

RIRA, Real IRA; CIRA, Continuity IRA; RSF, Republican Sinn Féin; ONH, Óglaigh ha hÉireann;32 CSM, 32 County Sovereignty Movement; NIFC, National Irish Freedom Committee; RNU, Republican Network for Unity.

Sovereignty Movement (32CSM) can be combined to show the membership of the Real Republican Movement. When this is done we see that at least 22 known members of the Continuity Movement and a further 20 known members of the Real Republican Movement have transitioned from PIRA involvement into dissident Republicanism. Although it is likely that the true figure for recidivism is larger than this, the data nevertheless show that in spite of the political advances of Sinn Féin and the PIRA, many of their former operationally active members (i.e., not simply supporters) have shown a continued belief in paramilitarism to achieve a 32-county Ireland.

■ THE ALLURE OF INVOLVEMENT

In addition to relying on experienced personnel in terms of both political and/ or operational acumen, the dissidents continue to attract new recruits. How young people come into contact with the dissidents and their "narrative" may be indicative of a broader legacy of the Troubles. In addition are the kinds of accounts that have emerged from socially disadvantaged areas of the Republic of Ireland, and how those areas have seen greater membership of 32CSM and other groups in the Republic.[26] Although we saw this in Chapter 4, the importance of children as a recruitment source for the next generation of Irish Republicans is evident in other respects. In November 1999, an RIRA training camp was discovered in a remote area of rural Ireland, in County Meath. The discovery of the camp provided insight not only into the kinds of training and weaponry in the possession of the RIRA at the time (including an armor-piercing RPG 18-mm rocket launcher, never before seen in the Republic) but also into its tactic of grooming teenagers for recruitment. One of the RIRA trainers picked up five young men (two of whom were aged 14 and 16 years) from outside a McDonalds in Dublin and drove them to the camp after following an elaborate trajectory that involved switching to different vehicles and walking some stages. The 14-year-old boy was "approached two days before his arrest at the training camp and told he would learn about Irish history, be shown guns and be allowed to fire blanks."[27]

Research by Jarman points to the "legitimizing impact of a wider culture of commemoration and celebration." The signs of this, he suggests, are not difficult to find, and include the following:

> [T]he annual cycle of parades that are held to mark the anniversaries of wars, battles, risings and martyrs. There is also a growing popular culture of paramilitarism and resistance which has been elaborated through the media of writing, song, music and the painting of elaborate murals and which is maintained through the numerous informal social clubs in working-class areas.

A challenge so often seen in attempts to find productive roles for ex-prisoners in their communities is that their role can be perceived from two very different perspectives. Former prisoners may well be seen as a critical force for good in their communities, but may also in some circumstances serve as a beacon for mobilization. Ex-paramilitary members are in this respect not unlike Arab Afghans who, in analysis from Hafez,[28] were dispersed following the defeat of al-Qaeda in Iraq, many of whom "went home and were treated as heroes."

Much more explicit and troubling, however, were problems highlighted by media reports in March 2011, when it emerged that a European Union-funded cultural center at Mullaghbawn in County Armagh encouraged children ("some as young as five or six"[29]) to pose for photographs. In the photographs, the children were dressed in paramilitary attire and masks and were brandishing replica weapons.[30] Some of the children were given AK-47 assault rifles and were encouraged to pose while aiming down the sights. Concerned parents first brought this activity to the attention of Families Acting for Innocent Relatives (FAIR), a group representing the relatives of terrorist victims. A local man reported to William Frazer of FAIR that his son "asked his father if he could join Sinn Féin Youth.... They had a heated discussion and, during this, the man discovered the photos on Facebook. He was distraught and was determined to make sure that no other child should face the same pressure."[31] Social Democratic and Labour Party (SDLP) member Dominic Bradley decried the *Ti Chulainn* cultural center as "an elaborate glorification of violence and Provo gunmen involving young children." Owen and Dutta[32] discovered that the children had been posed during an event to unveil a monument to dead PIRA members on the "South Armagh Roll of Honour." These examples resonate in other conflicts, in particular with how children are routinely paraded, often having been dressed as suicide bombers, in shows of strength by various Palestinian militant groups.

Shanahan[33] has explored in great detail the philosophical and psychological basis of Irish Republicans' "blood sacrifice." What is less obvious is how the Republican culture of martyrdom has been sustained since the end of the PIRA's campaign. A clue to this comes from Jarman's research. He explains the significance of marching bands, a regular feature of frequently controversial parades in Northern Ireland. So contentious are these events that a Parades Commission was established in 1988 to oversee them and, in some cases, impose restrictions in an effort to avoid sectarian tensions. Jarman explains that the bands are

…largely comprised of young males, although many are multi-generational…introduced at an early age by fathers or elder relatives. Many of these bands are also closely linked to paramilitary organizations and are prominent actors in the culture of commemoration and celebration of the culture of the gun. In some areas, belonging to the marching band brings with it social status and sex appeal, as well as the introduction to paramilitary life.

In Northern Ireland it is easy to see how historical commemoration and gun culture coexist. In May 2011, new reports were published of paramilitary murals reemerging in Northern Ireland. On the gable wall of a house on the Lower Newtownards Road in East Belfast, a traditional flashpoint for sectarian violence, rests a new mural "depicting UVF paramilitaries holding machine-guns." Those in favor of the mural instead describe it as merely a "tribute to the city's past."[34]

These qualities, each of which contributes to the allure of involvement in some aspects of militant culture, can be understood only in the broader context of the lasting legacy of the Troubles. To understand these realities, we should consider how the region has changed since the onset of the GFA. Jarman[35] draws attention to patterns of violence in Northern Ireland at the time of the peace process and during the period after the GFA. Likening Northern Ireland to South Africa in the post-Apartheid period, he notes that a recurrent problem of "post-conflict societies" is that conflict rarely comes to a complete end. He remarks that the sectarian violence in North and East Belfast (practically an annual event in the "interface" areas) in particular has led to a "general deterioration of community relations."[36] Such tensions are heightened by the continuing residential segregation of working-class areas. Perhaps surprisingly, the process of segregation has actually "continued throughout the transitional period and the tension of the summer months is one factor that has led to an increase in people either being intimidated, or feeling significantly threatened, that they choose to move home."[37] Jarman provides figures from the Northern Ireland housing executive that cite several thousand people requesting rehousing in the years from 1996 to 2002 and beyond.

A visit by British prime minister David Cameron to Northern Ireland in June 2011 drew attention to the stark reminders of this segregation. "Peace walls" are large concrete barriers, some of them 12 meters high, that separate Protestant and Catholic communities. Since the 2006 St. Andrews Agreement, the number of these "peace walls" increased from 37 to 48.[38] Visitors to Northern Ireland, especially those led on organized tours of areas previously associated with the worst atrocities of the Troubles, are stunned to see these symbols of segregation.

The societal challenges described in Jarman's research resonate elsewhere. In late 2010, the London-based conservative think tank, the Center for Social Justice (CSJ), released a long-awaited report on the legacy of the Troubles that presented an even bleaker portrait of postconflict society in Northern Ireland. The report described the following: "High levels of educational underachievement, long-term unemployment, welfare dependency, family breakdown, poverty, deprivation, mental illness, suicide, debt, alcohol dependence, illicit and pharmaceutical drug abuse, and anti-depressant use."[39] In one of many commentaries on the report,

Irish Times journalist David Adams summarizes the "meticulously researched" statistics and the depressing characterization of working-class communities in Northern Ireland in 2010:

- Nearly 50,000 people officially registered "unable to work" because of mental health or behavioral problems.
- Nearly 90,000 people use antidepressants on a monthly basis.
- Nearly 100,000 adults use alcohol every day, with 72% of males and 57% of females (aged 18–29) binge-drinking at least once a week.
- Highest teenage pregnancy rates in Europe.
- 25,000 domestic violence incidents reported in one year alone.
- Male suicide on the rise.

The report estimates that the approximately 14% of children in Northern Ireland who come from "workless households" are "more likely than their counterparts from working households to experience family breakdown, suffer low self-esteem, be socially excluded, do badly at school, become parents during their teenage years, be workless themselves in adulthood, or earn less if they do enter employment."[40]

The report portrays a society that remains profoundly damaged, struggling to break free of its past yet inextricably hampered in its progression by a still-misunderstood legacy of conflict. And yet despite all of these challenges, the CSJ report makes what David Adams describes as "no mention...of what effect the continuing existence of paramilitary groups may be having on public health." He asserts: "[The report] correctly contends that the Troubles cannot forever be blamed for every social problem, but all references to the conflict are decidedly in the past tense. Yet for many working-class communities the Troubles have never quite ended. They remain, in at least one important respect, an inescapable part of their everyday existence."

Nowhere are signs of conflict more evident than during the summer marching season. Some of the worst unrest in recent memory (overshadowed only by the level of trouble in 2010) occurred in 2011. More than 20 police officers were injured as a result of clashes with more than 200 young people. One 14-year-old boy was among those arrested for the violence.

Social tensions can easily be taken out of context to provide an overly simplistic explanation of dissident mobilization. They do not necessarily strengthen the existence of the dissidents but taken together they contribute to a social milieu in which anger, disaffection, and disenfranchisement combine with mythology in a way that can, at local levels, be effectively channeled into dissident activity, and eventually violence. One observer of the 2011 violence in Belfast, a former Irish National Liberation Army (INLA) member, viewed the children as guaranteed "future recruits" for the dissidents.[41]

The dissidents have sustained the intergenerational dynamic, so powerful a weapon for the PIRA's efforts to recruit young people in the past. An example of this is illustrated in arrest patterns. On 2 August 2011, four men were arrested in the Foyle Road area of Londonderry on charges of involvement in dissident

Republican activity. The men were aged 54, 42, 23, and 16 years.[42] Very similar patterns are revealed at arrests at training camps, mentioned earlier.

■ SUSTAINING COMMITMENT

The availability of a small but steady stream of youth has not been lost on the dissidents. In appealing across their communities, anti-GFA Republican dissidents claim to not only serve the community in tackling antisocial behavior, but also to reach out to "parents seeking help for their sons and daughters who may have a drug addiction [and] women suffering from domestic abuse." In several areas, the option of joining 32CSM is sold as a welcome alternative to the dangers of social decay. Reflecting on social problems in the Republic of Ireland that mirror those afflicting Northern Ireland, a 32CSM spokesman from Cork says that in addition to "a good mixture of experienced republicans, former members of Sinn Féin," 32CSM's "new young members" are "people lucky to have not gotten swallowed up by drugs culture which sweeps through our city." 32CSM in Cork and elsewhere fervently denies that involvement with the movement is damaging or dangerous for vulnerable youths, explaining: "All our young members have the support of their families." But the spokesperson added a key issue: "That is made clear to them when they are joining...to make their family aware of because as republicans...we do suffer at the hands of Special Branch harassment."

Suffering "at the hands of Special Branch" might normally be expected to be a deterrent to membership, but for Irish Republicans it is a badge of honor and a core principle used in a long-standing tradition of helping sell the prospect of membership. The allure and subsequent prestige of becoming a committed Republican outsider are reinforced in multiple public and private expressions of commitment to the group. The dissidents are locked in a battle to effectively position themselves between disaffected Nationalist youth and mainstream Republicans who would sooner divert frustration from feeding mobilization to their critics. The dissidents can provide not simply an identity but meaning in the form of noble suffering and righteous anger. Such issues are not necessarily critical for promoting initial involvement, but may be important in helping to sustain commitment to the group. In Northern Ireland, Loyalist leaders have also recognized these issues. There have been significant attempts by former paramilitaries, including Winston Rea and Jackie McDonald, to deglamorize conflict to young people as a means of reducing their vulnerability to involvement.[43]

The dissidents are, in more ways than one, building a community of practice in which being an outsider is not just a tool for recruitment but also a powerful, meaningful affirmation of identity and status. In the words of a 32CSM member: "We have been visible with our position of national sovereignty from day one in 1996 and formally since 1997. There is a difference between being visible and having the mainstream media ignore you." Frampton observes that "contemporary dissident republicanism, though characterised by organizational diversity, exhibits a certain level of ideological homogeny."[44] This homogeny, however, can be both a source of strength and weakness for the dissidents. The potential weakness is in their inability to distinguish themselves ideologically from other disaffected Republicans. Marian Price of 32CSM has delivered several important statements on behalf of 32CSM and the RIRA. In April 2010, she delivered the Easter oration on behalf of 32CSM, and her speech offers insight into how aware the movement is of falling into parodied cliché:

> We extend our hearty congratulations to all those republican activists, from various republican organisations that campaigned long and hard for this outcome. You have shown the way. More of our fellow country people remain incarcerated because the root cause of the conflict has not been addressed in the so-called peace process. Home Rule is not the issue that needs to be resolved. Pearse told us this in 1916. Devolution of limited powers to micro ministers is not the answer either. The 32 County Sovereignty Movement tells us this today. We do well to avoid clichés but the parallels of then and now are as stark as ever.

Price demonstrated something important though not obvious here: the role of cliché (and countercliché) in discussions about the persistence of militant Irish Republicanism. By acknowledging the risk of cliché, she is virtually accepting popular opinion, perhaps even within the wider anti-GFA Republican movement. In a common sense, cliché essentially is "frequently recycled expressions...looked upon as unquestionable truths."[45] The issue of cliché in the Irish Republican psyche is important for both attracting members as well as sustaining commitment. In citing Gramley and Patzold, researchers Ilie and Hellspong note that "clichés fulfill an important social function and can be assigned even a positive role in those areas of human interaction where consciously thought-out language is unusual, if not inappropriate, such as funerals, disasters, the writing of references and testimonials." Ilie and Hellspong add that because clichés make statements about the way things are, they, in doing so, "restrict...the possible ways of looking at a certain issue....Typically, a cliché is not questioned by its adherents. That does not mean that they might not see its problematic nature if it were pointed out to them. But basically they tend to treat the cliché as something that can be taken for granted and that is not a proper subject for a debate."

It may be useful to draw on Ilie and Hellspong's framework to work through an example from the dissidents. Let us first paraphrase a common line of argument from the dissidents: "The Sinn Féin leadership must not be trusted because a united Ireland cannot be delivered through the Good Friday Agreement." This type of argument is based on two critical clichés, which, although not self-evident in a strict sense, are unlikely to be critically examined by supporters. The first cliché functions as what Ilie and Hellspong characterize as the "suppressed major premise"—in this case, that the lack of a united Ireland is unsatisfactory and must be addressed. Naturally, a coherent argument can be made against this view, not least as epitomized through Unionist sentiment as well as recent survey results reported in Chapter 5. It remains a cliché, however, because, in the words of Ilie and Hellspong: "most people who share this view do not feel that it should be interpreted as a controversial view that needs to be defended." As they argue, followers "rest assured that all sensible people will agree...most people who think like this might not even have the impression that they are committed to a specific view but rather that they are just expressing an objective fact of life."

The "suppressed minor premise," in the words of Ilie and Hellspong, is a less obvious cliché in our context here—namely that Sinn Féin (in the eyes of the dissidents) is thwarting efforts to achieve a united Ireland. This is a slightly different kind of cliché with a different kind of function: "Many people who hold this view are definitely aware that it is not a neutral, but a politically loaded truth and that many others may completely disagree." The researchers conclude: "in such a case, two important functions are associated with the cliché: (a) it fulfills an ideological function by defining certain basic views about potentially controversial issues as being most accurate and relevant; (b) it functions as a device for strengthening group cohesion." Ilie and Hellspong make an important point here: "asserting them instead of presupposing them might even draw undue attention to them and consequently involve them in a debate as elements that can be scrutinized and questioned."

For our purposes here, understanding the role and functions of cliché can help us understand a series of characteristics we frequently associate with anti-GFA Republicans. It may well help understand the public emphasis the RIRA places on *not* negotiating, as well as frequent public statements that 32CSM is *not* a political party in the normal sense. Like much of what the dissidents say, this last statement is contradictory—officially, 32CSM members say that they are not a political group, yet alleged leading RIRA dissident John Connolly claimed (in denying his role in the RIRA to a reporter[46]) that he was "a member of the 32 County Sovereignty Movement, which is a legitimate political organisation."

The function of clichés is not just "to brainwash the audience."[47] They have both ideological and social objectives. The ideological function is important for rooting arguments in common ground, in order to guarantee their function as supporters of the general social claims articulated by the group using them. Thus, clichés help maintain a common perspective that is essential for efficient arguments—a point emphasized by Ilie and Hellspong. Nowhere is this more evident than in the national-level policy documents of RSF and 32CSM, which contain all the dissident clichés that have now become obvious. The groups view themselves as the "true" Republicans, acting in part with the knowledge and firm belief that previous "true" Republicans have died in vain for what the Provisional leadership has delivered. The dissidents see themselves as protectors of abandoned communities, pride themselves on their ability to identify what they see as hypocrisy (e.g., being told by the Provisional movement that their struggle is futile and not what people want), and (consistent with what Ilie and Hellspong's research suggests), view their clichés positively.[48] To paraphrase Ilie and Hellspong's framework in the context of the dissidents, faced with the abandonment of Republican principles by the Provisional movement, the dissidents have arrived at "ready-made conclusions," thus "inhibiting critical scrutiny"—in the case of the dissidents, this is particularly so in terms of how they resist any criticism from Sinn Féin.[49]

The counterclichés leveled at the dissidents include the common refrain that they must stop their violence because "they have nothing constructive to offer,"[50] that they "are not republican and offer our community nothing for the future,"[51] that "they're not going to succeed"[52] and are "futile"[53] or "wrong."[54] Such statements by Sinn Féin tend to be consistent, but are rarely described in terms stronger than these. This issue has great significance for the development of a counter-VDR strategy and will be discussed in more detail in the next chapter. The higher potential for truthfulness will likely require a greater and more systematic response to the dissidents from Sinn Féin. After all, Sinn Féin had those same counterclichés leveled against it and the Provisional IRA, and these had almost no negative effect either on the PIRA's belief in its ability to succeed or on the Republican leadership's decision to allow time for the ceasefires of 1994 and 1997 to bring dividends.

■ SUSTAINING ACTIVITY

Regardless of the dissidents' evident abilities to eloquently expose Sinn Féin "hypocrisies," for them to continue to denigrate those who have led the charge in abandoning "real" Republicanism, there can be no question that in the absence of any political engagement, they are likely to make significant efforts to sustain themselves through operational activity. The VDR groups' capacity to conduct successful operations remains key to their ability to attract new membership and to the ability of specific groupings (e.g., the CIRA and the RIRA) to distinguish themselves from other dissident or even "dissenter" initiatives. The following common question arises in analyses of the VDR threat: "How can we predict what they might do next, and what kinds of targets might they 'go' for?" As impossible and inappropriate as it is for open-source research to even attempt to provide answers to these questions, we can at least explore two very specific issues: (1) the possible level of attacks in which the dissidents might engage as a function of the relationship they have with the communities from which they seek to draw support, and (2) a lesson about what the frequency of those attacks *needs* to be in order to maintain relevance.

Certainly, in the absence of routine armed struggle, and despite their claims to not be particularly concerned about the media, the dissident groups struggle to exude a confident image. In a scathing portrayal of the Real IRA, *Belfast Telegraph* reporter Fionola Meredith characterizes dissident activity as a predictable combination of "the sinister" and "the shambolic":

> Take the time that veteran republican Marian Price held up a statement for a rather tubby guy in a balaclava to read out at a dissident republican rally in Derry on Easter Monday...the pages had obviously been folded several times, the sort of thing you would dig out from the bottom of your handbag when you were having a clear-out. Rather than a grand proclamation, it looked more like last week's shopping list. And then there was the question of why Price needed to hold the statement at all, in such an apparently deferential handmaiden move. Presumably, the idea was to confer a bit of pomp and ceremony on the occasion.... The combination of porky paramilitaries and crumpled statements made a mockery of this ostentatious attempt at dignity and ideological grandeur.[55]

It is a very well-established principle of organizational adaptation that all militant groups face the same basic inherent pressures to survive. As Martha Crenshaw has often said, terrorist organizations must not only offer real incentives to join, but have to prioritize "action over talk."[56] How *much* action (as well as what kind of action) takes place, however, is not merely an exercise in self-promotion of particular groups before the security forces. Sustaining activity also serves a critical function in attracting and sustaining adherents. After the 2002 split within the RIRA, dissident activity fell to a low. The dissidents' failure to sustain activity during this time, Frampton argues in detail, led to retreat and fragmentation.[57] The movement had to sustain itself during this time, and this led to significant internal strategic development by 32CSM. However, a clue to the psychology of the RIRA military strategy comes from a 2009 interview with reporter Suzanne Breen. As described in Chapter 5, when the RIRA claimed responsibility for the murder of Denis Donaldson, a member of the group's Army Council explained that RIRA strategy was to "engage in tactical use of armed struggle," adding that "The days of a campaign involving military operations every day or every few days, are over. We're looking for high-profile targets, though we'll obviously take advantage when other targets present themselves."[58]

No nonstate militant group, terrorist or otherwise, can maintain a fixed schedule of attacks. Because of limited resources, attrition, failure to replace lost members, and a host of other issues, a "variable" schedule typically characterizes the delivery of terrorist acts. For our purposes here, it helps to understand why, particularly in the self-imposed absence of community support and popularity, the dissidents require operational activity in the form of visible attacks to sustain themselves. Additionally, however, a variable schedule of attacks (whether strategically deployed or not) is also effective as a psychological tool in maintaining uncertainty on the part of those tasked with responding to the dissidents—in other words, the strategic value for the dissidents of their enemies not knowing when and where they are likely to strike next. This is a very fundamental quality of all terrorist groups. What makes the group *effective*, at least in the tactical and short-term to medium-term strategic sense, is its ability to continue to strike. The issue may not necessarily be "how many attacks are the dissidents capable of?" but rather what frequency is likely and what implications might that "spacing" of operations have on the kind of target chosen? A discussion of these issues is conspicuous by its absence from any kind of threat assessment of the dissidents.

Given this, we would do well to focus less attention on assessing the effectiveness of the dissidents based on the frequency of their attacks and more on the qualities of their targets. It was clear from the early days of the RIRA resurgence that the group placed value on hitting high-prestige targets. On 20 September 2000, only 2 years after the Omagh bomb, the RIRA made international headlines with an RPG attack on MI6 headquarters in London. Frampton describes other, equally audacious plans supposedly hatched by McKevitt, including a possible attack on a British Naval ship "inspired by AQ attack on US *Cole* in Yemen in Sept 2000"; as a result, McKevitt wanted to launch a remote-controlled bomb to counter the "absence of Irish suicide bombers."[59] In the absence of a convincing political plan at the national level, establishing a variable interval schedule of attacks may not be enough to raise any dissident group as a serious contender to the Republican throne, but at the very least, it will ensure that its activity will not simply be relegated to the inevitable postconflict acts of "residual" disaffected groups.

What will be increasingly important for thinking about the future of the dissident groups is the continued relationship they have within Republican communities. Psychiatrist Jerrold Post identified two major types of terrorist groups on the basis of the distinct relationships such groups have with their environments. He argues that each type may exert psychological influences on those members in dissimilar ways.[60] The first of these is the "anarchic-ideologue" group. These tend to be small, "revolution"-oriented, and committed to the overthrow of some current political or social regime, largely for ideological reasons. In the past, left-wing terrorist movements would have typified this type of group. Post argues that the members of such groups frequently suffer "alienation" from their families or immediate communities. The second type of terrorist group is the "nationalist-separatist" group; the PIRA, with its long historical tradition of resistance against British rule, was a typical example. Intergenerational dynamics were common, with family involvement (father, uncles, cousins, etc.) allowing the grooming and recruitment of young people to be presented as a rite of passage. From a psychological point of view, Post suggests that members of these kinds of organizations are not estranged from their families or communities.

The position occupied by the dissidents appears to be somewhere in the middle. They draw their inspiration from history and are buoyed on by what they predicted would be the inevitable compromise and selling-out by Sinn Féin, but at the same time (because of the contemporary context) are consequently alienated from the broader Republican family as well as the communities they ultimately claim to serve. They are more overtly ideological than the Provisionals ever were. Their refusal to entertain the view from outsiders that they need support to thrive is a testament to their self-imposed alienation yet simultaneous embracing of historical ideology as inerrant truth. An outsider might view this position as contributing to an estrangement from and insensitivity to the environment in which the groups operate if it were not for their highly localized efforts that appear supplementary and somewhat removed from national-level objectives. When it comes to targeting, these contradictory dynamics can contribute to an internal decision-making climate in the groups that has led in the past to indiscriminate activity such as the attack on Omagh. But the VDR groups have changed significantly since then. They still claim *not* to need a mandate from the communities in which they operate, yet at the same time have taken significant steps to offer services to those communities in the form of responding to antisocial behavior, bringing law and order to areas they claim the Police Service of Northern Ireland (PSNI) in the North and An Garda Síochána in the South have ignored.

Looking ahead, if the dissidents feel real pressure to signal their continued existence, it is not inconceivable that they may begin attacking their "near enemy" not just through more attacks on Catholic PSNI officers, but in the form of the Sinn Féin leadership. The propaganda they continue to build against Sinn Féin may not be limited to mere opportunistic efforts at gaining press coverage or attempting to sway disaffected former Provisionals into support of some kind. Because of an experienced leadership, the dissidents have the benefit of cherry-picking the best features of a terrorist campaign waged by the Provisionals. Tactical use of the armed struggle has been reborn and rejuvenated for the dissidents. Another atrocity against civilians on the scale of Omagh is improbable as a strategic choice because ideologically, the dissidents are fundamentally unable to justify such an attack.[61] The targeting of police officers is consistent with their ideological statements, whereas the targeting of the Sinn Féin leadership represents a hypothetical step that, although seemingly extreme, might appear logical in hindsight.

■ CONCLUSIONS

Despite intermittent efforts at unification, the promise of a united dissident front remains a fantasy. There are numerous examples of collaboration and coalescence, but these remain short-lived, typically for specific operations that cross geographic boundaries or hold the promise of disruption that may benefit the broader dissident cause. If anything, most of the dissident groups actually pride themselves on their distinctive features. Rowan asks, "when you scratch the surface of all of this, you wonder how much belief and confidence there is in the different wars; what they are really about and what those who are directing them think they can achieve."[62] The dissident groups are often so small that local variations and setting and fluidity are at the heart of any comprehensive effort to understand where they might be going.

Aside from wanting a united Ireland on their own terms, two specific issues consistently unite the disparate dissident groups: their hatred of the Sinn Féin leadership for selling out the Republican dream and, less significantly, the treatment of prisoners from the various dissident groupings. Beyond this, at a strategic level, and despite constant reminders of the possibility of a pan-dissident bridge-building effort by groups such as RNU, they remain deeply at odds with each other. Confronted with the reality of failed operations, lack of popular support, and increasingly successful counterterrorism responses, the VDRs cut a defensive pose. They face an inescapable truth now that they stand divided. They claim not only to not need support but actively shun it, priding themselves on their pariah status. It is that pariah status, however, that they use as part of their efforts to both attract and retain new support. Demonstrating sensitivity to multiple audiences (both internal and external), they have taken efforts to carefully choreograph expectations. Mindful of comparisons between themselves and the Provisional IRA, the violent dissident groups offer regular reminders that they should not be expected to detonate bombs every few days. This conflict, they tell us, is different, requiring different tactics, different strategies, and a different psychology.

Ironically, it may well be this unfailing pride that will ultimately herald the downfall of the dissidents. This is not lost even on distant supporters. "Panther," a poster to the online *Irish Republican Forum* (itself a petri dish of the doubts, splits, divisions, and recriminations that characterize the ever-porous dissident movement), remarked on 9 August 2011: "If we're not unified even in the smallest sense in which groups are capable of carrying out armed action allied together, then the

British government will be able to use these tensions to their advantage to target militants that are striving for liberation."

The dissidents have had multiple opportunities for mobilization and recruitment. They have attempted to exploit Nationalist rioting by inserting themselves between rioters and "mainstream" Republicans. It is too early to tell if the dissidents' successes in recruiting young people reflect real alienation or dissatisfaction in the latter, or whether this provides merely a convenient narrative, both for the dissidents as well as for Sinn Féin's efforts to placate the frustrations inherent in sections of the Nationalist and Republican communities. This deprivation is easy to associate with a perceived failure in the peace process.

Frampton's analysis is based on his exhaustive description of the dissidents' efforts to "keep the flame alive," but despite their own acknowledgment that confusion about the nature of the dissident campaign suits the leadership, this position is better understood as one of defensive posturing in the face of external and internal pressures. Rather than carrying on the flame through intermittent operational successes, the grand dissident campaign is better characterized as convenient (for now) tag-teaming. The dissident groups continue to lack the ability to choreograph their activity in a way that results in a clear systematic assessment of their capabilities, though, as this chapter has shown, we would do well to be cautious in assuming that this assessment should be understood in terms of the frequency of violent attacks.

■ **NOTES**

1. Horgan, J. 2009. *Walking Away from Terrorism: Accounts of Disengagement from Radical and Extremist Movements*. London: Routledge.

2. McDonald, H. 2011. "Militant Republicans 'Blamed for Second Night of Violence in Belfast." *The Guardian*, 13 July.

3. Orde, cited in Gilmore, M. 2009. "No Way Back? Examining the Background and Response to the Rise of Dissident Terrorist Activity in Northern Ireland." *The Journal of the Royal United Services Institute for Defence and Security Studies, 154*(2), 50–55.

4. Edwards, A. 2011. "When Terrorism as Strategy Fails: Dissident Irish Republicans and the Threat to British Security." *Studies in Conflict and Terrorism, 34*(4), 318–336.

5. Frampton, M. 2010. *The Return of the Militants: Violent Dissident Republicanism*. London: International Centre for the Study of Radicalisation and Political Violence.

6. Gilmore, 2009, p. 52.

7. Frampton, 2010, p. 24.

8. Henriksen, R., & Vinci, A. 2008. "Combat Motivation in Non-State Armed Groups." *Terrorism and Political Violence, 20*(1), 87–109.

9. Ibid., pp. 87–88.

10. White, R.W. 2010. "Structural Identity Theory and the Post-Recruitment Activism of Irish Republicans: Persistence, Disengagement, Splits and Dissidents in Social Movement Organizations." *Social Problems, 57*(3), 341–370.

11. Ibid., p. 359.

12. Ibid., p. 342.

13. Ibid., p. 360.

14. Ibid.

15. Ibid, p. 366.

16. Dwyer, C. D. 2007. "Risk, Politics and the 'Scientification' of Political Judgement: Prisoner Release and Conflict Transformation in Northern Ireland." *British Journal of Criminology, 47*, 779–797.

17. Shirlow, P., Tonge, J., McAuley, J., & McGlynn, C. 2010. *Abandoning Historical Conflict? Former Political Prisoners and Reconciliation in Northern Ireland.* Manchester: Manchester University Press.

18. Ibid., p. 159.

19. Ibid.

20. Dwyer, C.D. (2007). "Risk, Politics and the 'Scientification' of Political Judgement: Prisoner Release and Conflict Transformation in Northern Ireland." *British Journal of Criminology, 47*, 779–797.

21. Ibid., pp. 788–795.

22. Shirlow et al., 2010, p. 160.

23. Dwyer, 2007, p. 779.

24. Dwyer, 2007, p. 785.

25. Dwyer, 2007, p. 779.

26. BBC News Northern Ireland. 2010. "Northern Ireland's Grand Plan to Tackle Sectarianism," 28 July.

27. Wilson, J. 2000. "How the Real IRA Recruits Boys into a Life of Terrorism." *The Guardian*, 18 November.

28. Hafez, M. M. 2009. "Jihad after Iraq: Lessons from the Arab Afghans." *Studies in Conflict and Terrorism, 32*, 73–94.

29. *Belfast Newsletter.* 2011. "Probe Launched over Kids in IRA Guns Pose," 23 March.

30. Owen, J., & Dutta, K. 2011. "Children Pose as IRA Terrorists at EU-Funded Center." *The Independent*, 27 March.

31. Ibid.

32. Ibid.

33. Shanahan, T. 2009. *The Provisional Irish Republican Army and the Morality of Terrorism.* Edinburgh: Edinburgh University Press.

34. McAleese, D. 2011. "Loyalist Murals Return to East Belfast, and Few Welcome Them." *Belfast Telegraph*, 11 May.

35. Jarman, N. 2004. "From War to Peace? Changing Patterns of Violence in Northern Ireland, 1990–2003." *Terrorism and Political Violence, 16*(3), 420–438.

36. Jarman, 2004, p. 421.

37. Jarman, 2004, p. 426.

38. BBC News Online. (2011). "Rise in NI's Peace Walls 'Disappointing' says Cameron." *BBC News UK Northern Ireland*, 9 June. http://www.bbc.co.uk/news/uk-northern-ireland-13710969.

39. Adams, D. 2010. "Legacy of Troubles Can't Be Ignored in Northern Crisis." *Irish Times*, 9 September.

40. Ibid.

41. McDonald, H. 2011. "'Militant Republicans' Blamed for Second Night of Violence in Belfast." *The Guardian*, 13 July.

42. BBC News. 2011. "Four Dissident Suspects Arrested and Rifle Found in Derry," 3 August; also McDonald, H. 2011. "Northern Ireland Police Arrest Four Men and Recover Gun in Dissident Enquiry." *The Guardian*, 3 August.

43. Rowan, B. 2011. "How Can We Stop Our Young Rioters Ending Up in Prison?" *Belfast Telegraph*, 30 July.

44. Frampton, 2011, p. 280.

45. Ilie, C., & Hellspong, L. 1999. Arguing from Clichés: Communication and Miscommunication." In F. I. van Eemeren, R. Grootendorst, J. A. Blair, & C. A. Willard (Eds.), *Proceedings of the Fourth International Conference of the International Society for the Study of Argumentation* (pp. 386–391). Amsterdam: International Center for the Study of Argumentation.

46. *Belfast Telegraph*. 2011. "Face to Face with RIRA," 10 July.

47. Ilie, C. 2000. "Cliche-Based Metadiscursive Argumentation in the Houses of Parliament." *International Journal of Applied Linguistics*, 10(1), 65–84.

48. Ibid, p. 69.

49. Also see Ricks, C. 1980. "Clichés." In L. Michaels & C. Ricks (Eds.), *The State of the Language* (pp. 54–63). Berkeley: University of California Press; also see Redfern, W. 1989. *Clichés and Coinages*. Cambridge: Basil Blackwell.

50. Statement by Sinn Féin's Gerry Kelly to AP/RN 6 December 2007 on the targeting of Sinn Fein Councillor Briege Meehan.

51. Sinn Féin's Paul Maskey, speaking about the dissidents at a public event in Belfast 16 April 2009.

52. Sinn Féin's Martin McGuinness speaking to AP/RN on 30 April 2009.

53. Sinn Féin's Raymond McCartney speaking to AP/RN on 30 April 2009.

54. Sinn Féin's Gerry Adams speaking to AP/RN on 12 March 2009.

55. Meredith, F. 2011. "Pompous Paramilitaries Paint a Pathetic Picture." *Belfast Telegraph*, 29 June.

56. Crenshaw, 1985, p. 474.

57. Frampton, 2011, p. 192.

58. Breen, S. 2009 "Exclusive: Real IRA 'We Will Take Campaign to Britain." *Sunday Tribune*, 12 April.

59. Frampton, 2011, p. 120.

60. Post, J. M. 1986. "Group and Organisational Dynamics of Political Terrorism: Implications for Counterterrorist Policy." In P. Wilkinson & A. M. Stewart (Eds.), *Contemporary Research on Terrorism* (pp. 307–317). Aberdeen: Aberdeen University Press.

61. I am grateful to Liam Clarke for discussion on this issue.

62. Rowan, B. 2011. "Dissidents Beginning to Doubt Their Divided Fight." *Belfast Telegraph*, 9 August.

7 A (Short-Term) Counter-VDR Strategy

A popular acronym from U.S. strategic military vocabulary is VUCA: volatility, uncertainty, complexity, and ambiguity, a term often used to reflect particular situations, as well as the behavior of a broad variety of groups and organizations. Easily a term that can apply to the myriad of al-Qaeda affiliates, it is not one we would expect to use in the context of postconflict violence in Northern Ireland. Yet, it epitomizes the broad front of currently active Irish Republicans. Where the Provisional IRA (PIRA) was relatively well understood and identifiable, it remains a daunting task to decipher just who precisely the dissident groups are, and whether they even represent distinct and stable structures. In fact, it remains unclear whether they can truly be characterized as loose groups of affiliates, movements, or actual organizations. In an interview with Rowan,[1] a spokesman from Óglaigh na hÉireann (ONH) remarked that the confusion apparent in "media and security circles" about the origins and identities of these groups suited them "no end."

Despite the best efforts of the analysis presented in Chapter 2, it remains a challenge to accurately characterize the dissidents. Each of the dissident groups was born of a complex, messy, and mostly private history, the true story of which will probably never emerge (at least not publicly). Their respective histories are not linear, and owe much to the public and private activities of key personalities in ways that do not tend to emerge in the history books. In addition to their complete rejection of the term "dissident Republican"—it is Sinn Féin, from their perspective, that is "dissident"—they are currently united by their rejection of the Good Friday Agreement (GFA). However, for most currently active groups, this rejectionist stance neither explains their origins nor their ability to sustain themselves. In terms of the individual make-up of their members, the groups remain heterogeneous both individually and collectively. The overarching strategic positions of the groups may, in time, also prove to be more flexible than would otherwise be suggested by a reading of their stated objectives from Chapter 5. Today's potential bridge-builders [e.g., Éirígí, Republican Network for Unity (RNU)] may become tomorrow's spoilers and vice versa. And if the Violent Dissident Republican (VDR) groups do not deliver for their respective followers, the nonviolent dissenters may offer, in time, not just an effective voice for Republican dissident, but might become a potential unifying political platform, at least in some respects.

Though this chapter is concerned with responses to the dissidents, it is not the stance of "dissent" that is problematic; it is the continuing use of violence as a vehicle for expressing that dissent and the ensuing disruption of society and security that warrants an exploration of how to respond to VDR groups. Given this state of both complexity and confusion, if anything, a collective term such as "dissidents" (or rejectionists, or whatever single term we use) is barely appropriate to describe that intricacy or dynamism, and this has implications for avoiding a "one size fits all" strategy to counter any or all of the threats they pose. The membership of the violent groups is fluid, again, both between and within groups, and the extent to which they are able to engage in successful activity is most certainly a function of an increasingly assertive response from the security forces. What remains absent, however, is a clear political strategy that may help limit if not redirect the current tactical and strategic defining features of VDR groups.

Given all of this, it might appear premature to suggest strategies for responding to the dissidents (let alone to allow interpretations or explanations to be derived purely from an open-source analysis such as this). The complexity of that prospect mirrors the evolving character of the groups themselves, and as a result the task ahead borders on overwhelming. Let us begin then by asserting that this complexity should not deter us from identifying critical areas for further development. The threat of violence posed by the VDRs is very real, however intermittent the frequency of security threats may be, and those tasked with responding are not afforded the luxury of forever contemplating the nature of these groups or the reluctance of militant Irish Republicanism to fade away. As the hundredth anniversary of the 1916 rising draws nearer and the dissidents realize that despite the enthusiasm with which they reject attempts to describe themselves as "going nowhere," they will have to contemplate the urgency to remain relevant and functioning. Though they themselves would probably balk at the comparison, the dissidents share at least one similarity with religious groups, in particular millennial movements. Faced with what from their perspective is the reality that the forces of evil are conspiring to complete their mission (in their case, Sinn Féin and the continuing normalization of Northern Irish structures and society), there is an urgency to act and act now. The dissident groupings may be patient (whether of their choosing or not), but if they are unable to exert significant influence, individually or collectively, in the lead-up to 2016, it is possible that they may lose their one undeniable focal point for mobilization and recruitment in the face of increasing irrelevance. It is not unlikely that as 2016 approaches, the limitations and (from the dissidents' perspective) failures of the GFA will become more apparent and focused for them. They have time on their side, for now at least, and their ability to focus in the immediate years ahead is helped in no small part by what appears to be an economy in terminal decline (both North and South).

This chapter will consider several issues. It will examine how the police and security services in Northern Ireland and the Republic of Ireland have responded to the dissidents, what role there may be for Sinn Féin and for victims of ongoing terrorism in Northern Ireland, and will identify additional critical areas for future consideration as the dissident threat evolves. Finally, drawing on the data from the International Center for the Study of Terrorism (ICST) VDR project, this chapter will make a number of suggestions to help inform a strategy to counter the continuing violence of the dissidents and encourage them to reject violence and enter the political process.

A Short-Term Strategy

Let us begin by stressing basic principles. A successful counter-VDR (CVDR) strategy must be multilayered, making explicit factors that can help deescalate the immediate threat as well as preventing, or at least containing, the growth of violent dissident groups in the medium to long term. Such a strategy needs to address both local and national issues, and thus contain elements specifically targeted to both. Given the nature, variety, and scope of dissident activity, both violent and nonviolent, it is apparent that efforts to counter the dissident threat of violence cannot be the sole responsibility of any one agency. This makes it even more urgent that each has clear roles and responsibilities in tackling the growth of the groups in this direction. The cross-border nature of the threat emphasizes the necessity for the Gardaí and the Police Service of Northern Ireland (PSNI), as well as the intelligence services and politicians on both sides of the border, to work together closely.

The ultimate fate of the dissidents' violent campaign rests in part on the activities of those tasked with curtailing the threat posed by them. This includes not just the security services but also Sinn Féin and the wider Republican community. The existence of the dissidents is inextricably linked to the unfurling actions of Sinn Féin as well as the success or failure of the security forces. The double-bind position of Sinn Féin will be discussed below, but it is clear that it will have to face major responsibilities in playing its role to curb the growth of the dissidents' violence while at the same time doing so in such a way as to not reinforce the dissidents' agenda and any propaganda value they exploit from engagement by Sinn Féin in this role.

The very nature and history of dissident Irish Republicanism, and Irish Republicanism in general, have created an inherent distrust of the British intelligence services and the police. This distrust is manipulated by the dissidents to justify and gain support for their existence. In one sense, this is apparent in their continued dedication to vigilantism. In carrying out attacks on suspected criminals, particularly drug dealers, the VDR groups portray themselves as doing the job they say the PSNI cannot, and should not be allowed to, do. They want to show the Republican communities that they are the real guardians of those communities, not the PSNI. The deep-rooted nature of this distrust places great importance on the potential role of those who *do* have the trust of the communities.

It is probably within the ability of the security forces to neutralize (or at least contain) the bulk of the violent threat posed by the dissidents. But although violent activities can always be curbed in the short term, through arrests, crackdowns, and other measures, it is unclear if anything less than a united Ireland will ultimately satisfy those Republicans willing, in Martyn Frampton's words, "to keep the flame alive." The dissidents see violence as the inevitable response they need to make to signal their existence and their dissatisfaction with the very foundations of the GFA. Realistically, it is unlikely that they expect an overreaction from the state given the history of the consequences of doing so during the Provisional campaign, but the dissidents certainly do know how to slowly and steadily foster support. Their steadfast hostility to the compromise peace initiatives, which they see as contradictory to their strongly held and highly ideological positions, might indicate that a successful CVDR strategy should not necessarily aim to bring these dissidents into that same process.

The central aim of any strategy must be to reduce the dissidents' reliance on violence by redirecting their opposition into nonviolent protest. If this critical objective can be realistically met it is then possible to think about any possibility of at least partially aligning them with the democratic political process (in whatever shape that might take). The idea of engagement with the dissidents arises regularly, and in doing so spawns widely different positions. Despite the clichéd rejectionist stance shared by VDR groups, it is likely that there are secret negotiations of one kind or another going on between the highest levels of those same VDR groups and government representatives. Even if this is so, it should not detract from an exploration of how to undermine the legitimacy and attractiveness of the dissidents while they continue to engage in violence.

As stated throughout, there is nothing wrong with dissent. In fact, dissent is a healthy sign of democratic functioning in Northern Ireland. For Republicans, whose dissent in the past was stifled through a bullet or at the very least the promise of ignominy, such is the progress that dissenting nonviolent Republicans are able to engage in debate at all levels of the political process. Yet this has not been equal for all "dissenters," and the GFA rejectionists are well aware of the actions taken by the PIRA to stifle discord. The overriding concern is with the dissidents' continued adherence to violent means, and it is this defining feature that shapes a CVDR strategy to follow.

When the Provisional movement was gradually drawn into talks leading up to the peace process, the initial consultations that facilitated this process were with people from the Provisionals' own communities. In the aftermath of the dissident violence there have been a number of approaches to enter into talks made to the dissidents by people within the Nationalist communities, mainly Catholic priests and members of Sinn Féin. Given the diminished respect for the Catholic Church in Ireland, the latter has likely no role to play in this either now or in the future (at least not in terms of exerting moral authority). Effective interlocutors are not likely to come from the ranks of Sinn Féin, either; offers by Sinn Féin were rejected out of hand by Republican Sinn Féin, 32 County Sovereignty Movement (32CSM), and others. Republican Sinn Féin (RSF) president Des Dalton said in response to one such offer that Sinn Féin was "absorbed into the apparatus of British rule and we feel we have absolutely nothing to say to them on that basis."[2] Faced with this reaction, Sinn Féin has not wasted time pursuing other avenues, as we shall see below.

In addition, there is little point in engaging in speculation about the implications of microideological similarities and differences of the various dissident groupings. The core principle in shaping a short-term CVDR strategy must be to promote the capacity for a reduction in violence. This will include, but not be limited to,

1. undermining the legitimacy and credibility of those who engage in or ally themselves with violence
2. reducing the attractiveness of involvement in VDR groups to those vulnerable to mobilization, and related to this
3. building resilience to that vulnerability by addressing core social and economic issues that provide a mobilization context (mostly at a local level) for VDR groups
4. stripping the VDR groups of their ideological soundness by highlighting their continued, extensive involvement in criminality
5. illustrating and explaining the significance of the dissidents' efforts to generate support for alternative justice systems within Republican communities
6. continued effective and consistent police and intelligence operations to secure convictions of key violent personnel
7. not ignoring the potential for actionable response on social, political, or other critical issues that serve to unite the dissidents (e.g., treatment of prisoners)
8. developing a meaningful political strategy to engage the dissidents

What follows is an exploration of areas that might inform a short-term CVDR strategy. This is described by delineating potential roles for particular groups and communities. Although these are introduced and described separately, none of them alone ought to be considered the sole component in a CVDR "toolbox." As with any proposals for a strategy, these need to be concrete and practical while at the same time sensible enough to allow them to take root as accepted "principles" (the execution and delivery of which may take different forms, and be evaluated in different ways). What is thus presented here are some general aspirational themes, which hopefully avoid, as the dissidents themselves say, the risk of cliché, as well as some practical suggestions for action. What is being proposed is relevant to the present environment. However, with minor alterations it can be made relevant to the inevitable changes in the situation.

∎ POLICE, SECURITY, AND PRISON SERVICES

At the forefront of any effective counterterrorism initiative is the response by the security forces. The relationship between the PSNI and An Garda Síochána (Gardaí) is key to reducing the capacity for violence. As well as operational assistance this likely includes cross-border intelligence sharing. Although the data indicate that the majority of VDR attacks have occurred in Northern Ireland, the perpetrators are predominantly from the Republic. This suggests that a significant amount of the planning of attacks is taking place in the South. David Ford, the Northern Ireland justice minister, stated in February 2011 that "the work of the Gardaí is absolutely vital....all the information that I get is of the highest level of co-operation in terms of intelligence. It certainly seems to me that ...the security forces are bearing down on the dissidents."[3]

However, in that same interview Ford identified obstacles to cooperation and potential further steps to improve cooperation, both across the border and within individual districts in Northern Ireland: "I think even a few years ago if you wanted to communicate from Enniskillen's police station to Cavan Garda station [approximately 30 miles apart] you virtually had to be routed through Belfast and Dublin. Now officers can call straight from Enniskillen to Cavan station." In the absence of a serious crisis that invariably tends to focus interagency efforts, the inability to deal with such basic issues seems incredible.

The most obvious way to undermine the capacity for violence is through arrest and incarceration of known militant members of VDR groups. This is the quickest way to significantly weaken the operational capabilities of the groups, and may at times, but not always, deliver the parallel effect of deterrence. But this is easier said than done. Issues of arrest and incarceration must be considered carefully, as failure on issues relevant to this front may likely strengthen support for the groups. A prevailing attitude within disillusioned Republican communities is that suspected members of dissident groups are unfairly victimized and imprisoned for long periods without trial. This is portrayed by some as "internment without trial," a return to the controversial and explosively alienating strategy adopted at the birth of the Troubles. Unfortunately, the analogy is not entirely without substance, for two reasons.

First, there is a considerable length of time between arrest and trial for a large number of dissidents. This may well provide an impetus for the VDR groups to continue their search for support within those affected Republican communities. A vacuum of silence provides the dissidents with the opportunity to paint a picture of themselves as the victims of "human rights abuses." Therefore it is essential, especially in the high-profile cases, that there are clear and accessible explanations as to why such cases take so long to get to court. In their absence, conspiracy theories reinforcing historical stereotypes of the state security and judiciary continue to gain momentum.

Second, and more obvious, is the disparity between the numbers of those arrested and charged with VDR offenses compared to those successfully convicted. Table 7.1, a recreation of a PSNI table, shows the gap between the number

TABLE 7.1. *Number of Persons Arrested under Section 41 of the Terrorism Act and Subsequently Charged (February 19, 2001–July 31, 2011)*[4]

	Persons Arrested	Persons Charged
2001 (from 19 February)	180	51
2002	236	80
2003	359	121
2004	230	69
2005	249	73
2006	214	61
2007	145	44
2008	150	28
2009	163	40
2010	205	48
2011 (up to 31 July)	92	19
Total	**2223**	**634**

of people arrested under Section 41 of the Terrorism Act and those subsequently charged (let alone convicted). This disparity, we should note, is not just particular to Northern Ireland, but there are special ramifications in the context of what it might mean for how support for VDR groups is generated.

These statistics encompass those arrested and/or charged under Section 41, not all of whom are suspected VDR personnel. PSNI statistics (rather than ICST VDR data) are used here because ICST's open-source data focus only on personnel who are named in two or more media sources, and reports of arrests or charges often do not name the individuals in question. In light of this fact, and the resultant possibility of duplication of data, the project concentrated only on publicly named personnel. Although Table 7.1 comprises all people arrested and charged under Section 41, the fact that the VDR groups were the most active terrorist groups throughout this period would suggest that suspected VDR personnel should in turn make up the majority of those included in it. This is particularly true within the third wave of activity (between 2007 and the present day), in which there has been no reported illegal activity by the PIRA, sustained ceasefires by the majority of the Loyalist paramilitaries, and a decrease in activity by the Irish National Liberation Army (INLA).

Within Wave 3 the percentage of those charged compared with those arrested is a mere 23.7%, or less than one in four. What these data do not reveal, but the VDR project does, is the subsequent number of people who either have their charges dropped or are acquitted. To date (and excluding the significant numbers of those arrested in 2010 and 2011) the VDR project data have recorded a total of 54 suspected VDR personnel who have either had their charges dropped or have been acquitted. This represents a further 8.52% of all those charged according to the PSNI statistics. When the non-VDR groups are factored out this percentage will be higher.

Several complex factors may contribute to this seeming inability to successfully convict people charged with violent dissident activity. Some may relate to the nature of the evidence used to secure a conviction, whereas others may relate to the circumstances in which that evidence was collected and how that may negatively impact the possibility of a successful prosecution. Other far less obvious reasons may relate to the intricacies of ongoing counterterrorism operations. In any event, however, and despite an arrest–conviction gap typical outside of Northern Ireland, it is clear that a failure to narrow the gap between arrests and convictions may reinforce the dissident view of the security forces as conspiring to stifle legitimate dissent by falsely imprisoning those who (from the dissidents' point of view) are not doing anything illegal.

Related to this is the perception of prisoner treatment and what is viewed by the dissidents as the severe inadequacy of the prison service on the whole. A major sustaining factor for the dissidents has been the inability of the prison service to quickly and sufficiently defuse and contain the intermittent protests within Maghaberry prison. These have a major potential to gain further momentum and support within the dissident Republican communities. In fact, the failure to redress these problems may serve as a unifying force between otherwise fractious VDR groups. Though the significance of the prisoners probably fluctuates, there are sufficient historical examples to suggest the potential catalyst that prisoner rights issues can be in Northern Ireland. Although it is unlikely that any of these protests will gain the levels of support their predecessors achieved in the 1970s and 1980s, the longer they continue the more potential they have of increasing sympathy for the dissident movement and, in turn, reinforcing a narrative that contributes to mobilization and eventual recruitment. If these problems cannot be resolved, it is especially important to explain why not in the public eye. As with the latency between arrest and trial, silence provides opportunities for the dissidents to portray themselves, and their prisoners, as victims of human rights abuses. Any opportunity they are given to take the moral high ground provides them with a chance to deflect attention from their own activities and take comfort in victimization.

The power of leadership arrests was displayed in the aftermath of the Omagh bombing. The RIRA was unable to ride out the outrage that followed the bombing and suffered a major blow when Liam Campbell was arrested in 2000 on charges of membership in an illegal organization. McKevitt's dream of a resurgent campaign was instantly dashed. A series of additional arrests proved devastating until the RIRA reached its all-time low in 2002. As Frampton[5] explains: "[It] could take small pride in its accomplishments. There was little on its balance sheet to counteract the accusation that it was merely a pale imitation of the Provisional IRA, unable to pose a serious threat to the British state." By the end of 2002, Frampton[6] believes that a second phase of dissident Republican militancy "appeared to have drawn to a close." The Real IRA that was "still in existence was now a shadow of itself: to its critics, a pale imitation of a pale imitation." In comparison, the second wave of activity identified here goes from the aftermath of the Omagh bombing in 1998 to Sinn Féin's support for the PSNI in 2007. However, as the data depicted in Chapter 3 show, similar to Frampton, we observed a significant drop in activity levels, from the height of 56 violent events in 2001 to just 22 in 2007. From that year until the end of the wave the levels of annual activity were sporadic and never again reached the heights of 2001. This is best illustrated by analyzing the bombing data.

Chapter 3 showed that from 2001 until the end of Wave 2 in 2007 there was a significant drop in the number of VDR bombs that were successfully detonated. The most significant factor from 2003 until the end of the wave was that the numbers of bombs defused consistently exceeded those successfully detonated. Up until that point in the wave, detonated bombs exceeded those defused every year (apart from 1999, when no attempted bombings were recorded). One possible explanation for this could be the targeting of the *right* individuals for arrest, i.e., those who had the most influence on the group's survival and ability to sustain armed action. Targeting the right personnel—or perhaps, more appropriately, the right roles and functions—includes the targeting of those with very specialized skill sets essential to armed action.

Role-specific intelligence gathering and targeting are common in counterterrorism investigations. In the context of the VDRs, an obvious example is the case of bombmakers. Although there is danger involved, it does not take great skill to either plant or transport a bomb. Members able and willing to do so (when they actually have a choice in the matter), although still considered a loss if arrested, tend to be dispensable. Those with the ability to consistently produce sophisticated bombs are a different matter. As we saw upon the arrest and conviction of the Patterson twins in 2001, described in Chapter 4, a single bombmaking team may end up developing and supplying improvised explosive devices (IEDs) for a wide range of operations by the group. The police stated in the aftermath of Pattersons' convictions that the twins had developed a sophisticated bombmaking factory in Louth that was believed to have supplied bombs for campaigns in both Northern Ireland and Great Britain. In the years after the arrest and conviction of the Pattersons, the bombing data suggest that there was a significant decline in the number of successful VDR bombings for Wave 2. The inability to successfully carry out bombings, in addition to the obvious improvements in public safety, can also have a negative impact on the support levels and membership confidence in the groups. A drop in confidence can and does lead to people leaving the group and/or switching allegiance.

Another interesting statistic deserves exploration. The ICST VDR data suggest that 7% of those convicted of VDR offenses were given suspended sentences. This is generally the case for young members with no prior involvement who are convicted of low-level VDR activity and/or "membership" in an illegal organization, but who show remorse for their actions. Given the troubled history of the "Supergrass" trials in Northern Ireland, there is an uncomfortable contemporary resonance with young members expressing regret and remorse for their actions. Although not always popular, offering suspended sentences for public expressions of remorse represents a creative opportunity recognized by the courts. These young males are given the chance to disengage from their respective VDR groups or face an inevitable alternative: entering prison and sharing a floor with other convicted Republicans. Though decisions to suspend sentences may be made for reasons other than those described here, considering this a possible preventive element of CVDR strategy contributes a valuable opportunity to disrupt potential terrorist careers at their outset. To be effective in the long term, however, and learning the lessons from other countries, particularly where terrorist "deradicalization" programs are practiced (also often encompassing young people on the cusp of serious involvement but appearing before the courts for a more minor offense), significant sanctions would be expected for breaching the conditions of the suspension.

This has not necessarily been the case so far. A 14-year-old boy arrested at an RIRA training camp discovered in 1999 (described in the previous chapter) was described by officers as "emotionally overcome" when he was removed, crying and shaking, from the training bunker. At his sentencing, at age 16, the court delivered a 3-year suspended sentence, but detectives who gave evidence in the case said that the "youth still had very strong leanings towards extremist Republican organisations and had been seen in the company of leading dissidents since his arrest."[7] Another young man arrested at the same time, and 18 years old at the time of sentencing, was given a 7-year suspended sentence. The judge ruled that despite the seriousness of the charge, the court "had taken into account the fact that he had no previous convictions and came from a good family."[8]

Given that it is Republican communities that are most negatively affected by dissident violence, these communities also provide opportunities for the police, as well as peaceful Republicans, to draw support and possibly membership away from the violent groups. There is an argument to be made here to move beyond the "either/or" nature of prison or suspended sentence and include community service as an additional option at the point of sentencing. This should not just be an alternative to the existing sentencing options but could be considered as an add-on to these punishments for young offenders. A well-structured, rigorously supervised community service program can emphasize to these young recruits the negative effects VDR groups have on their communities. This may also include an educational element from influential individuals within the community promoting peaceful Republicanism, i.e., one that emphasizes the negativity of violence. Though these recommendations are general in nature, and certainly more aspirational in the context in which they are presented here, on one level they are not unlike some of the community intervention programs developed as part of the PREVENT strategy in the United Kingdom. At the very least they deserve further consideration.

Though arrests and secure convictions provide the obvious important step of containing the dissidents, there are important lessons for effective communication strategies. Ironically, prison sentences provide members, young and old, with an opportunity to publicly display (and receive recognition for) the "sacrifice" they have made in seeking a united Ireland. Although being arrested and convicted obviously means that they have been caught, it somewhat counterintuitively raises their stature within the movement. For an overall CVDR strategy to have any degree of long-term success it must go beyond arrests and convictions and must also involve a positive alternative to illegal violent dissident activity.

The scale of the difficulties facing the PSNI in combating the dissidents is not to be underestimated. Within the present wave of attacks they are the number one target of politically motivated dissident violence, followed closely, until recently, by prison officers. This is particularly true for the Catholic members of the force as was illustrated by the murder of Ronan Kerr in 2011 and the near fatal attack on Peadar Heffron in 2010 (not to mention the multiple other attacks and attempted murders of PSNI officers). There is widespread agreement in the ranks of the PSNI that a sign of the dissidents' weakness is that more PSNI officers have not been killed.

A positive result of the peace process has been the dramatic deescalation of the British army presence in Northern Ireland. The withdrawal of the army and the overall effects of the peace process have brought in much-needed reforms in policing structures and operations. However, this reformation has brought with it considerable challenges for the police's attempts to counter the dissidents. Frampton has identified some complications for the police. Prominent among these is a "skills gap," which Frampton argues is the result of both the peace process and the "dismantling of the [RUC's] counter-terrorist infrastructure."[9]

The economic downturn has seen cuts in spending across the board both north and south of the border. However, due to the growing dissident threat it was announced in February 2011 that the PSNI would be provided with £245 million in extra funding to help implement a 4-year plan. PSNI Chief Constable Matt Baggott explained that "after years of change and difficulty, we now have the ability to plan into the long term and sustain all that is good. The money will be spent on investigation, on more detectives, on more equipment, transport, air-support, [and] in sustaining our street presence in neighborhoods."[10] However, even with this funding in place Terry Spence, the chairman of the Northern Ireland Police Federation, described the perceived necessity to add more police to the force. He stated that the PSNI "are languishing at around 7,000 front-line full-time officers and the threat level now is worse than it was in 1998 [when] we had 13,000 officers."[11]

Amid politicized and acrimonious discussions about budgets, a successful counterviolence strategy needs to not only address the dissident threat directly, but also tackle wider issues. There have been not unreasonable fears that a heightened campaign by the dissidents might serve to reengage the Loyalists paramilitaries. The Independent Monitoring Commission (IMC) has routinely warned of the difficulties the Loyalist groups have had in successfully disengaging from terrorism. In part this is due to a failure to "articulate clearly how they want to move forward or to recognize, as one day they must, that as paramilitary groups they have neither role nor legitimacy ... the PIRA, however slowly, transformed itself under firm leadership and has gone out of business as a paramilitary group while loyalist groups, lacking comparable direction, have struggled to adapt."[12] Recent riots in East Belfast have shown the potential reemergence of violent sectarianism. Unless addressed, these developments provide opportunities for the dissidents to carve out an important role for themselves, not just as defenders of law and order against drug dealers and joyriders but an implicit role of "defenders." Giving the lingering legacy of sectarian divisions across Northern Ireland, visible mostly in urban areas, the ramifications of this could be substantial during particular periods.

The perception that VDR groups provide policing and protection must certainly be forcibly countered. There must be a concerted and visible effort by police forces and community agencies North and South to tackle the drug problems that affect a variety of urban areas. This is certainly already taking place across Ireland. To many, the drug problem may seem an issue very separate from VDR activity. However, by tackling it the police indirectly weaken the legitimization of a VDR group's existence at a local level, at least in terms of this specific role they claim to fulfill. Parallel to this must be a direct challenge from peaceful "dissenting" Republicans about the sincerity of the dissidents' vigilantism. They need to be challenged on why they are targeting specific individuals and what is the true purpose of these attacks. Sporadic increases in visible patrolling in the wake of individual attacks on police officers are welcome, but will not do enough to quell the dissidents' march to harness greater control and legitimacy within Nationalist and Republican areas. Amid all of this, it is increasingly evident that the logic of the dissidents' pursuit of this activity is not without historical precedent. They are, after all, following in the footsteps of the Provisionals and recognizing that there is, on some levels, a real appetite for this kind of informal justice in these same communities.

■ **THE REPUBLICAN COMMUNITY**

Although the clear face of nonviolent Republicanism is now Sinn Féin, one of the most defining characteristics of the VDR groups is their disdain for the continuing politicization of that movement. They believe that the Sinn Féin leadership has abandoned and betrayed Irish Republicanism. For many of the members of VDR groups, especially those older, more experienced members, there is no way in which Sinn Féin can possibly be seen as a viable alternative to VDR membership. A more likely alternative for channeling disaffected Republicans into exclusively nonviolent dissident Republicanism may well be by exploring ways to strengthen the position and capacities of those referred to as "the dissenters." Though this is not without its own challenges, the promotion of nonviolent dissidence in very specific ways deserves closer consideration.

Disengagement from terrorist activity is often, though not always, a gradual process. Although people may no longer subscribe to the tactical and strategic use of violence to achieve their aims, this does not mean that they no longer believe in the cause they were fighting for. Therefore, if there is a viable alternative in place, one that continues to provide them with opportunities to address their perceived injustices, then this provides both a possible step away from violent activity or, for others, a possible step toward affiliation that is non-VDR-related. The ambiguity around the use of violence that is often associated with those same avowed "nonviolent" dissidents is also an important consideration. But if a focus here is on identifying paths to a deescalation of violent activity, we should consider what can be offered to dissidents by dissenters such as Éirígí or an affiliation with active independent dissenters such as Anthony McIntyre or Richard O'Rawe. This, again, might seem easier said than done. It is unclear how the governments and institutions of the states involved could actively promote involvement in these groups as an alternative to violence, and therefore this requires more exploration.

However, one practical first step here is for state institutions to help make a clearer distinction between "dissidents" and "dissenters"—between those willing to work within the state functions and those who reject them outright. Being "dissident" to Sinn Féin can truly be acknowledged as the "badge of honor" that dissenters suggest it is without embracing militant activity. If local and national government bodies actively show that they hold nothing fundamentally against dissent per se, that their opposition is focused on *violent* dissident Republicanism, then they will not only promote active alternatives for disaffected Republicans, but also reduce opportunities for the VDR groups to continue to promote themselves as "victims." This suggestion is consistent with the acknowledgment from Chapter 4 that not everyone involved in VDR groups necessarily has any real sense of ideological or strategic acumen. The idea of non-Sinn Féin Republican "alternatives" may represent an anathema for older and politically minded members of VDR groups, but not for young recruits (or those on the fringes).[13]

Extending this argument further, there must be visible and active support from both governments and positive nonpolitical role models and influential individuals from within the dissidents' own communities. This kind of support was apparent in the last Irish government, notably with Michael Martin as minister for foreign affairs. When Martin declared that dissident "is a completely inappropriate term"[14] he was visiting Lurgan's Kilwilkie estate. He was there to demonstrate the government's support for the young people of the area who had "resisted the lure of the dissidents." His visit was specifically connected to a project that saw 14 young people from the area work with a professional film crew to make a film portraying the struggles young people have with alcohol, drugs, and "dissident activity." This project, run by the cross-border body Cooperation Ireland, is one of many examples of how the young people of the worst-affected areas can be provided with alternatives to violence to express their frustrations and grievances.

As highlighted by Currie and Taylor's volume on the dissident Republican movement,[15] in a time when the current economic downturn and cuts in public spending may "add to the potential for recruitment both of new and experienced members, and may also widen facilitatory community support," these issues are of critical importance. Going hand in hand with these alternatives is an emphasis for the young Republicans on the negative impact illegal Republican activity will have on the rest of their lives. The deterrent effect of understanding that membership or activity in an illegal organization such as the Continuity IRA (CIRA) or the RIRA will severely restrict opportunities for travel—and especially work in countries such as the United States—should not be underestimated. In any event, alternatives and deterrents such as these must not only be in place within the Republican communities from which young people are currently being groomed for recruitment, but must be in place in those communities with the growing potential for recruitment.

A CVDR strategy must involve nonpolitical groupings such as various sporting, business, and religious organizations. The role such groups can and should play is illustrated clearly when we consider the Gaelic Athletic Association (GAA). When Peadar Heffron, a Gaelic football-playing Catholic PSNI officer, was badly injured by an ONH car bomb, the GAA's reaction was one of silence. Heffron was nearly killed by dissident Republicans, yet his GAA club was unwilling to condemn the attack. Almost a year later in Omagh, Ronan Kerr, also a Gaelic football-playing Catholic PSNI officer, was murdered by the explosion of a VDR bomb. On this occasion the GAA both locally and nationally took the lead in the cross-community condemnation of the attack. The day after the murder, Tyrone GAA issued a statement strongly critical of the killing and the wider specter of dissident violence. Speaking about the murder, the GAA said that "his death demeans humanity and is detrimental to the development of a shared future based on mutual respect. In a rights conscious society there is no greater right than the right to life and the need to protect it."[16] This and similar statements were followed by the powerfully symbolic funeral of Constable Kerr. Although there remain significant questions (and likely, tensions) about which bodies or individuals ought to coordinate such activity, it would seem likely at least in the short term that these groupings are inevitably going to remain responsive rather than proactive forces for deterrence.

▪ SINN FÉIN

The role of Sinn Féin in countering the dissidents is one of the most subtle, complex, and vital in ensuring a reduction in violence. Within the party's current ranks and support base, there are unquestionably many potential future violent dissident Republicans. As the emergence of the Tyrone-based "IRA" would suggest, there are people within the Provisional movement who are not content with the progress, or lack thereof, made by Sinn Féin since the Good Friday Agreement. Some of those discontents are now willing to disengage from the political process and reengage with armed action. In his analysis of the gradual politicization of the Provisionals, Morrison[17] illustrated that the number one priority of any political group at a time of significant change is the retention of its base. Without the approval of its base any changes made by a leadership are irrelevant. Although the slowness of Sinn Féin may at times be perceived as "dragging their feet," it may often be the case that members are making sure that they still have this support and possibly preventing (though this would be difficult to verify) an even bigger change and direction of support. What is becoming increasingly clear, however, is that the ability of Sinn Féin to "drag their feet" will likely be reduced in time, as others realize that the party can play a broader, more proactive role in responding to the dissident threat.

The current and likely future role of Sinn Féin in quelling violence by the dissidents goes far beyond the continuation of its politicization. Even though VDR groups discount the Sinn Féin leadership, recent elections have shown that the majority of Northern Irish Republicans support the party. Therefore Sinn Féin remains the group with the largest political influence on the overall Republican community. Although the dissenters may pose one kind of alternative to VDR activity, Sinn Féin's role is to retain its membership and support through the aforementioned political process, but also through *delegitimizing* VDR groups and their activities. The party can continue to do this through its constant promotion of what Sinn Féin and other groups have achieved for the Republican communities through exclusively peaceful methods but also by displaying the damaging effect that armed activity can and will have on this very same community in a modern-day Northern Ireland. Its actions and statements can and do show the irrelevance of, and the true nature of, the VDR groups.

Counternarratives

In their analysis of VDR activity, Currie and Taylor[18] emphasize the critical need to encourage the development of counternarratives in the struggle to contain the growth of the dissidents, at least in the direction of violent activity. As they suggest, this issue permeates the entire civil society of Northern Ireland. They recommend the development of a counternarrative that exposes the "criminality, cruelty and hypocrisy of dissident communications and activity, to undermine the appeal of fictionalized accounts of violent attacks and to promote understanding of the significant achievements of the peace process and the injustices and suffering that went before."[19] Some of the greatest potential will be what develops from within Sinn Féin.

A critical sustaining factor for dissident protest, and at least one issue that could serve to unite the dissidents, is the perceived treatment of prisoners. The dissidents' position is that the Sinn Féin leadership does nothing for the prisoners and that leaders have "forgotten those from within their own community." Sinn Féin may have an important role in countering that narrative by highlighting exactly what it is doing for prisoners. It can, and probably will, use the recent example of the release of Brendan Lillis from prison to hospital through peaceful politics, negotiations, and campaigning. Alongside Lillis' family, members of Sinn Féin and the Social Democratic and Labour Party (SDLP) had actively campaigned for his release on compassionate grounds due to a debilitating illness. The Sinn Féin-led campaign actively demonstrated to its base that it is sensitive to prisoner issues and is not reluctant to investigate perceived injustices against fellow Republicans. This is vital for Sinn Féin both in retaining its base while also preventing drift to the dissidents. In the inevitable tit-for-tat, it is highly likely that the dissidents will counter by arguing that Sinn Féin campaigns only on behalf of its "own" members (though still having been seen by the dissidents as "dragging their feet") who have been imprisoned and turn a blind eye toward injustices against other dissident prisoners.

This provides a conundrum for Sinn Féin. If it appears to do nothing to campaign against perceived injustices against Republican prisoners (including dissidents) it risks losing the support of extreme elements of its support and membership. However, if it appears to be too enthusiastic about these prisoners it risks undermining the confidence of its partner in Stormont, the Democratic Unionist Party (DUP).

Sinn Féin has slowly begun to occupy its important though (from its own position) carefully choreographed role in emphasizing the negative impact VDRs have on Republican communities. Between January 2007 and March 2011, Sinn Féin officials published 43 responses to the Real IRA and Continuity IRA. The regularity of these responses peaked in 2009, when 19 statements denouncing VDR actions were issued. The majority of the denunciations (86%) were published in the immediate wake of a physical attack, but six were not related to specific attacks; instead, they were prepared statements that included mention of violent dissident Republican activity. Among Sinn Féin's statements in *An Phoblacht*, 67.4% were in response to dissident attacks against non-Sinn Féin targets—PSNI personnel, British military, or civilians. For example, on 12 March 2009, *An Phoblacht* published a statement by Gerry Adams condemning a Real IRA attack on the Massereene barracks that killed two British soldiers and wounded four others (including two pizza deliverymen). In the statement, Adams referred to the event as "an attack on the Peace Process" and added that

…the vast majority of people are opposed to what happened. In the days when there was no peaceful or democratic way forward for those who wanted basic rights—civil rights—or for those who wanted national rights as well, Sinn Féin spokespersons, including myself, defended the IRA's armed struggle. We didn't accept everything that was done and in most instances the case we made was in defence of the legitimacy of IRA actions in the context of British Army occupation. There is no such legitimacy today. Our political position was based also on the absence of any alternative way to bring about positive change. Today there is an alternative.

Attacks or threats against Sinn Féin officials have also prompted public reactions against the dissident groups—eight of the released statements in *An*

Phoblacht between January 2007 and March 2011 were made in response to such events. For instance, in April 2009, Martin McGuinness was informed by the PSNI that there was a threat against his life by dissident Republicans. In response, *An Phoblacht* published a statement by McGuinness mocking members of the dissident Republican groups as "a set of impostors who are trying to hijack the Republican cause for their own purposes." He added: "they're not going to succeed. Sinn Féin has a job to do, it is a difficult job and it may be a dangerous job, some of us may lose our lives, but we're not going to be intimidated." Sinn Féin has regularly challenged the dissidents to, in the words of senior Republican Bobby Storey, "outline ... their strategy for achieving a united Ireland," adding that "they routinely fail to even provide a public explanation or justification for their actions. They fail to outline their political vision of what kind of society they want to build and the only point they agree on is the use of physical force."[20]

These statements appear designed not only to disregard the dissidents, but to reassert Sinn Féin's mandate, legitimacy, and capability to effectively achieve the goals of Irish Republicanism and unity. Although each of the statements released by Sinn Féin is slightly different, at least one of those three themes is present in nearly every one.

Sinn Féin's attempts to attack and undermine the dissident campaign have not been limited to the ideological battlefield. Frampton describes the "reticence periodically shown by members of the PIRA when it came to 'challenging the dissident narrative.'"[21] However, Sinn Féin appears to have gradually increased its efforts to undermine the credibility of the dissidents, with a particular focus on the relationship between dissident groups and drug-related crime. A common theme throughout Sinn Féin's statements has been the emphasis on the "criminal" nature of dissident activity. Surely cognizant of how it was previously linked to criminal activity by its political opponents and the negative impact this had, Sinn Féin has (though it might not describe it as such) helped develop a potentially crushing counternarrative about the dissidents, increasingly highlighting the "criminal" nature of much of what the dissidents do.

For example, in late April 2009, Sinn Féin member and MLA Daithí McKay emphasized the links between "antisocial" and criminal groups and the dissidents: "Republicanism is nothing more than a flag of convenience for these people."[22] Sinn Féin politician and former PIRA volunteer Martin Ferris stated that "nobody ... can use the Republican cause as a cloak for criminal activity. If they attempt to do so, they will be repudiated and should face the full rigours of the law."[23] But looking closer, it is clear that Sinn Féin knows it is walking a dangerous line, and has been careful in attributing the label of criminality to the dissidents. Often, instead of unambiguous and outright declarations condemning dissidents as criminals, the party has delivered statements arguing how the dissidents have been, in the words of Sinn Féin's Martina Anderson, "infiltrated ... by criminals."[24]

Despite the frequency of Sinn Féin's statements, the ambiguity remains. In 2008 and 2009, only "some" or "others" were "involved in undisguised criminality."[25] More recently, however, and in particular in light of dissident threats made against former PIRA members and Sinn Féin community workers, Sinn Féin members have accused the dissidents of outright "extortion and criminality" more frequently.[26]

The role of Sinn Féin, and the wider Provisional community, goes beyond current efforts to counter the dissidents. More than any other group it knows what it takes for a Republican paramilitary group to move from an armed campaign toward exclusively peaceful methods. These experiences must not be forgotten, as they may provide a template for a modern-day CVDR strategy. We need to learn from both the mistakes and the positive steps that were made in tackling the Provisional threat. Although the two situations are not identical there are clear and striking similarities. As we saw in earlier chapters, at their birth the Provisionals were a dissident Republican group that rejected the political strategy of the leadership of Cathal Goulding. They, like the VDR groups of today, were steadfast in their promotion of the utility of armed action to achieve a united Ireland. However, through a gradual process that began in the mid-1970s,[27] the Provisionals succeeded in moving away from armed action and toward the fully politicized Sinn Féin of today. This gradual but still dramatic change of strategy required the resolution of several issues. Although actions by state agencies on both sides of the border were important, the most vital steps were taken by those within the group.

All of this, reiterated from the lessons of Chapter 2, demonstrates that regardless of the CVDR policies that are put in place, they will require a parallel effort by internal actors within the paramilitary organizations if they are to bring an end to the armed strategy. Although arrests and incarceration may bring a short-term end to the violence, history has shown that only internal change can bring about long-term success. These and other lessons of the past must not be forgotten. The achievements and failures of the past may point the way to successfully countering the dissident threat. Although the VDR threat is not identical to that posed by the PIRA, there are too many similarities to ignore. Therefore consultation with those who were at the forefront, both internally and externally, of bringing the PIRA away from violence can provide valuable insights into how to deal with this current threat. At present, there remains a worrying absence of any clear political effort (at least publicly) to bring about this engagement with the dissidents.

■ **VICTIM GROUPS**

On the subject of counternarratives, one of the most powerful groups in countering the dissident threat, and historically the wider paramilitary threat, has been victims' groups. Frampton describes a group of bereaved friends and family members of the Omagh victims as one of the most effective and "pugnacious"[28] responses to the RIRA. As he explains, that the RIRA tried unsuccessfully to distance itself from the atrocity was in no small part because of the Omagh Support and Self-Help Group (OSSHG). The group eventually brought a civil action against five key Republicans: Mickey McKevitt, Liam Campbell, Colm Murphy, Seamus Daly, and Seamus McGrane. It did so because nobody had been convicted of involvement in the Omagh bombing (Murphy, the only man charged in connection with Omagh, was found guilty in January 2002;

however, his 14-year sentence was overturned in January 2005 and he was subsequently found not guilty).

Bringing a civil case meant that even if the accused were found guilty, he would not face a criminal conviction. But the families stressed that their actions were specifically engineered to put "as much information as possible into the public domain about the bombing and the men they claim were involved."[29] They were successful. In 2009, Murphy, McKevitt, Campbell, and Daly were found "liable" in the civil case of responsibility for Omagh.[30] The Omagh families were awarded limited financial damages, but they were the first to successfully sue a terrorist group.

The power of victim groups to undermine the credibility and legitimacy of violent groups is well illustrated with the case of Robert McCartney. McCartney, a resident of the Republican Short Strand area of East Belfast, was not aligned to any political or paramilitary group. He was murdered by the Provisional IRA in the Markets area of East Belfast in January 2005. In the months before his murder Sinn Féin had to respond to allegations of its knowledge and sanctioning of the Northern Bank robbery as well as face challenges to supply photographic evidence of PIRA decommissioning. But those pressures, which were significant, paled in comparison to the challenges the PIRA leadership faced in the wake of McCartney's murder.

Locally, the McCartney family knew within a few hours who had committed the murder and who had engaged in the forensic cleanup, but realized quickly that no one was willing to approach the police. In the days and weeks that followed, McCartney's sisters and fiancée approached the media to wage a high-profile publicity campaign aimed, in their words, at bringing justice to their brother's memory. In turn the local community emerged in public solidarity with the sisters, something that had never before happened when the PIRA had decided to kill one of its "own" community. The campaign generated by the sisters attracted enormous attention, and their remarkable courage was important in keeping the campaign alive. Sinn Féin was once again embarrassed and its responses were derided as arrogant and hypocritical: 5 weeks after the murder, Gerry Adams explained that "Sinn Féin is not in a position to carry out an investigation which would adequately establish the facts that surround the killing of Robert McCartney." However, the party would not support calls to encourage witnesses to come forward to the police. This and other surrounding events resulted in significant pressure being placed on Sinn Féin, nationally, internationally, but, most importantly, locally. The backlash that was growing within the Nationalist community left Sinn Féin with no choice but to issue carefully worded statements in support of the McCartney family.

In the weeks that followed, the pressure on Sinn Féin became so great that the Provisional IRA contacted the McCartney family actually offering to shoot those responsible. To widespread condemnation and disbelief, the Republican party's fundamental inability to accept the rule of law was exposed for all to see. This was the only way in which a desperate PIRA could deal with the crisis. Also exposed at this time were Sinn Féin's efforts to stifle dissidence from independent Republicans who drew attention to the attempted cover-up.[31] In January 2007, due in large part to the persistence of the McCartneys, Sinn Féin finally publicly encouraged anyone with any information on any case to go to the police. This was an historic announcement, and although not solely a result of the campaigns of the McCartneys, their role in the process was critical.

There are valuable lessons to be gained here that may provide opportunities to quell support for VDRs. Small-scale attacks do not command the media attention of a large bomb, but in terms of their effects on the communities in which they occur, they have profound impact. As a party that needed to maintain the trust of the British and Irish governments as well as Nationalist and Unionist politicians, Sinn Féin was forced to respond to the national and international pressure created by the McCartney murder with a series of strong reactions, even if these were much delayed. At the time it was not impossible to imagine that the culmination of these events could have been the complete collapse of the already burgeoning peace process. These same constraints are not in place for the VDRs. As they are not involved in any peace process, and are not political representatives for any community, they do not face the same external pressures the Sinn Féin leadership encountered in 2005. It will therefore be more difficult for victims groups comparable to the McCartneys to bring about similarly significant advances. This is not to say that victims groups do not have anything to add to the CVDR strategy—the centrality of the OSSHG clearly suggests otherwise. However, any changes they bring about may need to be even harder fought for than those of the McCartneys.

▪ CONCLUSIONS

The fluid and dynamic nature of the dissident threat probably renders recommendations for a long-term counterviolence strategy premature. The same cannot be said, however, for what can be done in the short to medium term. Tactics and strategies involved in countering the violent dissident threat must be multilayered and must be tackled by a variety of credible groups. It will take time for these roles and responsibilities to be recognized, let alone fulfilled, but there is a serious urgency to develop a CVDR strategy. There are some hard choices that need to be made in responding to the dissidents. The meaningful development of a CVDR strategy must look beyond the dissidents themselves and focus on the relevant factors within wider Northern Irish society, factors that can indirectly dissipate the VDR threat. This can involve, among other areas, a strengthened antidrugs strategy and the continued normalization of Northern Irish political and social life.

Close observers of the dissidents are most concerned with the growing inevitability that Sinn Féin will probably play the most prominent role in providing a counternarrative. In Republican areas, and despite short-term gains by the dissidents, Sinn Féin effectively *is* the voice of civil society. What the party continues to do will significantly affect the dissidents' ability to sustain themselves in the longer run. In those same communities, Sinn Féin's voice will continue to remain loudest. But outside violent actions prompted by the dissidents (e.g., high-profile attacks) the party has demonstrated a (not atypical) reluctance to effectively realize its potential in a CVDR strategy. Whatever the future brings, it is likely that Sinn Féin will continue to be the major potential figure in such a strategy. Cognizant of its own politicization process, a central aim of the CVDR strategy need not be an attempt by Sinn Féin at the outset to draw these individuals into an acceptance of the peace process. Instead, the first priority of political efforts must be quelling the violence. Only then, and not unlike the same process that marked a watershed moment for the Provisionals, will any negotiated cessation of violence allow the time for political initiatives (in whatever form) to develop.

■ **NOTES**

1. Rowan, B. 2010. "Dissidents: Interview with Terror Splinter Group." *Belfast Telegraph,* 3 November.

2. BBC News. 2010. "Dissidents Reject Sinn Féin Talks Offer." 9 August.

3. McManus, G. 2011. "Gardai Saving Our Lives—NI Justice Chief." *Evening Herald,* 8 February.

4. http://www.psni.police.uk/persons_arrested_and_charged_cy.pdf. Accessed August 16, 2011.

5. Frampton, M. 2011. *Legion of the Rearguard: Dissident Irish Republicanism.* Dublin: Irish Academic Press. P. 145.

6. Frampton, 2011, p. 148.

7. Wilson, J. 2000. "How the Real IRA Recruits Boys into a Life of Terrorism." *The Guardian,* 18 November.

8. BBC News. 2000. "Real IRA Camp 'Trainee' Freed." 2 March.

9. Frampton, 2010, p. 3.

10. BBC News Online. 2011. "Matt Baggott Welcomes Extra £245m for Police." 18 February. http://www.bbc.co.uk/news/uk-northern-ireland-12500020. Accessed August 19, 2011.

11. Ibid.

12. Independent Monitoring Commission. 2011. *Twenty-Sixth and Final Report of the Independent Monitoring Commission: 2004–2011 Changes, Impact and Lessons.* London: The Stationery Office. P. 14.

13. Morrison, J. F. 2010. *"The Affirmation of Behan?": An Understanding of the Politicisation Process of the Provisional Irish Republican Movement Through an Organisational Analysis of Splits from 1969 to 1997.* Ph.D. dissertation submitted to the University of St. Andrews.

14. Simpson, M. "Visit Part of New Anti-Dissident Strategy." BBC, October 12, 2010. http://www.bbc.co.uk/news/uk-northern-ireland-11521483. Accessed April 18, 2011.

15. Currie, P. M., & Taylor, M. (Eds.). 2011. *Dissident Irish Republicanism.* London: Continuum. P. 173

16. Tyrone GAA. 2011. "GAA Statement on Ronan Kerr Murder," 3 April. http://www.tyronegaa.ie/2011/04/gaa-statement-on-ronan-kerr-murder/. Accessed August 19, 2011.

17. Morrison, 2010.

18. Currie & Taylor, 2011.

19. Ibid., p. 173.

20. AP/RN, July 2010, p. 16.

21. Frampton, 2011, p. 140.

22. AP/RN, 30 April, 2009, p. 3.

23. AP/RN, 29 February 2009, p. 4.

24. AP/RN, 4 March 2010, p. 2.

25. Statement by Declan Kearney, AP/RN, 2008.

26. See, for example, AP/RN, March 2011, p. 14.

27. Morrison, 2010.

28. Frampton, 2011, p. 133.

29. Kearney, V. 2009. "Judgement Due in Omagh Civil Suit." BBC News, 8 June.

30. RTE News. 2009. "Four Found Liable for Omagh Bombing," 8 June.

31. McIntyre, A. 2008. *Good Friday: The Death of Irish Republicanism*. New York: Ausubo Press. P. 166.

8 Conclusions: Doomed to Fail?

The hundredth anniversary of the 1916 Easter Rising will soon be upon us. A swarm of Republican and Nationalist parties and groups are likely to scramble to depict themselves as the heirs apparent to their Republican forefathers. Although the dissidents have a tendency to look to the past for answers, there is no doubt that they may look to the future to help focus an otherwise divided stand against their enemies. The level and nature of dissident activity since 2008 are testaments to the false sense of security felt by Northern Ireland's distant observers, but the next 4 years may shatter any illusions that the dissidents represent a dwindling threat.[1] Despite a series of dangerous "near misses" through attempted murders, failed and foiled bombings, and an intermittent schedule of successful attacks, the data suggest that dissident violence and related activity are on the rise.

Perhaps the most frequently asked question is whether the dissidents have a future, and if so, if that future will continue to be highlighted by violence? Liam Clarke,[2] in late 2010, described the dissidents as "stranded by the tide of history" and a "mass of contradictions. Like the Provos they are doomed to fail." He concludes: "Tactically it knows what it is doing, but strategically it is whistling in the dark." Clarke's assessment of tactical effectiveness is supported by the data presented in Chapter 3, and more generally by the data presented in these chapters. Furthermore, Rowan notes that the dissidents have succeeded in regaining the media spotlight and announcing their resurgence to the world. The recent upsurge has ensured that across Northern Ireland, the police are "again wearing flak-jackets and mounting frequent checkpoints...undercover soldiers of the Special Reconnaissance Regiment have been deployed in the province, bomb-disposal experts have been recalled from Afghanistan and the drift towards the visible deployment of military resources may prove unstoppable."[3] That the dissidents have not only returned but are on the march is a reality.

A more pressing question, and one worth asking at the conclusion of this book, is whether they are likely to survive. It remains unclear whether the dissident groups have a strategic direction to help sustain their tactical effectiveness into the medium- to long-term future. Assessing the strategic capabilities of terrorist groups can be a dangerous and foolhardy exercise. It can be as easy to overestimate them as it is to underestimate them, with or without access to data from multiple private and public sources. As Kydd and Walter[4] remind us: "terrorists are not always the rational, calculating individuals we assume, and terrorist violence is certainly not always aimed at breaking down peace negotiations. Simple revenge or retaliation may explain some of the violence." Given how the broader dissident campaign is buoyed on by each successive signal of Sinn Féin's "normalization," revenge and retaliation would certainly appear to be at the immediate heart of what drives the dissidents. There certainly are identifiable strategic positions, but the extent to which national-level policies are apparent or even relevant to the dissidents' day-to-day activities remains unclear. If the dissident leadership has a strategic plan to enable them to grow beyond simply being an armed protest movement and instead becoming a militant organization(s), it has yet to emerge.

Despite their unification on several issues, the dissidents remain as divided as ever. But time has shown us that this should not necessarily be equated with low risk or an inability to cause continued disruption to peace and security in Northern Ireland. Whenever we think they are starting to fade away, they bounce back to remind us that they are still here. Though they have not been able (or perhaps, from their perspective, have deliberately decided not) to engage in frequent attacks, they have managed to give the impression that lasting peace in Northern Ireland is under threat, which has allowed them to sustain the belief and self-righteousness of what they seek to do.

In addition, there are certainly dynamic qualities associated with their ongoing strategic development. Speaking about the split that threatened to herald the Real IRA (RIRA)'s demise in 2002, RIRA member Declan Carroll asserted that the decision to withdraw allegiance from outside leadership was the right move *at that time*. Lamenting the lack of a "genuine republican alternative" to that of the Provisional leadership, Carroll decries the "*current* strategy of the main dissident groups" [emphasis mine] as "futile." Despite the ideological dogma frequently attributed to the 32 County Sovereignty Movement (32CSM) and Republican Sinn Féin (RSF), the groups are not as desensitized to strategic adaptation as we might like to believe. Though that adaptation may not be apparent in their policy documents, we should not assume it is not happening in ways we have yet to detect. Understanding the factors that give rise to and sustain ongoing strategic development is critical. Development of strategy signals vitality, and the dissidents' ability to sustain that adaptation may ultimately signal the effectiveness of some particular factions over others. Although there is no statistical correlation between the duration of a terrorist group and ideological motivation, economic conditions, regime type, or the breadth of the group's goals, there is at least some correlation between the group's size and its duration; put simply, larger groups tend to last longer than smaller groups.[5]

The assessment that the dissidents are, in the long term, doomed to failure arises from the judgment that they cannot possibly hope to gain the level of support the Provisional IRA (PIRA) grudgingly commanded. However, the dissidents themselves repeatedly and consistently indicate that this lack of support will not deter them from their mission. In the words of the RIRA leadership:

> No guerilla can exist without a support base—ours is considerable, certainly sufficient, principled and politically aware. The disillusionment felt in relation to the present political path of the Provisional leadership is clearly evident in the sharp decline in those registering to vote in certain constituencies.... Eamon de Valera is on record as having said in relation to the Treaty of 1921 that "the Irish people did

not have the right to vote for treachery." We believe that just as in 1921 a war-weary Irish nation in 1998 was bombarded, hoodwinked and confused by a pro-British and West Briton media into voting for a political package which deprived them of their right to self-determination and subverted the Republic established by them in 1918. If we as Republicans who oppose the sell-out enshrined in the 1998 Agreement are a minority in the population of today we follow a long and noble tradition stretching back to the Fenians, the men of 1916, Republican Volunteers of the '30s, '40s and '50s, who had no electoral mandate but were convinced of the rightness of their cause and had the physical and moral strength of their convictions.

So central is cliché for the psychology and strategy of Violent Dissident Republicans (VDRs) that it might seem redundant to conclude this book on a cliché, but one thing is certain. Violent Dissident Republicans know that they have 4 years to prove whether they really are here to stay.

■ NOTES

1. This view is consistent with Frampton who argues that many of the "lucky misses" by dissident groups were "largely ignored by the mainstream media, giving a false impression of stability in Northern Ireland." P. 2. Frampton, M. 2010. *The Return of the Militants: Violent Dissident Republicanism*. London: International Centre for the Study of Radicalisation and Political Violence.

2. Clarke, L. 2010. "Dissidents Stranded by the Tide of History." *Belfast Telegraph*, 3 November, p. 33.

3. Ibid.

4. Kydd, A., & Walter, B. 2002. "Sabotaging the Peace: The Politics of Extremist Violence." *International Organization*, 56(2), 263–296.

5. Jones, S. G., & Libicki, M. C. 2008. *How Terrorist Groups End: Lessons for Countering al Qa'ida*. Santa Monica, CA: RAND Corporation, MG-741-1-RC. On the web: http://www.rand.org/pubs/monographs/MG741-1.html.

■ APPENDIX

Database Structure and Fields

VDR Events Database Headings

1. Timing
   - Month
   - Day
   - Year
   - MM/DD/YYYY
2. Location
   - Region
   - County
   - City/Town
   - Street
   - Policing District/Division
   - LAT/LONG
3. Responsibility
   - VDR Group
   - Claimed
   - Perpetrator's Name
4. Event Type
   - Violent/Nonviolent/Threat of Violence
   - Event Type
   - Weapon
   - Number of Devices
   - Number of Locations
   - Other Events Possibly Connected to
5. Direct Victims
   - Dead
   - Wounded
   - Hostage
   - Total
   - Victim/Target Type
   - Age of Victims
6. Summary and Sources
   - Event Summary
   - Sources

VDR Personnel Database Headings

1. Biographical Data
   - ID Number
   - Name

- Gender
- Date of Birth
- Month of Birth
- Day of Birth
- Year of Birth
- Date of Death
- Age as of December 31, 2010
- Age Range as of December 31, 2010
- Marital Status
- Children

2. Residential Data
   - Place of Birth
   - Policing District/Division (Place of Birth)
   - North/South
   - Known Addresses
   - Policing District/Division (Known Address)
   - County

3. Occupational and Educational Data
   - Occupation
   - Socioeconomic Status
   - Education Level Attained

4. VDR Affiliation
   - VDR Group
   - Prior Affiliation
   - Convicted/Charged/Political

5. VDR Activity and Position
   - Age at Recruitment
   - Year of Recruitment
   - Age Range at Recruitment
   - Year of First Known Activity
   - Year of First Known Illegal Activity
   - Age Range at First Known Illegal Activity
   - Type of First Known Illegal Activity
   - Year of First Known Current Group Activity
   - Age Range at First Known Illegal Group Activity
   - Type of First Known Current Group Activity
   - Type of First Known Current Group Illegal Activity
   - Year of Last Known Illegal Activity
   - Type of Last Known Illegal Activity
   - Age at Last Known Illegal Activity
   - Subgrouping
   - Position in Movement
   - Role in Illegal Activities
   - Period of Illegal Activities

6. Status
   - Current Status
   - Place of Arrest

- Policing District/Division of Arrest
- Length of Sentence
- Plea
- Number of VDR Convictions
- Length of Sentences
- Date of Charges
- Date of Convictions
- Ordinary Criminal Convictions
- Date of Status Update

7. Acquaintances
    - ID Number of Family
    - ID of Acquaintances Prejoining
    - ID of Acquaintances Postjoining
    - Operational Acquaintances
    - Immediate Family
    - Relatives

8. Summary and Sources
    - Information
    - Sources

GLOSSARY

32 County Sovereignty Movement (32CSM)—A dissident Irish republican political movement created in 1997 by a section of the Sinn Féin membership that did not support the acceptance of the Mitchell Principles. This group is widely believed to be the political wing of the Real IRA, a belief regularly refuted by 32CSM. It was originally known as the 32 County Sovereignty Committee (32CSC).

Abstentionist Policy—A policy historically adopted by the Irish Republican Movement whereby elected representatives do not take their seats in Dáil Éireann (Irish parliament), Westminster, or Stormont. This was adopted due to the belief that these three parliaments actively promoted the partition of Ireland and it was a major factor behind some of the most significant splits in Republicanism. Sinn Féin still retains its abstentionist policy to Westminster but abolished the similar policies with respect to Dáil Éireann in 1986 and 1998, respectively.

British Labour Party/Labour Party—The center-left democratic socialist political party of the United Kingdom.

Conservative Party—A center-right British political party that actively supports British unity. They unsuccessfully fielded joint candidates with the Ulster Unionist Party in the 2008 European election and 2010 general election under the banner Ulster Conservative and Unionist New Force (UCUNF).

Continuity Irish Republican Army (CIRA)—A dissident Irish republican paramilitary organization created in 1986 by senior Provisional IRA (PIRA) members dissatisfied with Sinn Féin's decision (under Gerry Adams) to abandon its abstentionist policy, and the PIRA's support of this. It is widely believed to be the paramilitary branch of Republican Sinn Féin. Among its most recent activity has been the murder of Police Service of Northern Ireland (PSNI) officer Stephen Carroll in Craigavon in March 2009.

Democratic Unionist Party (DUP)—A Northern Irish unionist party founded by Rev Ian Paisley, Desmond Boal, and fellow members of the Protestant Unionist Party in 1971. It withdrew from the negotiations that resulted in the Belfast Agreement because Sinn Féin was allowed to participate (despite the PIRA continuing to retain its weapons). The party campaigned against the passing of the agreement but eventually accepted the St. Andrews Agreement in 2006.

District Policing Partnerships (DPP)—These are partnerships between the district council, councilors, and local communities in Northern Ireland created to monitor the effectiveness of policing in each area. They also act as a consultative forum on matters concerning policing in the districts. This is not to be confused with the Director of Public Prosecutions (also DPP) in the Republic of Ireland, Great Britain, and Northern Ireland.

Éirígí—A socialist republican political movement in Ireland formed in Dublin in 2006. It opposes the British presence in Northern Ireland and seeks the establishment of a united Ireland. It is not considered a paramilitary organization, but is based on revolutionary socialist principles. The word "**Éirígí**" is Irish for "rise."

Fianna Éireann—The former youth wing of PIRA. This name has been used by numerous Irish Republican organizations for their youth wings in both the twentieth and twenty-first centuries.

Fianna Fáil (FF)—One of the two main political organizations, alongside Fine Gael, in the Republic of Ireland. It was established in 1921 in opposition to the "Treaty." Traditionally it is the largest Irish political party; however, after the 2011 general election it was for the first time in its history the third largest party behind Fine Gael and the Labour Party.

Fine Gael (FG)—One of the two main political organizations in the Republic of Ireland. It was originally formed in 1921 from the wing of Sinn Féin that supported the "Treaty." It is traditionally the smaller of the two main parties; however, in the 2011 general election it became the largest party in Dáil Éireann for the first time in its history.

Garda Síochána/Gardaí—The police force of the Republic of Ireland. The name means "Guardians of the Peace" in Irish.

Good Friday Agreement/Belfast Agreement/Stormont Agreement—A political agreement in the Northern Ireland peace process that signified the end of the Troubles. The agreement represented the culmination of 2 years of multiparty negotiations. The agreement sought to create a representative Northern Ireland Assembly and develop a doctrine for the disposal of paramilitary weapons. This was ratified by two separate referenda in Northern Ireland and the Republic of Ireland on May 23, 1998. Among other provisions this saw the abolition of the Republic of Ireland's territorial claim to Northern Ireland via the alterations of Articles 2 and 3 of the Irish Constitution.

Independent International Commission on Decommissioning (IICD)—A group established in the 1990s to oversee the decommissioning of the weapons of paramilitary groups, both Republican and Loyalist, in Northern Ireland. The IICD disbanded in 2010. Only days before its disbanding the INLA and OIRA announced the decommissioning of their weapons.

Independent Monitoring Commission (IMC)—A group created by the Irish and British governments in 2004 to help promote the establishment of stable and inclusive government in Northern Ireland by reporting on the activity of paramilitary groups and security normalization measures.

Irish Free State—The Irish Free State came into existence in 1922 under the Anglo-Irish Treaty (also known as The Treaty). The Free State ceased to exist in 1937 when a referendum was voted through to replace the 1922 constitution. The Free State was succeeded by the sovereign state of Ireland, and in 1949 under the Republic of Ireland Act the office of President of Ireland replaced the King of England as head of the state, thus cutting the final tie to British rule. Although the Free State is no longer in existence the term is often used, sometimes in a derogatory manner, by Republicans to refer to the 26 counties of the Republic of Ireland.

Irish Labour Party—A center-left political party in the Republic of Ireland.

Irish Republican Socialist Party (IRSP)—A movement formed in 1974 after breaking away from Official Sinn Féin. It was considered to be the political wing of the Irish National Liberation Army (INLA), a paramilitary group decommissioned in 2010. It supports the establishment of a 32 county socialist republic in Ireland and opposes both the Good Friday Agreement and the Peace Process. In 2009 it ordered an end to the armed struggle.

Loyalist—A term referring to an individual who gives tacit or actual support to the British Crown and state for the union of Northern Ireland with Great Britain (i.e., the United

Kingdom). "Loyalist" sometimes is used to describe those who support the use of paramilitary force to defend that union.

MI5—The British internal security service, otherwise known as the "security service."

MLA—Member of Legislative Assembly. The Northern Ireland equivalent of MP or TD.

Nationalist—A term used in Northern Ireland to describe those who support the reunification of Ireland, the majority being from the Catholic community. However, not all Nationalists support republican groups.

Office of the First Minister and Deputy First Minister (OFMdFM)—This is one of 11 devolved Northern Ireland departments created in December 1999 under the Northern Ireland Act. It has the overall responsibility for running the Northern Ireland Executive and is run by the First Minister and deputy First Minister. The two positions share equal power.

Official Republican Movement (ORM)—This is the collective term used to refer to the Official IRA and Official Sinn Féin from which the Provisional Republican Movement split away in 1969. It has also more recently been adopted by a small grouping that split from the Worker's Party in 1991 when it viewed the party as drifting away from its Republican heritage.

Óglaigh na hÉireann (ONH)—Irish republican paramilitary organization that formed in 2006 and is believed to be a faction of the Real IRA. It recruits and trains members in Northern Ireland, and has been responsible for high-profile attacks on the PSNI and British Army. This is a name used by a number of Irish Republican paramilitary organizations, including the splinter group of the CIRA that broke away in 2006. It is also a name used by the legitimate army of the Republic of Ireland.

Progressive Unionist Party (PUP)—A loyalist political party with links to the paramilitary group, the Ulster Volunteer Force (UVF).

Provisional Irish Republican Army (PIRA)—The main republican paramilitary group, founded in January 1970 after a split within the Republican movement.

Real Irish Republican Army (RIRA)—Dissident Irish republican paramilitary organization formed in 1997 by disaffected senior Provisional IRA members. It is opposed to the Good Friday Agreement and is believed to be, in effect, the military wing of the 32 County Sovereignty Movement. This group was primarily responsible for the Omagh bombing in 1998, the murder of two British soldiers at the Massareene Barracks in 2009, and multiple additional operations.

Republican—In the Northern Ireland context, the term traditionally refers to an individual who supports the use of violence to establish a United (32 county) Ireland.

Republican Action Against Drugs (RAAD)—An Irish republican vigilante group targeting alleged drug dealers largely via paramilitary attacks, intimidation, and arson. They are most active in Northern Ireland across Derry, Strabane, and Newry.

Republican Network for Unity (RNU)—A coalition of dissident Republicans opposed to the twenty-first-century direction of Sinn Féin. Although it does not have a military wing it did send "comradely greetings to Óglaigh na hÉireann" at their 2011 Ard Fheis.

Republican Sinn Féin (RSF)—An Irish republican political party that broke away from Sinn Féin in 1986 out of opposition to its policy to end abstention from the Dáil. RSF opposed both the PIRA ceasefire and the Peace Process, and it is widely regarded as the political wing of the Continuity IRA.

Royal Ulster Constabulary (RUC)—The police force of Northern Ireland from 1922 to 2001. It has been succeeded by the heavily reformed Police Service of Northern Ireland (PSNI).

Sinn Féin—The left-wing republican political party, advocating Irish unity and self-determination. It is widely regarded as the political wing of the PIRA, though the leadership of the party denies these claims.

"Six Counties"—The term Republicans use to refer to Northern Ireland, since they do not acknowledge it as a state. The counties include Antrim, Armagh, Derry (Londonderry), Down, Fermanagh, and Tyrone.

Social Democratic and Labour Party (SDLP)—Nationalist political party in Northern Ireland that has traditionally opposed the violent campaign of the PIRA, though it is committed to the unification of Ireland through political means.

St. Andrews Agreement—This 2006 agreement was the result of multiparty talks held between the British and Irish governments and the main Northern Irish political parties. The most significant outcomes of this agreement were the restoration of the Northern Ireland Assembly, the formation of a new Northern Ireland Executive, and the acceptance by Sinn Féin of the PSNI. The signing of the Agreement saw the DUP and Sinn Féin entering into a power sharing agreement with Ian Paisley and Martin McGuinness, elected First Minister and deputy First Minister, respectively.

Ulster Unionist Party (UUP)—Traditionally the largest Unionist part in Northern Ireland, but it has recently been surpassed by the DUP. It is considered to be the most centrist of the Unionist parties and has strong ties with the British Conservative party.

Unionist—A term in Northern Ireland that refers to those who support the union of Northern Ireland with Great Britain.

■ SELECT BIBLIOGRAPHY

Alonso, R . (2001). The Modernization of Irish Republican Thinking Toward the Utility of Violence. *Studies in Conflict and Terrorism*, 24, 131–144.

Bass, C., & Smith, M. L. R. (2008). The War Continues? Combating the Paramilitaries and the Role of the British Army After the Belfast Agreement. In J. Dingley (Ed.), *Combating Terrorism in Northern Ireland*. London: Routledge. Pp. 258–279.

Baxter, I., & Crowcroft, R. (2010). The Troubles in Northern Ireland: Conflict Resolution and the Problem with Being "Reasonable. *Small Wars Journal*, September 21, 2010.

Bean, K. (2007). *The New Politics of Sinn Fein*. Liverpool: Liverpool University Press.

Bew, P. (2007). *Ireland: The Politics of Enmity 1789–2006*. Oxford: Oxford University Press.

Bew, P. (2007). *The Making and Remaking of the Good Friday Agreement*. Dublin: Liffey Press.

Bjørgo, T., & Horgan, J. (Eds.) (2009). *Leaving Terrorism Behind: Individual and Collective Disengagement*. London: Routledge.

Boyne, S. (1998). The Real IRA: After Omagh, What Now? *Jane's Intelligence Review*, August 24.

Bueno de Mesquita, E. (2008). Terrorist Factions. *Quarterly Journal of Political Science*, 3, 399–418.

Coogan, T. P. (2002). *The IRA*. London: Palgrave.

Cronin, A. K. (2009). *How Terrorism Ends: Understanding the Decline and Demise of Terrorist Campaigns*. Princeton: Princeton University Press.

Currie, P. M., & Taylor, M. (Eds.) (2011). *Dissident Irish Republicanism*. London: Continuum Press.

De Breadun, D. (2008). *The Far Side of Revenge: Making Peace in Northern Ireland*. Cork: The Collins Press.

Dingley, J. (2001). The Bombing of Omagh, 15 August 1998: The Bombers, Their Tactics, Strategy, and Purpose Behind the Incident. *Studies in Conflict and Terrorism*, 24(6), 451–465.

Dingley, J., & Kirk-Smith, M. (2000). How Could They Do It?: The Bombing of Omagh, 1998. *Journal of Conflict Studies*, 20(1), 105–126.

Dudley Edwards, R. (2009). *Aftermath: The Omagh Bombing and the Families' Pursuit of Justice*. London: Harvill Secker.

English, R. (2004). *Armed Struggle: The History of the IRA*. New York: Oxford University Press.

Evans, R. (2002). Real IRA Indicates Willingness to Intensify Terror Campaign. *Jane's Intelligence Review*, 14, 22–23.

Fay, M., Morrissey, M., & Smyth, M. (1999). *Northern Ireland's Troubles: The Human Costs*. London: Pluto Press.

Frampton, M. (2009). *The Long March: The Political Strategy of Sinn Fein, 1981–2007*. London: Palgrave Macmillan

Frampton, M. (2010). *The Return of the Militants: Violent Dissident Republicanism*. London: The International Centre for the Study of Radicalisation and Political Violence.

Frampton, M. (2010). *Legion of the Rearguard: Dissident Irish Republicanism*. Dublin: Irish Academic Press.

Galamaga, A. (2009). *Today's Political Landscape in Northern Ireland as an Aftermath of the Troubles*. Norderstedt, Germany: GRIN Verlag.

Gilmore, M. (2009). No Way Back? Examining the Background and Response to the Rise of Dissident Terrorist Activity in Northern Ireland. *The Journal of the Royal United Services Institute for Defence and Security Studies*, 154(2), 50–55.

Harnden, T. (1999). *Bandit Country*. London: Hodder & Stoughton.

Hayes, B. C., & McAllister, I. (2001). Sowing Dragon's Teeth: Public Support for Political Violence and Paramilitarism in Northern Ireland. *Political Studies*, 49, 901–922.

Horgan, J. (2009). *Walking away from Terrorism: Accounts of Disengagement from Radical and Extremist Movements*. New York: Routledge.

Jarman, N. (2004). From War to Peace? Changing Patterns of Violence in Northern Ireland, 1990–2003. *Terrorism and Political Violence*, 16(3), 420–438.

Knox, C. (2002). "See No Evil, Hear No Evil": Insidious Paramilitary Violence in Northern Ireland. *British Journal of Criminology*, 42, 164–185.

Maillot, A. (2005). *New Sinn Fein: Irish Republicanism in the Twenty First Century*. London: Routledge.

McDonald, H. (2008). *Gunsmoke and Mirrors: How Sinn Fein Dressed Up Defeat as Victory*. Dublin: Gill and Macmillan.

McInerney, L. (2011). Real IRA (Irish Republican Army). Presented at the Annual Meeting of the International Studies Association Annual Conference "Global Governance. Political Authority in Transition," Montreal, Canada, 16 March, 2011.

McIntyre, A. (1995). Modern Irish Republicanism. The Product of British State Strategies. *Irish Political Studies*, 10, 97–122.

McIntyre, A. (2008). *Good Friday: The Death of Irish Republicanism*. New York: Ausubo Press.

McKearney, T. (2011). *The Provisional IRA: From Insurrection to Parliament*. London: Pluto Press.

McKittrick, D. (2001). *Lost Lives: The Stories of the Men, Women, and Children Who Died as a Result of the Northern Ireland Troubles*. London: Pluto Press.

Moloney, E. (2002). *A Secret History of the IRA*. London: Norton.

Monaghan, R. (2004). "An Imperfect Peace": Paramilitary "Punishments" in Northern Ireland. *Terrorism and Political Violence*, 16(3), 439–461.

Mooney, J., & O'Toole, M. (2003). *Black Operations: The Secret War against the Real IRA*. Duboyne, Ireland: Maverick House.Moran, J. (2008). *Policing the Peace in Northern Ireland: Politics, Crime and Security after the Belfast Agreement*. Manchester: Manchester University Press.

Potter, S. J. O . (2000). The Omagh Bombing: A Medical Perspective. *Journal of the Royal Army Medical Corps*, 146, 18–21.

Sanders, A. (2011). *Inside the IRA: Dissident Republicans and the War for Legitimacy*. Edinburgh: Edinburgh University Press.

Sluka, J. A. (1990). *Hearts, Minds, Fish, and Water: Support for the IRA and INLA in a Northern Irish Ghetto*. London: JAI Press.

Sluka, J. A. (2009). In the Shadow of the Gun: "Not-War-Not-Peace" and the Future of Conflict in Northern Ireland. *Critique of Anthropology*, 23(3), 279–299.

Tonge, J. (2002). *Northern Ireland: Conflict and Change* (2nd ed.). London: Longman.

Tonge, J. (2004). "They Haven't Gone Away, You Know": Irish Republican "Dissidents" and "Armed Struggle." *Terrorism and Political Violence*, 13(3), 671–693.

White, R. W. (2006). *Ruairi O Bradaigh: The Life and Politics of an Irish Revolutionary.* Bloomington: Indiana University Press.

White, R. W. (2010). Structural Identity Theory and the Post-Recruitment Activism of Irish Republicans: Persistence, Splits, and Dissidents in Social Movement Organizations. *Social Problems*, 57(3), 341–370.

White, R. W., & Fraser, M. R. (2000). Personal and Collective Identities and Long-Term Social Movement Activism: Republican Sinn Fein. In S. Stryker, T. J. Owens, and R.W. White (Eds.), *Self, Identity, and Social Movements* (pp. 324–346). Minneapolis: University of Minnesota Press.

Wilford, R., & Wilson, R. (Eds.) (May 2009). *Northern Ireland Devolution Monitoring Report.* London: The Constitution Unit.

■ INDEX